T0367596

UNDENIABLE
TRUTHS

UNDENIABLE TRUTHS

The Clear and Simple Facts Surrounding the Murder of President John F. Kennedy

ED SOUZA

UNDENIABLE TRUTHS
The Clear and Simple Facts Surrounding the Murder of President John F. Kennedy

iUniverse books may be ordered through booksellers or by contacting:

iUniverse
1663 Liberty Drive
Bloomington, IN 47403
www.iuniverse.com
1-800-Authors (1-800-288-4677)

ISBN: 978-1-4917-3642-5 (sc)
ISBN: 978-1-4917-3697-5 (hc)
ISBN: 978-1-4917-3643-2 (e)

Library of Congress Control Number: 2014910275

Print information available on the last page.

iUniverse rev. date: 05/22/2015

In the search for truth and decency regarding the murder of President John F. Kennedy, many true patriots have emerged in the last five decades to help uncover the facts of this case. In my opinion, one of these warriors deserves special honor and recognition: Mark Lane. Lane was one of the first whistle-blowers to the Warren Commission's whitewash and withstood many character attacks in those initial years after the assassination. Lane stood his ground and provided solid information for future researchers like myself. His groundbreaking work *Rush to Judgment* is still a classic today, and his ability to interview many vital witnesses to the murder on video who were later killed or died cannot be underestimated; this was pure genius on his part.

Mark Lane, thank you for being a true role model for my generation and your unwavering pursuit of truth and justice in this case.

"The search for truth and knowledge is one of the first attributes of a man, though often it is most loudly voiced by those who strive for it the least."

—Albert Einstein

Contents

Preface

"The truly educated man is that rare individual who can separate reality from illusion." —Unknown

For many decades, my friends, students, and family members have all tried to convince me to write a book on the murder of President Kennedy and the subsequent cover-up of the assassination. I somehow resisted that request–until now. I do not know why, other than to say that so much has already been written on the subject up to this point. Most people consider it overkill. There has also been a significant amount of misinformation released on this subject, which is undocumented and just mere speculation. The events surrounding the shooting, combined with the evidence still available today, clearly indicate that the official government story was simply a massive cover-up of information.

My training with the Los Angeles Police Department (LAPD) and my twenty five years of experience as an investigator, researcher, and educator were not needed to come to that conclusion. After visiting the location of the shooting on several occasions and seeing the actual dimensions and dynamics of where this horrible act took place, it is simple to determine that one man with one rifle could not have committed this crime alone. If anyone ever tries to convince you of this fact, and many, such as Bill O'Reilly, will still try (see chapter 14), just do me a favor and laugh, and then finish my book.

When I was young, my father was fascinated with the murder of President Kennedy, and this has rubbed off on me. My father had two heroes: Arnold Palmer and President Kennedy, both of who he believed were men of great character. My father was a champion golfer in our local town. He truly loved Arnold Palmer, whom I had the pleasure of meeting. With regard to President Kennedy, my father shared many of his traits as well. Both were World War II veterans; both valued truth, honesty, and decency; and both were true Americans who fought for their country. My father was brokenhearted after the murder of President Kennedy, and he never got over the incident throughout my entire childhood.

He would, on occasion, bring home books and magazines about the assassination and store them in a cabinet downstairs in my childhood home in Rhode Island. I, being the most inquisitive child, wondered just what this incident was all about. Granted, I was maybe eight at the time, so it was the pictures in the books and magazines that fascinated me the most. It was not until a couple of years later that my father began to discuss this subject openly with me on a regular basis. After having gone through his materials for so long, I was already so familiar with much of the information that he was somewhat impressed. Of course, after I became interested in printed materials, Mark Lane's book, *Rush to Judgment: A Critique of the Warren Commission's Inquiry into the Murders of President John F. Kennedy, Officer J. D. Tippit, and Lee Harvey Oswald*, helped me a great deal. By this time, Bobby Kennedy and Dr. King had also been gunned down in the same year. The 1960s were what I would term the "decade of death" for our country, not only the death of these three great men, but also the death of our freedoms as well as the concepts of truth and liberty. This is how it all started: me with a flashlight downstairs, trying to figure out just what my father was so deeply concerned with that it consumed most of his free time.

My objective for providing the reader with that background information is partly to highlight the fact that even a ten-year-old boy could look at the evidence in this case and determine that we were not told the truth. You do not need a great mind, a forensic lab, and thousands of pages of material to prove that point. One of the most dramatic points in my life came when my uncle Joe taught me how to shoot a rifle. He was an avid hunter and a true NRA man who wanted his nephew to know how to handle weapons and not be afraid of them. My father, although a combat veteran from

World War II, was not into marksmanship or hunting. I guess he saw enough shooting and killing during the war, so this task was left to Uncle Joe. We would shoot out in the country areas, of course, with plenty of room and in a location where they would shoot skeet as well, which is where I learned to shoot at moving targets.

I later became a competitive shooter myself, shooting on the LAPD Police Olympic shooting team, which I still miss to this day. If you have ever shot at a moving target, whether moving slowly or quickly, you were probably humbled the first time you tried. This type of shooting requires the shooter to have knowledge of angles, wind speeds, and how to lead a target, which means to shoot where one feels the target will be when the bullet arrives at the target. One weapon we used was a bolt-action rifle, which requires the shooter to eject the bullet casing from the rifle with a manual bolt action, pulling back on the bolt and pushing it back into place. The manual action reloads another round in the chamber. This is the same type of weapon the Warren Commission says was used by Lee Oswald the day President Kennedy was killed.

What a valuable lesson I learned the first day I shot that weapon. I knew more than ever that we were simply lied to by President Johnson and the Warren Commission. I was just a ten-year-old boy, and I understood that one man with a rifle like my uncle Joe's could not have done the shooting from that building–firing through obstacles at a moving target with a bolt-action rifle. As Senator Richard Russell once said, "That dog don't hunt." It was not until much later, after I gained more understanding of the situation, that all the lights came on, but I understood enough to know then: we had been fooled. I remember the first time a teacher brought up the killing of President Kennedy and spouted out the official mind-control version of the shooting. He got much more than he bargained for from his young student when I asked him if he had ever fired a rifle. His answer was no. I asked him, "What was Oswald's motive for wanting to kill the president?" He had no effective answer. This is simply because Oswald had no motive, a fact even confirmed in Bill O'Reilly's new book, which I will discuss in depth. Do not feel bad, Mr. O'Reilly. The Warren Commission could not answer that question either, so I cannot expect anyone else to.

For years, I read almost everything that came out on the assassination, and I became an expert on what did not happen. If someone wrote a book on the subject, I could see quickly if his or her thesis held any water, having studied the facts for many years. I am not going to tell you that I know every fact and detail, which would be ridiculous, but the shooting is truly a simple case. The motives behind the shooting and the cover-up that took place are separate issues altogether and do require some serious thought. I will discuss those thoughts in this book, but for now please keep in mind a famous saying which states that, "truth can be stranger than fiction"; you are about to discover how true this is. Remember also that, "Knowledge is power."

I leave you now with an excerpt from Michael Kurtz's book, *The JFK Assassination Debates, Lone Gunman versus Conspiracy:*

> A final aspect of the case for conspiracy lies within a simple question. If Oswald did it all by himself, with no conspiracy, why was there a massive cover-up of the evidence? Newly released documents from the inquiry by the [Assassination Records Review Board] reveal that a deliberate, concerted effort to suppress the truth occurred. Documents were altered, such as Gerald Ford's raising the actual location of the wound in Kennedy's back to his neck so it would fit the single bullet trajectory. Material evidence such as John Kennedy's brain was either destroyed or simply disappeared. Critical witnesses, such as Jack Ruby, were not allowed to testify. Autopsy photographs and x-rays, as well as other vital medical evidence, were suppressed or even altered. The Secret Service, the FBI, and the CIA all withheld hundreds and thousands of crucial materials from the public record. All this smacks of a concerted effort by various agencies

of the federal government to conceal the truth about the assassination; none of this would have been necessary if it indeed had been the result from the action of a deranged, misguided social misfit. (Kurtz 2006, 101–102)[1]

1 Kurtz, M. (2006). *The JFK Assassination Debates: Lone Gunman versus Conspiracy*. Lawrence: University Press of Kansas.

Introduction

As you read through this book, please keep in mind that it is written as an introduction to the facts of the case. I wrote this book for the layperson that may have an interest in what the facts truly were and not to explain every fact, detail, or theory. (That would take a lifetime.) That is why I decided to configure the book as an easy read while allowing further research–if one so desires. Keep in mind that there is a truly vast amount of information on the JFK assassination, which really is very surprising when you consider the shooting, if handled properly and without deceit, could have been investigated and solved by a rookie officer and a decent crime lab. The problem was that they simply did not want us to know the facts–except for those that concluded it was a lone assassin, Lee Oswald, who did the shooting.

This book will not go into the subject of every conspiracy theory; I plan to write other volumes that will cover the subject of theories more deeply. Until then, I just wanted to make a few quick points. Point one is, do not try to think of this murder as having one set of conspirators, such as just the CIA, only the Mafia, just the Texas connection, Lyndon Johnson, or whatever group you feel had the stronger motive to murder the president. When people learn that I have expertise in this subject, they always ask the same question: who killed JFK? This is a great question for sure, but as I have said, my goal for this book was not to solve every issue surrounding the murder of President Kennedy. My goal was to develop a quick book that was easy and enjoyable to read that contained the true and real facts in this case, not the media spin we have heard for the past several decades. Many books on this subject are long, overly detailed, and sometimes so boring that most people get lost in all the details. After all, most people are not as addicted to this subject as the researchers are. I hope you enjoy this fast-paced and detailed examination of the murder of John F. Kennedy; feel free to use the references to further investigate this case. It truly was the murder of the century and perhaps the millennium. In future books, I will examine the effects of this disastrous event and how we are all children of a fallen king who may never receive their full inheritance because of this tragic event.

Also, this book is my attempt to allow you to investigate this incident as a police investigator would have. I have deferred to many experts in various fields of criminal justice to answer particular questions, such as ballistics, photography, and medical procedures and practices. Law enforcement professionals are a community of experts, and we work as a team, deferring to each other while conducting investigations. It is truly a team effort to get a conviction in any case, and any good investigator will admit to that fact. For example, while I have a solid understanding of ballistics because of my law enforcement background and other training, I am not an expert on this subject. Although I teach forensics, which covers the subject of ballistics, it is not one of the subjects that I teach within criminal justice. Based on this fact, I would then locate an expert, much like the police and district attorneys do when they are investigating crimes; they simply call in the experts. In the LAPD, most of our experts come out of the Scientific Investigation Division (SID); they are typically called out on all major crimes. Too many times, I read about authors who speak on topics they are not experts in, and they have no business trying to convince us that they are. You may be better off going down to the local Panera Bread and having a discussion with a random customer; I do that a lot and have a great time as well!

Before we continue, please consider this famous statement by Albert Einstein: "The world will not be destroyed by those who do evil but by those who watch them without doing anything."

Chapter 1

First Things First

"Beware lest you lose the substance by grasping at the shadow."

—Aesop

There are many undeniable truths surrounding the murder of President Kennedy. The reason I started this project was to write a simple, compact book that explains some of the many details of this investigation with all the pertinent information. I say "investigation" because we are simply investigating a crime. During my time with the LAPD, I encountered several hundred murder victims. Working in Los Angeles as a police officer quickly exposes a person to a large body count out on the streets, sometimes daily. I have personally seen many murder victims–most of them having been shot with rifles, shotguns, and pistols.

When you begin an investigation, you must start with securing the scene; in Dallas, the scene of the assassination was never secured. Evidence was destroyed by both the Dallas police and the Secret Service, who took buckets of water and washed out the back of the president's limo within minutes of the shooting. Any hope of reconstructing the crime scene or conducting a proper forensic investigation of the evidence in that vehicle was destroyed. Just think of the evidence we could have had if a proper crime scene investigation had occurred. The School Book Depository was not locked down and secured until almost thirty minutes after the shooting. Considering that the Dallas Police believed this was where some of the shots came from, the depository should have been locked down right away. In fact, if Oswald was the real suspect, the Dallas Police allowed him to walk right out the front door of the depository after the shooting. But even after Secret Service agents washed much of the evidence out with water buckets, there were still several bullet fragments recovered in the presidential limo; the problem for the Warren Commission was there were too many to have come from one round.[2]

According to the official investigation, the throat and back wounds of President Kennedy and the chest, wrist, and thigh wounds of Governor Connelly were all caused by one bullet, the so-called magic bullet. So how would it be possible for them to have recovered all of these bullet fragments, enough for almost three bullets, if there was only one bullet fired after the magic bullet?[3] In their new book, *They Killed Our President,* Jesse Ventura and his fellow authors, Russell and Wayne, point out what most of us researchers and investigators have known for years: that "fragmenting bullets that explode on impact—also known as 'frangible' bullets or 'hot loads'—are not consistent with the rifle alleged to be used in the assassination. 'Oswald's rifle'—as the authorities like to call it—was not of the type that handled frangible ammo." Experts have looked over the photos of the bullet fragments found in the presidential limo, and as the authors point out, "numerous bullet fragments were found inside the president's limo; some were standard ammo, others were apparently from frangible bullets" (Ventura, Russell, and Wayne 2013, 167).[4]

---

2 You can view digitally enhanced photos of the bullet fragments and many other items related to the assassination through the National Archive website: http://www.archives.gov/research/search/

3 The authors also point out that a frangible or hollow point bullet obviously exploded inside the president's head because traces of several bullet fragments and other metals can be seen in the x-rays of his skull; a full metal jacket round like the ones supposedly fired by Oswald could never have broken apart or exploded in such a way. Numerous tests have conclusively proven this. This then indicates that the fatal head shot *could not* have come from the Oswald rifle.

4 Ventura, J., Russell, D., and Wayne, D. (2013). *They Killed Our President: 63 Reasons to Believe There Was a Conspiracy to Assassinate JFK.* New York: Skyhorse Publishing.

Also, consider the fact that the governor still had bullet fragments in him when he died in 1993, and the Parkland medical team said they took more fragments out of the governor's wrist than was missing from the magic bullet—something has to give here; does any of this make sense to you? Even more absurd is that no one in the Warren Commission considered this ridiculous set of facts sufficient enough to explain them to the public. With one pristine bullet missing only two grams of weight, and with all those wounds and all those bullet fragments collected, well, I think we deserve a better explanation for sure, and as we will see later, there is one.[5]

Because the Warren Commission said that all three shots came from behind, it is strange that the Secret Service agents in the front seat had no blood on them, nor were the back of their seats in the front of the car covered or sprayed with brain and blood matter. As I stated in my introduction, simply use your childlike intelligence as you consider this case. If JFK was truly shot from behind, where would the blood and brain matter have been sprayed? Right! It would have been sprayed in front of him, and not behind or beside him, like we find in this case. These facts make it clearly obvious that President Kennedy was shot from the right front of the vehicle, possibly from one of the locations behind the grassy knoll. [6]

---

5 The magic bullet: never in the history of ballistics has there ever been such a ridiculous claim made about any bullet.

6 Go to http://www.youtube.com/watch?v=eqzJQE8LYrQ to watch the assassination

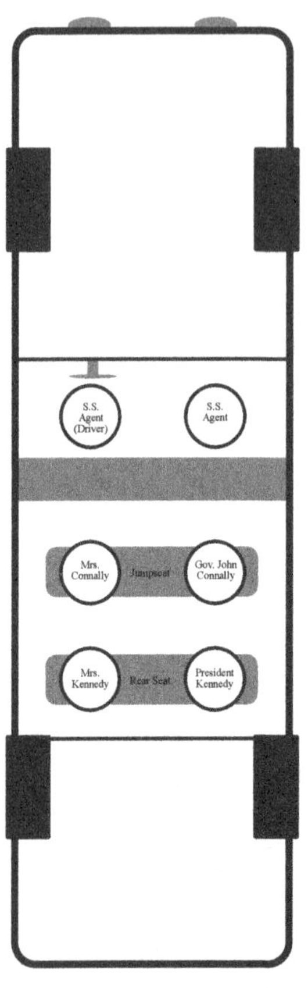

Figure-2 The Presidential Limo- This is the interior layout, and passenger locations in the Kennedy Limo on November 22nd as it drove through Dealey Plaza. Notice that the governor is sitting directly in front of the president, not to the left, or to the right as many would have you believe in order to facilitate the fictitious magic bullet scenario; no clearly Governor Connally was squarely in front of the president which is verified by the videos that day. (Limo graph is courtesy of Valerie Eldridge-Casey)

View from behind the picket fence. Photo Credit: Author.

This is a very unique view through the trees from behind the fence; notice the perfect view of the street right where the limo came by and right where many witnesses saw smoke coming out. Photo Credit: Author.

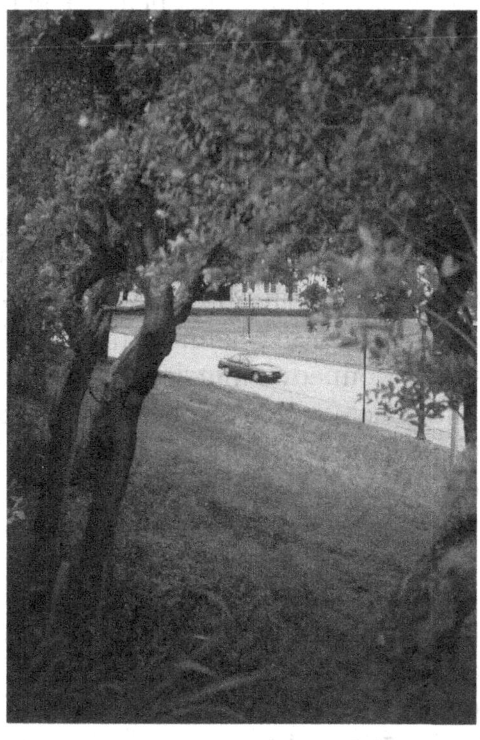

Now it should be noted that in all the time I was a member of the LAPD, I never saw the laws of physics violated, and I am certain that none of you have observed such an anomaly. Do not fall for the smoke and mirrors put out by recent computer reenactments found on certain cable channels. Use the common sense that God gave you, because this is not brain surgery. For example, if I punched you in the back of the head, which way is your head going to move? Correct, forward. It is as simple as that. I think a guy named Newton figured that out already. Certain television shows are crazy; they do everything possible to prove that the head shot came from behind. Such shows discuss the wind, the direction of the vehicle, and all kinds of nonsense. Do not fall for this ridiculous, made-up, junk science. Instead, do what we officers of the LAPD did, and *keep it simple, stupid (KISS).*

Furthermore, the Warren Report itself even admits that all of the attending medical personnel at Parkland Hospital clearly acknowledged President Kennedy's head wound as a massive wound to the rear of his head.[7] The hospital personnel concluded that, without a doubt, it must have been an exit wound and not an entrance wound, as the Warren Commission would have us believe. In his book, *The Killing of a President*, Robert Groden does an excellent job of providing visual images of all the witnesses to the president's wounds.[8] Describing what they saw on pages 86–88 of his book, it is then amazing that the Warren Commission would conclude that the shot that caused the head wound came from behind the vehicle. Based on the overwhelming information available regarding President Kennedy's injuries, I cannot imagine how anyone could conclude that the head wound and the throat wound came from a bullet fired from the rear. These days, I suppose people feel they can run anything through a computer and the masses will believe the outcome.

The official pictures of President Kennedy's autopsy are evidence that the head shot could not have come from behind. If a shot had entered the rear of his head moving forward, how could his face have still been intact?[9] With a bullet traveling at 2,500 feet per second, the front part of his face would have been destroyed. I think it is simply insulting for investigators, as well as some modern-day authors, to make the assertion that the president was shot from behind and leave us no concrete evidence of this fact. How could a high-powered bullet enter the rear of his head and explode in a forward direction without taking out part, if not all, of his face and eye socket? Let us see what other discrepancies we find with the official version of the story.

---

7 This will be covered extensively in the next chapter.

8 Groden, R. J. (1993). *The Killing of a President.* New York: Penguin Books.

9 What is really crazy is the official x-rays show the blow-out in the front forehead area, but all the autopsy photos show the president's face and forehead in *perfect condition.* This is clear deception; you simply can't have it both ways.

Dealey Plaza is the small area of downtown Dallas where the shooting occurred. I have been to Dealey Plaza many times, and each time I go, I am reminded of how different it looks in person.

Here I am in the early 1990s behind the infamous grassy knoll picket fence. Photo Credit: Author.

Now here is a view looking up at the Book Depository; notice how thick the trees are. Photo Credit: Author.

View from the center of Dealey Plaza. Photo Credit: Author.

One thing to note is the sharp angle from the sixth floor window; this angle is much too steep to have caused any of President Kennedy's wounds as described by the autopsy doctors. Also, as we just discussed, the head shot from this location would have blown the front of the president's head into the front seat of the car. There would have been major damage to his face, forehead, and eye sockets, and he had no such injuries. Another powerful point was that for most of the shooting area, the trees, which are clearly seen in the above photo, would have been blocking the view of the president in the limo, certainly for the first two shots (one being the throat wound). When the first shots went off, it would have been impossible for the shooter to have seen anyone in the vehicle. This tells the logical person that there must have been another shooter located somewhere in the plaza.

View from the railroad bridge overpass toward the School Book Depository. Photo Credit: Author.

The view of the grassy knoll from Elm Street, where at least one gunman was hiding behind the white wall; it was perhaps the last thing JFK ever saw. Photo Credit: Author.

Another interesting note: there are some facts that the Warren Commission and many private researchers agree on, and one of those facts is that a bystander, James Tague, was hit with a bullet fragment while standing under the triple underpass. If you looked out of the sixth floor window, you could see the triple underpass in the distant background, where Tague was struck. Now ask yourself, how bad of a shot was Oswald? If he did fire that first shot, he not only missed the car, which again the Warren Commission agrees was the first shot, he also missed the entire plaza as well, a shot that was at least sixty yards off its mark. So considering that point, the Warren Commission then wanted the world to believe that the next two shots were fired by the same assailant with world-class accuracy, killing President Kennedy, when he missed the entire street with his first shot? Please do not insult our intelligence.

Nevertheless, it should be noted that Lee Oswald was considered a poor marksman by many of the marines who served with him, including Sergeant Nelson Delgado, who claimed that Oswald was a terrible shot, one of the worst he had ever seen on a Marine Corps firing line (see his testimony[10]). Oswald did make it through boot camp as a marksman, but that is the lowest rating for a marine, falling below the sharpshooter[11] and expert ratings. I doubt that even Oswald though was so bad as to miss the entire street. Actually, the shot that hit James Tague might have come from the grassy knoll fence line and not the Book Depository, which was his original explanation to Mark Lane in *Rush to Judgment*. It should be further noted, as I stated in my introduction, that hitting a moving target is different from hitting a stationary one; it is like night and day. Oswald had no formal training shooting at moving targets that we know of; certainly, he did not receive that kind of training in the marines, where he was a radar operator. Also, as I stated earlier, there was a large Texas live oak tree that would have obscured any view of the back of the president from the sixth floor window, when we consider even the Warren

---

10 See Sergeant Delgado's statements: http://www.youtube.com/watch?v=nS9Zi0B60lw

11 Oswald did receive this rating once, but never again, and according to Delgado, Oswald never had any interest in weapons or shooting; he always had to be told when to clean his rifle.

Commission's version of when the first shot was fired. If someone did shoot from the depository, they would have had to do so from another window to get a clear shot of the limo (unless, of course, the sixth floor window was just a diversionary shot). Among the observers in Dealey Plaza that morning was a law enforcement officer, who stated in an affidavit that he did not see anyone in the sixth floor window at the time of the shooting, or anything protruding from the sixth floor window, but that is not true of the fourth and fifth floor windows; two men were seen in one of those windows by a very powerful eyewitness, Carolyn Walther (Benson 1993, 470).[12]

The real irony involving the Texas School Book Depository is that none of the shots from that building, more than likely, ever hit the president. It appears that two of them might have missed completely, and one possibly hit James Tague with a ricochet. As mentioned, there is even reasonable doubt regarding that shot, which may have come from the grassy knoll, although one shot that struck the governor could have come from the west side of the depository. According to many experts, both of the shots that hit Governor Connally, nearly killing him, were fired from the opposite side of the building, the west side rather than the sixth floor sniper's nest. Again, because of the angles of the shots from the Texas School Book Depository and the fact that there were too many trees blocking the view of the limo, it would have been a very poor choice for any assassin.

12 Benson, M. (1993). *Who's Who in the JFK Assassination: An A-Z Encyclopedia.* New York: Carol Publishing Group.

This is a view of the School Book Depository from Houston Street. Photo Credit: Author.

One excellent shooting location for a trained sniper would have been the Dal Tex Building; from this location, a shooter could have done some real damage. In fact, one of the bullet wounds noted by doctors Humes and Boswell during the autopsy was located near the center of President Kennedy's back; according to their notes, it was low enough to have come from this location, (See Figure-1 page 19). This wound can be seen in one of the official autopsy photos, which also depicts a second wound in the middle of the president's back, below the one indicated above.

The Dal Tex Building, which was directly behind the limo and where many feel at least one shot was fired from. Photo Credit: Author.

I do believe President Kennedy was hit from the Dal Tex location, this shot can be seen in the Zapruder film pushing the president downward and forward in his seat, just before he received the throat wound.

I have been to the sixth floor of the School Book Depository where there is a museum; it follows the single-shooter theory that Oswald acted alone. What is most interesting, though, are the huge blow-ups they have of the occupants during the shooting. One of them clearly shows—and I say *clearly* because they are very large—that Governor Connelly was not hit by the same bullet or the so-called magic bullet, because President Kennedy was already grabbing his throat and slumping over. The governor was not even struck yet and can be seen still holding his hat while trying to look behind himself. The governor stated many times that he was attempting to turn around to see if the president was injured. The picture shows him a split second before he was struck with a bullet, which is clear evidence that it was at least two different projectiles that hit the two men. Go look for yourself if they have not been taken down, or you can just watch the Zapruder film in slow motion to see what so many of us have always known. There was clearly more than one gunman. I remember the first time I went to the museum; I stood right near those pictures and showed several people what I had observed. Most people walking through the museum did not have much knowledge of the incident, so I filled in the blanks for them. They all got the message because it was simple; there is no evidence that they were hit by the same bullet, and these blow-up pictures, along with the film of the assassination, clearly and unequivocally prove that point beyond any reasonable doubt.

Chapter 2

Parkland Hospital: What They Saw

"All truth passes through three stages. First, it is ridiculed. Second, it is violently opposed. Third it is accepted as being self-evident."
–Arthur Schopenhauer

The grassy knoll has become infamous because many researchers (and most of the witnesses) believe this is where the final and fatal shot came from.

View facing the grassy knoll. This is the exact spot of the fatal head shot; there is actually a white "X" on the street to mark the location. Photo Credit: Author.

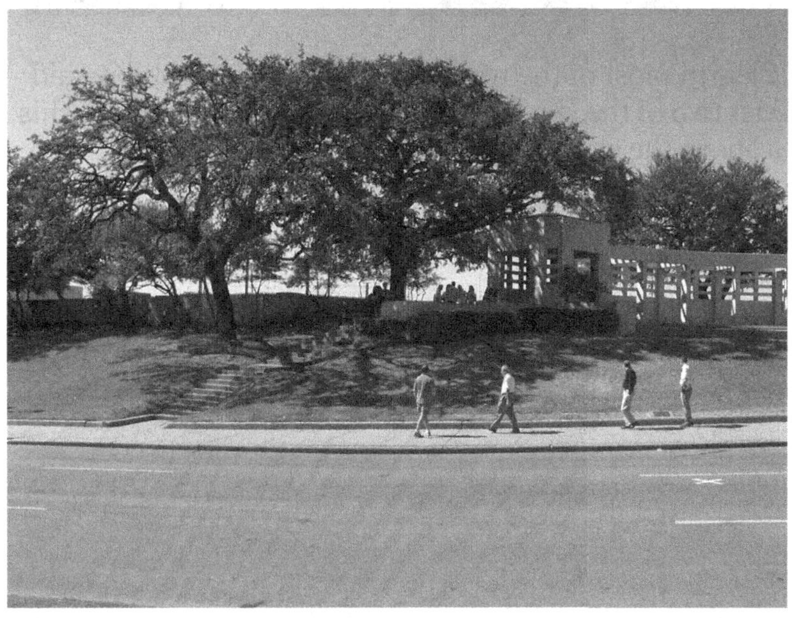

View driving down Elm Street coming around the curve. Photo Credit: Author.

Clearly, most of the witnesses in the plaza that day said at least two of the shots fired in the ambush came from this area above the grassy knoll.[13]

---

13 This is the exact location where the railroad men saw the smoke coming out from the trees and where several witnesses say they saw the shooter firing from.

Looking down from the railroad bridge overpass: the exact spot where Mr. Holland and his crew were standing. Photo Credit: Author.

A look behind the grassy knoll. Photo Credit: Author.

The parking lot behind the grassy knoll, circa 1990. Photo Credit: Author.

When conducting a proper and professional investigation, witness statements are extremely important, although many people see an event in different ways; their descriptions of the incident should be taken at face value, unless, of course, they are later discredited by solid physical evidence. It seems the Warren Commission investigators were not held to the standards of a proper criminal investigation. These so-called investigators would not have qualified for the Los Angeles Police Department (or the Mayberry Police Department, for that matter). As an example, here are several interviews conducted by the late Pennsylvania Senator Arlen Specter and others who were members of the Warren Commission staff.[14] Reading these interviews will open your eyes to many of the facts in this case, but doing so will certainly convince you that the president received at least two of his wounds from the front of the motorcade. It is a verifiable fact that *all* of the medical personal who treated President Kennedy on November 22, 1963, came to the same conclusion: that both of

14 Mr. Specter actually passed away while I was writing this book; another piece of history has moved on, although I consider his actions in this investigation to border on the criminal.

his wounds were frontal entrance wounds. These conclusions have been described in many books and interviews over the years; this also includes the Bethesda Hospital witnesses as well. Here now are their Warren Commission testimonies:

Figure-1- Here are the actual and verified gunshot wounds to President Kennedy, witnessed by the Parkland doctors and nurses, the medical staff at Bethesda, and the FBI agents present during the autopsy; also note that the bullets which entered the neck, and the back, did not exit the president's body, there were only entrance wounds in those locations indicated by the Bethesda doctors on their medical charts, and the President's actual death certificate. (Chart is courtesy of Valerie Eldridge-Casey)

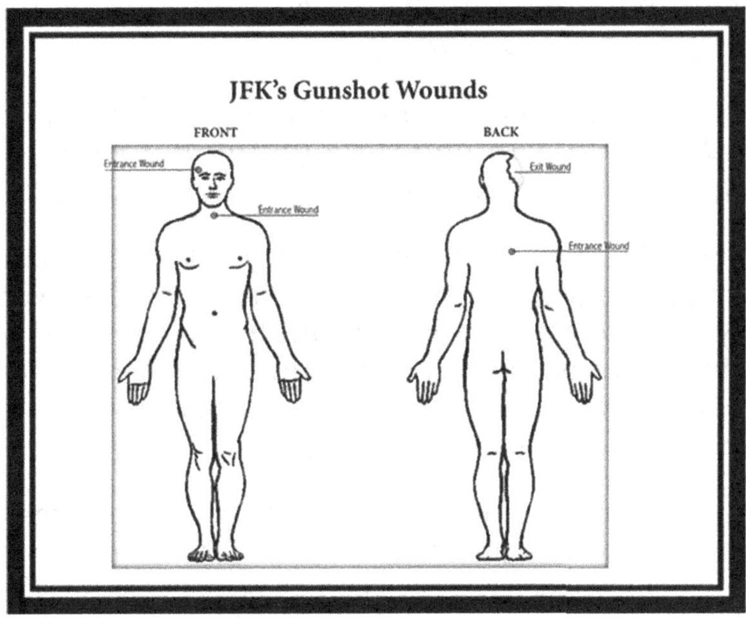

The testimony of Dr. Gene Coleman Akin was taken at 11:30 a.m., on March 25, 1964, at Parkland Memorial Hospital, Dallas, Texas, by Mr. Arlen Specter, assistant counsel of the President's Commission.

Mr. SPECTER: What did you observe as to the president's condition?

Dr. AKIN: He looked moribund in my medical judgment.

Mr. SPECTER: Did you observe any wounds on him at the time you first saw him?

Dr. AKIN: There was a midline neck wound below the level of the cricoid cartilage, about 1 to 1.5 cm. in diameter; the lower part of this had been cut across when I saw the wound; it had been cut across with a knife in the performance of the tracheotomy. The back of the right occipital parietal portion of his head was shattered, with brain substance extruding.

Mr. SPECTER: Returning to the wound which you first described, can you state in any more detail the appearance of it at the time you first saw it?

Now it should be clear that Dr. Akin has described both the throat wound and the head wound of the president with clarity. He believes, as we will see, that the throat wound was an entrance wound, much like all of the doctors in attendance that day (Fiester 2012, 271),[15] and the rear head wound was an exit wound, both of which are true.

Having worked in law enforcement in many capacities, I have seen my fair share of gunshot wounds and murder victims, but I will defer to an expert on ballistics at this time to give you a very clear distinction between an entrance wound and an exit wound, a distinction which is not missed very often by medical experts, and is certainly not missed by physicians working in a trauma unit at a main hospital such as Parkland.

> *It is not a difficult matter to distinguish the difference between a gunshot entry wound and a gunshot exit wound. All high-power rifle bullets are supersonic.*

---

15 Fiester, S. P. (2012). *Enemy of the Truth: Myths, Forensics, and the Kennedy Assassination.* Southlake, TX: JFK Lancer Publications.

Some such as the 5.56 mm (caliber .223) or 7.62 mm (caliber .308) fly at over twice the speed of sound. When a bullet is fired from a high-powered rifle it creates a supersonic column of air at its nose as it displaces the air on its way to the target. The atmospheric expansion of this air jet is unhindered before the bullet strikes the target. As the bullet enters the target at a very high rate of speed, it causes this air jet to slam into the wound cavity. With its expansion suddenly restricted by the surrounding tissue, the air jet causes a shockwave. This shockwave violently displaces the tissue in the wound, causing it to flare and expand at the bullet's exit point. This shockwave effect, and whatever tissue is forcibly displaced, is precisely why bullet exit wounds are always larger than entrance wounds, and thus readily distinguishable (Martin 2010, 69).[16]

I felt it necessary to give you that full explanation from Orlando Martin's book, *JFK: Analysis of a Shooting*, to show just how ridiculous it would be for an emergency room doctor to not know whether a wound was an entrance wound or an exit would; trust me, they know. As an example, the doctors in Los Angeles knew the difference. We would ask them all the time if a gunshot victim's wounds were entrance or exit wounds. The doctors would then provide their expert opinions. Clearly, emergency room physicians treat so many gunshot victims on a regular basis, especially in larger cities like Dallas, they know the difference between an entrance wound and an exit wound; to think otherwise would be simply illogical.[17]

---

16 Martin, O. (2010). *JFK Analysis of a Shooting: The Ultimate Ballistics Truth Exposed.* Indianapolis: Dog Ear Publishing.

17 Chief Jesse Curry made this comment about Parkland doctor Malcolm Perry: "By his later testimony, he stated he had previously treated from 150 to 200 gunshot wounds. The doctors were so absorbed by treatment of the massive head wound that his other wound (back or upper neck) was never noticed since he was lying on his back.... Dr. Perry insisted that the president was shot from the front" (Curry 1969, 34).

Now read in this passage how Specter tries to lead and manipulate the witness into giving him the answers he is looking for:

Mr. SPECTER: Dr. Akin, permit me, if you will, to give you a set of facts which I will ask you to assume for the purpose of giving me an opinion, if you are able to formulate one. Assume that the president was struck by a 6.5 ram. missile which had a muzzle velocity of approximately 2,000 feet per second at a time when the president was approximately 160 to 250 feet away from the weapon. Assume further that the bullet entered the president's body in the upper right posterior thorax just above the upper border of the scapula at a point 14 cm. from the tip of the right acromion process and 14 cm. below the tip of the right mastoid process. Assume further that the missile traveled through or in between, rather, the strap muscles without penetrating either muscle but going in between the two in the area of his back and traveled through the fascial channel without violating the pleura cavity, and that the bullet struck the side of the trachea and exited from the throat in the position of the punctate wound which you have described you saw; would the wound you saw be consistent with a wound of exit under the factors that I have just outlined to you?

Okay, what kind of ridiculous line of questioning is that? This is right out of the Warren Commission Report; talk about leading the witness. But the most incredible aspect to this interview remains to be seen; look at the final statement by Dr. Akin: he clearly states, unequivocally, that he believed that the president was struck from the front and that the head wound was a point of exit, not entrance.

Mr. SPECTER: Did you have any opinion as to the direction that the bullet hit his head?

Dr. AKIN: I assume that the right occipital parietal region was the exit, so to speak, that he had probably been hit on the other side of the head (obviously meaning the front of his head).[18]

So even with Specter's ridiculous antics, the doctor stood his ground and clearly stated for the record the clear and certain facts that were completely ignored by the commission. We further see that by the Warren Commission's own tactics and efforts, they tried to relegate all of the medical experts at Parkland Hospital to some menial group of individuals of low intelligence and that they were all incorrect in their observations regarding President Kennedy's wounds. A tactic, I should state, that unfortunately seemed to work in the realm of public opinion when it came to the commission's final conclusion.[19] Of course, the only two people in the country who seemed to have read the entire Warren Report at that time were Mark Lane and Jim Garrison.[20]

The testimony of Diana Hamilton Bowron was taken at 2:05 p.m., on March 24, 1964, at Parkland Memorial Hospital, Dallas, Texas, by Mr. Arlen Specter, assistant counsel of the President's Commission.

Now we come to the official testimony of Diana Hamilton Bowron, a nurse at Parkland Hospital who assisted in removing the president from the limo; read her testimony as to the condition of the president's head wound:

18 Warren Commission Report (1964).

19 Keep in mind the Warren Report was twenty-six volumes long, and to top it off, it had *no* index; that's correct: no index. It was a very disorganized investigation.

20 Mark Lane, of course, came out with his book *Rush to Judgment* in 1966, a serious, groundbreaking study into the murder of President Kennedy that allowed the *true facts* to come out, as well as Jim Garrison's study, which collimated in the trial of Clay Shaw in 1968.

Mr. SPECTER: And what, in a general way, did you observe with respect to President Kennedy's condition?

Miss BOWRON: He was very pale, he was lying across Mrs. Kennedy's knee, and there seemed to be blood everywhere. When I went around to the other side of the car, I saw the condition of his head.

Mr. SPECTER: You saw the condition of his what?

Miss BOWRON: The back of his head.

Mr. SPECTER: And what was that condition?

Miss BOWRON: Well, it was very bad ... you know.

Mr. SPECTER: How many holes did you see?

Miss BOWRON: I just saw one large hole.

Mr. SPECTER: Did you see a small bullet hole beneath that one large hole? **(**Another leading question**)**

Miss BOWRON: No, sir.

Nurse Hamilton clearly stated that the large hole was in the *rear* of the head and was an exit wound for sure; notice once again how Specter asks about a second smaller hole to try and get a statement to back up his ridiculous non-scientific theories. But she spoke the truth about what she saw: no second hole, only a large gaping hole that blew out the president's brains. It is impossible that the wound in the back of his head was anything other than an exit would; that is a fact based on professional observations and some of the true and factual, untouched photos of his autopsy.[21]

Let's move on to Dr. Charles J. Carrico's testimony; he was the first doctor to treat the president upon his arrival at Parkland Hospital.

THE TESTIMONY OF DR. CHARLES J. CARRICO WAS TAKEN AT 9:30 A.M. ON MARCH 25, 1964, AT PARKLAND MEMORIAL HOSPITAL, DALLAS, TEXAS, BY MR. ARLEN SPECTER, ASSISTANT COUNSEL OF THE PRESIDENT'S COMMISSION.

The first point of interest with regards to Dr. Carrico's testimony to the Warren Commission should be Arlen Specter's attempt, once again, to extract only the information he wanted and to stay away from anything that would indicate a second shooter.

Mr. SPECTER: Would you continue to describe your observations of the president?

Dr. CARRICO: His—the president's—color, I don't believe I said, he was an ashen, bluish, grey, cyanotic; he was making no spontaneous movements, I mean, no voluntary movements at all. We opened his shirt and coat and tie and observed a small wound in the anterior lower

21 I should note that some researchers feel it is possible that the president was also shot in the rear of his head a fraction of a second before the shot from the right front struck him. They claim that just before the final head shot you can see the president pushed forward after possibly being struck from behind by another head shot. I think the jury is still out on that one based on two points; one- most of the evidence was covered up so well from the autopsy it is hard to say if this is fact or fiction, and two- the large rear exit wound from the shot from the grassy knoll eliminated any physical or visual evidence of such an additional wound. What is certain in the video was the violent head snap that threw the president to the rear and across the car onto the floor board, a shot clearly fired from the right front.

third of the neck, listened very briefly, heard a few cardiac beats, felt the president's back, and detected no large or sucking chest wounds, and then proceeded to the examination of his head.

Mr. SPECTER: Approximately how many missile wounds, bullet wounds, have you had an opportunity to observe in your practice, Doctor?

Dr. CARRICO: I would guess 150 or 200.

Mr. SPECTER: Would you describe as precisely for me as possible the nature of the head wound which you observed on the president?

Dr. CARRICO: The wound that I saw was a large gaping wound, located in the right occipitoparietal area. I would estimate to be about 5 to 7 cm. in size, more or less circular, with avulsions of the calvarium and scalp tissue. As I stated before, I believe there was shredded macerated cerebral and cerebellar tissues both in the wounds and on the fragments of the skull attached to the dura.

Mr. SPECTER: Did you notice any other opening in the head besides the one you have just described?

Dr. CARRICO: No, sir; I did not.

Mr. SPECTER: Specifically, did you notice a bullet wound below the large gaping hole which you described? **[There is this question again, fishing to see if there was a smaller hole thereby providing evidence from a shot from behind]**

Dr. CARRICO: No, sir. [22]

---

22 Warren Commission Report (1964).

The testimony of Dr. William Kemp Clark was taken at 11:50 a.m., on March 21, 1964, at Parkland Memorial Hospital, Dallas, Tex., by Mr. Arlen Specter, assistant counsel of the President's Commission.

Mr. SPECTER: What did you observe the president's condition to be on your arrival there?

Dr. CLARK: I then examined the president briefly. My findings showed his pupils were widely dilated, did not react to light, and his eyes were deviated outward with a slight skew deviation. I then examined the wound in the back of the president's head. This was a large, gaping wound in the right posterior part, with cerebral and cerebellar tissue being damaged and exposed.

Mr. SPECTER: What, if anything, did you say then in the course of that press conference?

Dr. CLARK: I described the president's wound in his head in very much the same way as I have described it here. I was asked if this wound was an entrance wound, an exit wound, or what, and I said it could be an exit wound, but I felt it was a tangential wound.

Mr. SPECTER: Which wound did you refer to at this time?

Dr. CLARK: The wound in the head.

Mr. SPECTER: Did you describe at that time what you meant by "tangential"?

Dr. CLARK: Yes, sir; I did.

Mr. SPECTER: What definition of "tangential" did you make at that time?

Dr. CLARK: As I remember, I defined the word "tangential" as being [sic] striking an object obliquely, not squarely or head on.

Mr. SPECTER: Will you describe at this time in somewhat greater detail the consequences of a tangential wound as contrasted with another type of a striking?

Dr. Clark then went on to explain what he meant by a tangential-type wound; read how his expertise was simply overlooked and disregarded by Specter and the other commission members.

Dr. CLARK: The effects of any missile striking an organ is a function of the energy which is shed by the missile in passing through this organ; when a bullet strikes the head, if it is able to pass through rapidly without shedding any energy into the brain, little damage results, other than that part of the brain which is directly penetrated by the missile. However, if it strikes the skull at an angle, it must then penetrate much more bone than normal; therefore, it is likely to shed more energy, striking the brain a more powerful blow.

Secondly, in striking the bone in this manner, it may cause pieces of the bone to be blown into the brain and thus act as secondary missiles. Finally, the bullet itself may be deformed and deflected so that it would go through or penetrate parts of the brain, not in the usual direct line it was preceding.

Mr. SPECTER: Now, referring back to the press conference, did you define a tangential wound at that time?

Dr. CLARK: Yes.

Mr. SPECTER: And what else did you state at the press conference at 2:30 on November 22?

Dr. CLARK: I stated that the president had lost considerable blood, that one of the contributing causes of death was this massive blood loss, that I was unable to state how many wounds the president had sustained or from what angle they could have come. I finally remember stating that the president's wound was obviously a massive one and was not survivable.

Mr. SPECTER: What did Dr. Perry say at that time, during the course of that press conference, when the cameras were operating?

Dr. CLARK: As I recall, Dr. Perry stated that there was a small wound in the president's throat, that he made the incision for the tracheotomy through this wound. He discovered that the trachea was deviated so he felt that the missile had entered the president's chest. He asked for chest tubes then to be placed in the pleural cavities. He was asked if this wound in the throat was an entrance wound or an exit wound. He said it was small and clean so it could have been an entrance wound. [23]

Okay, here we have, once again, the clear and simple fact that the throat wound was an entrance wound; those of us involved in homicide investigations understand that a clean and smooth wound generally means that is a point of entrance, indicated by doctors Clark and Perry, of course. As additional evidence, here is the information that Dr. Clark gave to the *New York Times* only five days after the president was killed: "On his part according to the *New York Times* of November 27, Dr. Kemp Clark, who signed the Kennedy death certificate, declared that a bullet hit him right where the knot of his necktie was. He added, 'This bullet penetrated into his chest

[23] Warren Commission Report (1964).

and did not come out.'[24] The surgeon went on to say that the second wound of the president was 'tangential' and that it had been caused by a bullet which hit the right side of his head."

This testimony clearly shows beyond any doubt that Dr. Kemp Clark, who signed the death certificate, believed that the president was shot from the front when referring to both the throat wound and the head wound. **Why did the Warren Commission hide all of these facts in their final conclusion, you might ask?** Because they were simply dishonest and were fulfilling an agenda for those who covered up this crime; they also knew that very few people would ever read all twenty-six volumes of the Warren Report like I have done, and like Jim Garrison and Mark Lane did, long before I could even read (no offense, Mr. Lane). They were the first warriors to see through all the deception in this case.

The testimony of Margaret M. Henchliffe was taken at 2 p.m., on March 21, 1964, at Parkland Memorial Hospital, Dallas, Texas, by Mr. Arlen Specter, assistant counsel of the President's Commission.

In this exchange with Specter, Nurse Margaret Henchliffe sets him straight on whether the wound to the president's neck was an exit or an entrance wound.

Mr. SPECTER: Did you see any wound on any other part of his body?

Miss HENCHLIFFE: Yes; in the neck.

Mr. SPECTER: Will you describe it, please?

---

24 I would love to have had that bullet, but of course I'm sure it remained in the president's body and was buried with him (or was covertly removed and disposed of); clearly, that round did not come from the so-called Oswald rifle and would have indicated another shooter in the plaza, if it was ever thoroughly examined.

Miss HENCHLIFFE: It was just a little hole in the middle of his neck.

Mr. SPECTER: About how big a hole was it?

Miss HENCHLIFFE: About as big around as the end of my little finger.

Mr. SPECTER: Have you ever had any experience with bullet holes?

Miss HENCHLIFFE: Yes.

Mr. SPECTER: And what did that appear to you to be?

Miss HENCHLIFFE: An entrance bullet hole it looked to me like.

Truly, Miss Henchliffe was extremely clear about what she had observed; read on and see how Specter questions her further:

Mr. SPECTER: What experience have you had in observing bullet holes, Miss Henchliffe?

Miss HENCHLIFFE: Well, we take care of a lot of bullet wounds down there. I don't know how many a year.

Mr. SPECTER: Have you ever had any formal studies of bullet holes?

Miss HENCHLIFFE: Oh, no; nothing except my experience in the emergency room.

Mr. SPECTER: In what?

Miss HENCHLIFFE: In the emergency room is all.[25]

---

[25] Warren Commission Report (1964).

I wonder if Mr. Specter had ever seen even one gunshot wound in his life, so what made him qualified to question these emergency room professionals on their observations?

The testimony of Ronald Coy Jones, chief resident of surgery at Parkland Hospital. Jones stated his expert opinion regarding the president's wounds, the Throat wound, and the head wound.

The hole was very small and relatively clean cut, as you would see in a bullet that is entering rather than exiting a patient. If this were an exit wound, you would think that it exited at a very low velocity to produce no more damage than this had done, and if this were a missile of high velocity, you would expect more of an explosive type of exit wound, with more tissue destruction than this appeared to have on superficial examination.... [There] appeared to be an exit wound in the posterior portion of the skull.... There was a large defect in the back side of the head as the president lay in the cart with what appeared to be brain tissue hanging out of his wound with multiple pieces of skull noted next with [sic] the brain and with a tremendous amount of clot and blood (Benson 1993, 226).[26]

In final consideration of the medical testimony provided by the personnel at Parkland Hospital, I pointed out that many of them were truly experts on gunshot wounds. This included twenty-one doctors and nurses who all agreed and stated to the Warren Commission members that there was clear and unequivocal damage to the rear of the president's head but not to his face. Most of them stated that the head wound appeared to be an exit wound, concluding that brain

---

26 Benson, M. (1993). *Who's Who in the JFK Assassination: An A-Z Encyclopedia.* New York: Carol Publishing Group.

matter from the back of the head had been blown out of the rear of the skull. It is simply insulting and ignorant to conclude that these medical professionals were all wrong in their observations that day, especially since they were interviewed within a short time of the shooting.

Read what Dr. James H. Fetzer stated in his book, *Murder in Dealey Plaza:*[27] "Over twenty Parkland witnesses repeated neurosurgery professor Kemp Clark's description of a right-rearward, 'occipital,' skull defect. Among the Parkland witnesses who described JFK's skull defect as rearward, eight participating physicians used the term occipital in documents published by the Warren Commission: Doctors Kemp Clark, Robert McClelland, Marion Thomas Jenkins, Charles J. Carrico, Malcolm Perry, Gene Akin, Paul Peters, and Charles R. Baxter: Seven of them described having seen cerebellum, a very different looking portion of brain only found at the rear" (Fetzer 2000, 197).

Fetzer went on to point out that the official autopsy photographs, which show a large blown-out wound in front of the right ear, apparently contradict all of the hospital doctors' eyewitness statements. Of course, now we know that the conspirators who had complete control of the investigation back in 1963 and 1964 had inserted forged autopsy photos, as well as forged x-rays of the autopsy, into the official report. The statements you just read by the doctors, in combination with some untouched photos that surfaced years later, point to a clear and massive cover-up in this case; you just can't see it any other way.[28]

So the Parkland Hospital doctors, many of whom were experts with gunshot wounds, clearly noted that the

---

27 Fetzer, J. (2000). *Murder in Dealey Plaza: What We Know Now that We Didn't Know Then about the Death of JFK.* Chicago: Catfeet Press.

28 Paul O'Conner, the autopsy assistant at Bethesda, stated for the record many times that these pictures of the president were absolute fakes and not what he observed at the autopsy; he is featured in both *The Men Who Killed Kennedy* and *The Best Evidence* documentaries, stating the facts surrounding these fraudulent photos.

president's throat wound was an entrance wound, so much so that they never even once considered any other viewpoint regarding that wound. According to Lifton (1980), "The Dallas doctors saw the president for about twenty minutes. According to the clinical summary prepared by Dr. Kemp Clark, the neurosurgeon who pronounced Kennedy dead, the doctors saw only two wounds, one at the front of the throat, and a large head wound at the right rear. Because it was small, round, and punctuate, most of the Dallas doctors evaluated that the throat wound as a point of entrance" (Lifton 1980, 41).[29] Further evidence that the throat wound was an entrance wound would come from news reports made that day that quoted the Parkland doctors: "Dr. Malcolm Perry, thirty-four, said, 'There was an entrance wound below the Adam's apple.... Dr. Perry, an attending surgeon, and Dr. Kemp Clark, chief of neurosurgery at Parkland Hospital, gave more details. Mr. Kennedy was hit by a bullet in the throat, just below the Adam's apple, they said. This wound had the appearance of a bullet's entry" (Lifton 1980, 56). David Lifton's book, *Best Evidence,* is one of the most intelligent and in-depth books ever written on the assassination; you should read it as many times as possible; the truth shall make you free.

Could the Fatal Head Shot Have Come from Behind?

Research efforts and tests have been conducted over the years to try and duplicate the efforts of a lone gunman in this case. James Fetzer (2000) describes two of these tests: "Two different shooting tests have demonstrated that had JFK in fact suffered skull damage from shots fired from Oswald's alleged perch, the most visible blow-out wound would have been toward the front of his skull, perhaps involving JFK's forehead and eye socket. There is no evidence of any such wounds. Thus neither witnesses nor JFK's autopsy photographs give evidence that JFK had skull damage that fits well with the experiments that were performed to duplicate JFK's wounds by firing at skulls from Oswald's alleged seat" (Fetzer 2000, 196).

---

29 Lifton, D. S. (1980). *Best Evidence.* New York: McMillan.

Other points to consider: there were several broadcasts going out with eyewitnesses clearly stating that they saw or heard shots being fired from behind the fence on the grassy knoll. Then we have *all* of the Parkland doctors reporting the president's wounds as frontal points of entry; therefore, there should be no reasonable doubt that at least two shots originated from in front of the motorcade. Even one of the president's press secretaries, Malcolm Kilduff, made this point very clear, indicating just where the bullet entered the president's head: "right in the temple area," he said, pointing to that exact spot on his own head. He told the public he had received this information from not only the Dallas doctors, but also the president's own Surgeon General, George Berkley.

Once again referring to Lifton's noteworthy *Best Evidence* (1980), even the Secret Service stated in their official report that they saw the president struck by bullets fired from in front of him. Agent Sam Kinney, the driver of the follow-up car, reported: "I saw one shot strike ... the right side of the head. The president fell to the seat to the left toward Mrs. Kennedy." Agent George Hickey, sitting in the left rear of that same vehicle, wrote: "I heard what appeared to be two shots and it seemed as if the right side of his head was hit" (Lifton 1980, 43).[30]

The police and the press moved quickly to control what was being dispensed to the public. In my experience investigating crimes, the first information you get can be the most valuable and is many times the most accurate. This is the case with the JFK assassination; we have dozens of witnesses reporting shots from the front, bullets flying over people's heads, holes in the windshield of the presidential limo, the president's head flying backwards. But the Warren Commission still did their very best to find the two people who saw something in a window of the School Book Depository Building; [31] they then concluded that all the shots came from that building and

---

30 We also have Chief Jesse Curry stating that he felt at least some of the shots came from in front of the presidential limo; he was riding in the lead car during the motorcade.

31 This, I am sure, is true as well; we have witnesses that even saw two men in one window and one man in a window on the west side of the building.

from behind the president. This, of course, is simply bogus information and shows that the initial investigation was a fabrication of the facts right from the start. In my professional opinion, this investigation was more of a cover-up than an inquiry into the true facts. In Los Angeles, I saw the murders of prostitutes and pimps investigated more thoroughly and effectively than the Warren Commission's investigation into the murder of President Kennedy.

Let me make this one point vividly clear: when conducting a proper and lawful investigation, you never try to manipulate the statements and testimony of the witnesses. This is all part of trying to find out what the true facts of the case were. In any criminal investigation, you must allow the chips to fall where they may; this means allowing the free flow of information, not only from the professionals but also from the witnesses; after all, being an investigator is not a sales job. Of course, this type of proper investigation is time consuming, but you must turn over every stone, you must follow the evidence wherever it leads, and then base your conclusions on those facts alone. This was simply not the case with the Warren Commission's investigation; they concluded the facts *before* the investigation began, thereby guaranteeing the outcome they desired.

Of course, by now we know that the final and fatal shot came from the front, driving the president back and to the left; you will read evidence to this fact in the next chapters. This was a point made ever so clearly in Oliver Stone's masterpiece, *JFK*. In the film, Jim Garrison, played by Kevin Costner, makes this point vividly clear when he critiques the famous Zapruder film, pointing out over and over again to the jury that the president was driven back and to the left by the head shot. Costner repeats this line over and over: "Back and to the left, back and to the left, back and to the left." This movie should be on your must-watch list.

Additionally, we also know that the president's throat wound must have occurred from a point in front of the vehicle, most likely from the fence line to the right of Elm Street behind the grassy knoll; this wound was never truly explored, because the medical examiners at Bethesda chose not to investigate its track, or any other details regarding this wound.[32] If, however, the Parkland personnel were correct, and the throat wound originated from the right front, then we must conclude this to be a fact. We can also see the point of impact of this shot with the president's reaction when he reaches up and grabs his throat; the shooter was obviously attempting to strike him in the head but missed by a few inches.

The grassy knoll, seen from across Elm Street. Photo Credit: Author.

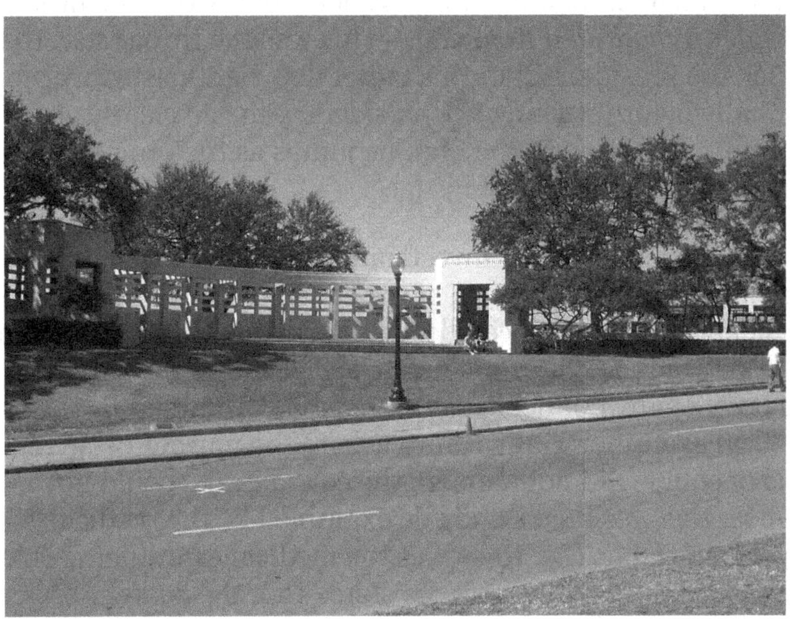

It is my opinion that the shooters did not want to take that grassy knoll head shot; it was an extremely risky shot when you consider that so many people were in that area. This risk became clear when the police caught the shooters in the

---

32 It should be noted that many people have said that the doctors at Bethesda never knew about the wound to the president's throat, which is why they never examined it, but Dr. Robert Livingston, who was the president of the National Institute for Mental Health, stated that he called Dr. Humes personally prior to the autopsy. Dr. Livingston had heard a description of that wound from the Parkland doctors and advised Dr. Humes of the exact location of this wound, telling him that it should be probed and fully examined (*The Men Who Killed Kennedy*, Episode 7, *Smoking Guns*, 2003).

parking lot, but they were able to weasel their way out using fraudulent Secret Service credentials. They only took that shot as a last resort because the president had to be killed; the chances of the conspiracy unraveling if the president had survived was completely overwhelming.

Other evidence of the frontal shot is backed up by still another witness from the Parkland Hospital staff. Dr. Evalea Glanges stated that she clearly saw a through-and-through bullet hole in the president's limo after the shooting; see her statements in *Smoking Guns,* episode 7 of the documentary, *The Men Who Killed Kennedy.*[33] This was the throat shot that struck the president first; this bullet flew right past Governor Connally before striking the president, you can clearly see Connally's reaction in the film: he jumps as the projectile comes close to the side of his face.

The next step in this investigation should then be to examine the cover-up stage of the conspiracy; once the president was pronounced dead at Parkland, his body should have stayed in Dallas, under state law at that time. In Texas, the body of any homicide victim must be examined by the medical examiner in the county where the murder occurred. This of course did not happen; the conspirators could not have let the president's body be examined by the medical experts in Dallas (Dr. Rose was the medical examiner at that time). There are witnesses who stated that the Secret Service actually pulled their weapons on Dr. Rose as they ripped the president's body away from him, committing the crime of obstruction of justice. They then took the body to *Air Force One,* destination, Washington, where the story continued.

On a final and most critical note, because of their actions by removing the president's body from Dallas, the case against Oswald was undermined; had he not been assassinated by Jack Ruby, he could not have been convicted. One reason is that state law would have prevented the prosecution from using the president's body as evidence

---

33 *The Men Who Killed Kennedy*, Episode 7, *Smoking Guns* (2003).

against Oswald. Yes, you read correctly: by removing the body and not having it properly examined and documented by medical authorities in Dallas, the president's body would have been excluded from the prosecution's case against Oswald. There would have been no continuity in the chain of evidence with respect to the body. You see, this is because the courts operate within the law, not within cover-ups and conspiracies (most of the time, of course). But truly I believe, given the true and factual evidence, along with the testimonies of the medical doctors, that the body of President Kennedy might have ultimately helped Oswald if the case had actually gone to trial.

Chapter 3

The Civilian Witnesses

"It is difficult to say what truth is, but sometimes it is easy to recognize a falsehood."
—Albert Einstein

The Warren Commission's Stance

The Warren Commission made two ridiculous statements with regards to the location of the gunfire in Dealey Plaza; they are listed here below:

"No credible evidence suggests that the shots were fired from the railroad bridge over the Triple Underpass, the nearby railroad yards, or any place other than the Texas School Book Depository."

"In contrast to the testimony of the witnesses who heard and observed shots fired from the depository, the commission's investigation has disclosed no credible evidence that any shots were fired from anywhere else."

—The Warren Commission Report, 1964[34]

Now here is the whole story.

The Warren Commission had many critics right in its own ranks who felt that the whole truth was not coming to the surface; here is a statement from the assistant counsel to the Warren Commission, Judge Burt W. Griffin: "I don't think some agencies were candid with us. I never thought the Dallas police were telling us the entire truth. Neither was the

---

34 Lane 1966, 36.

FBI" (Oglesby 1992, 96).[35] That is a pretty stunning statement indeed, and coming from the commission's assistant counsel, it carries an even larger impact.

In his book *Rush to Judgment,* Mark Lane stated the following: "To conclude that 'no credible evidence suggests' that shots came from any place other than the Book Depository is to ignore the evidence of Miss Mercer, Bowers, Price, Holland, Deputy Constable Weitzman, and the railroad yardman who spoke with them. Yet the statements of these six corroborate and are consistent with each other. For testimony to be so compatible, the common denominator—bar perjury—must be truth. The commission's apparently arbitrary rejection of such testimony reflects more damagingly upon itself than upon the credibility of the witnesses, for, in fact, nearly 100 other persons believed that the shots came from the knoll" (Lane 1966, 36).[36] This statement is very well articulated; as a former police officer, I always looked for witnesses to corroborate each other's stories and also to see if there were consistencies within their statements. This, as Lane states so correctly, is exactly what occurred with the witnesses to the JFK assassination.

One of the most astounding things about the murder of our thirty-fifth president is there were hundreds of witnesses to the incident.[37] In law enforcement, we call these witnesses "wits"; it is a common term heard day in and day out on the job. If you study the wits in this case, you might be shocked to

---

35 Oglesby, C. (1992). *The JFK Assassination: The Facts and the Theories.* New York: Penguin Books.

36 Lane, M. (1966). *Rush to Judgment: A Critique of the Warren Commission's Inquiry into the Murders of President John F. Kennedy, Officer J. D. Tippit, and Lee Harvey Oswald.* New York: Holt, Rinehart & Winston.

37 Around four hundred, to be exact; of the ninety witnesses contacted by the police, the FBI, and the Warren Commission, fifty-eight said that shots came from the direction of the grassy knoll and not from the Book Depository Building (Lane 1966, 37).

learn what they saw.[38] They include law enforcement officers, railroad workers, housewives, and businessmen. What is also clear is the Warren Commission's complete disregard for these eyewitness statements. As I mentioned in the previous chapters, it is vital that you take accurate and complete statements from your eyewitnesses, because many times they become the cornerstone of your investigation. When you consider all the evidence available in this case, such as the home movies, the still photos, and the hundreds of witnesses, it should have been no problem to piece together what actually occurred. If the Warren Commission had compared and contrasted all of the statements together, they would have understood what actually occurred at the time of the shooting. Let's take a good look at the witnesses in this case and see what they all have in common with each other (much of this information was kept from the pubic for decades).

We begin with the thirteen railroad workers who were standing on the railroad overpass above Elm Street. These gentlemen had a complete view of the whole plaza on the day of the shooting. All of them saw or heard shots coming from the grassy knoll, some saw smoke, and many heard the shot at the same time that they saw the smoke coming out from the fence line.

S. M. Holland

S. M. Holland, who was first interviewed on camera by Mark Lane back in the 1960s for *Rush to Judgment*,[39] was one of the best witnesses of the assassination that I have ever heard on camera, and he clearly saw the shooting in Dealey Plaza in great detail. He was what I would call Johnny on the spot; he was standing on the railroad overpass with several of his coworkers, watching the president's motorcade go by, when he

---

38 I must note here that no witness, group of witnesses, medical personnel, or law enforcement personnel have ever described the assassination in the way the Warren Commission did, not even one witness; it was simply amazing how they got away with their astounding lies in their conclusion.

39 *Rush to Judgment*, http://www.youtube.com/watch?v=cHaMxA5w4_Y

saw something he would never forget. It should be noted that Mark Lane, as far as I know, never paid any of the witnesses for their statements, so Holland had absolutely nothing to gain by telling his story. I have included the YouTube link to *Rush to Judgment* in the footnotes; I highly recommend you watch this whole documentary. Lane does a fantastic job in this video, considering this was only two years after the murder.[40] S. M. Holland's statements to Mark Lane were chilling, and totally contrary to the Warren Commissions conclusions. S. M. Holland said he was standing on the triple underpass and had one of the best views of any of the eyewitness, he said he heard four shots, and clearly not all of them originated from behind the motorcade, he said without a doubt the third one definitely came from behind the wooden fence. There was a puff of smoke under the trees like someone had thrown out a Chinese firecracker; the sound was entirely different from the one which was fired from the Texas School Book Depository building.[41]

---

40 Mark Lane is one my personal heroes in this whole ordeal, and we all owe him a tremendous debt of gratitude for bringing forth information regarding the murder of President Kennedy that may have been lost forever to history. He had the fortitude to stand up and give a rather large part of his life for truth and decency, which were both completely lacking in the official investigation.

41 This is another important point simply overlooked by many: the witnesses who heard the shot from the grassy knoll, including S. M. Holland, Chief Curry, and Lee Bowers, said that the last couple of shots sounded very different than the first ones; well, of course they did, because they were fired from totally different locations and with different weapons. It makes complete sense as well because a shot high up and much farther away will sound very different than a shot fired much lower and at a shorter distance. It could also have been that the firearms used for the closer shots were not as high powered as the ones fired from a longer distance, possibly because they needed more controlled fire up close in order not to hit the ladies riding in the car. You can just imagine if JFK had survived this shooting but Jackie had been murdered; just think of the madness that would have ensued. JFK would have left no stone unturned to find the conspirators.

Once again, a look through the trees behind the fence where the smoke came out. Photo Credit: Author.

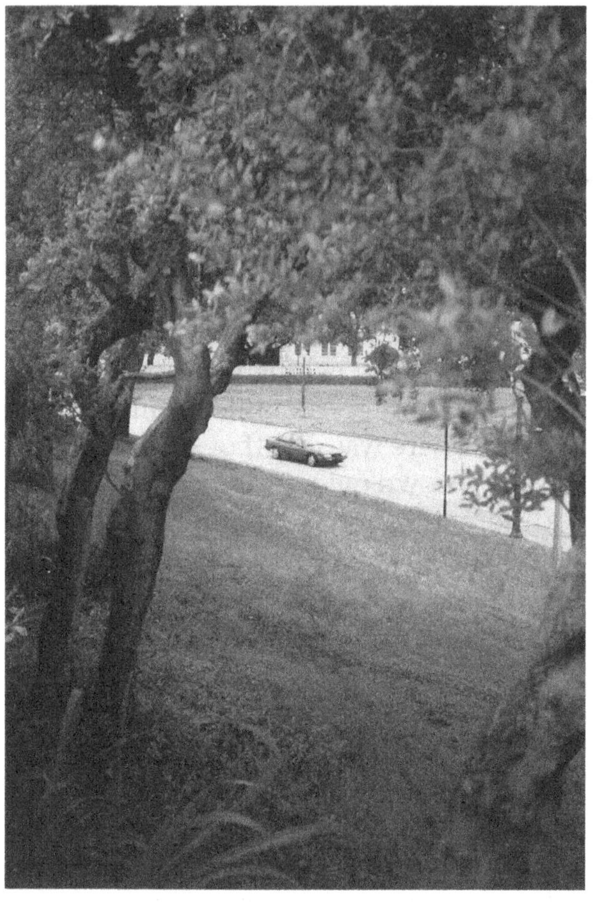

According to Holland then, the third shot came from the grassy knoll,[42] and he was determined to locate the shooter. He and his team headed in the direction of the shot. When Holland and his men reached the area behind the grassy knoll, they found a station wagon and a sedan parked behind the fence. On the bumper of the station wagon, there were two muddy marks, as if someone had stood there to look over the fence. At least seven other witnesses on the overpass saw smoke rising from the same area and also smelled the

[42] *What They Saw: S. M. Holland*, http://www.youtube.com/watch?v=o8LnoCA0qR0

gun powder from the shot as well.[43] Many other witnesses thought the shots came from behind the picket fence. One Dallas policeman, J. M. Smith, even claimed to have caught the smell of gunpowder behind the wooden fence (A Primer of Assassination Theories).[44]

Richard C. Dodd

Richard Dodd was another railroad worker and witness to the shooting who was standing with Holland on the railroad overpass. He also gave some powerful testimony to authorities as well as to Mark Lane, who interviewed him for *Rush to Judgment*. Dodd stated to Lane, "We all seen about the same thing, there was a puff of smoke that came out, the shot came from behind the hedge on the north side of the plaza" (Lane 1967). [45]

It is hard to imagine that the FBI, the Dallas police, the Warren Commission, and all of the other law enforcement agencies involved totally and willfully ignored these key eyewitness statements. As a former law enforcement officer myself, this is totally inconceivable to me. The witness list continues with James Simmons, another railroad worker.

James Simmons

While Simmons was looking down from his perch on the railroad overpass with his coworkers, he said he heard the shots ring out from in front of them. He stated, "The shot sounded like it came from in front of us, and to the left, there was a puff of smoke that came underneath the trees, the

---

43 Many people riding in the motorcade, including Senator Yarborough and several law enforcement officers, also reported smelling gun smoke in the air; how could the smell of gun smoke have come all the way down from the depository in just seconds? Simply put, it couldn't have.

44 *A Primer of Assassination Theories*. Retrieved from http://kenrahn.com/JFK/Conspiracy_theories/Primer/Primer_of_assassination_theories.html

45 *What They Saw: Richard Dodd*, http://www.youtube.com/watch?v=OgTWNmMcnFQ

smoke was right directly in front of the wooden fence" (Lane 1967, 40).[46]

Lane, interviewed all of the railroad workers and said, "Six other men on the overpass saw smoke in the same area. Austin L. Miller stated in an affidavit on November 22, 'I saw something which I thought was smoke or steam coming from a group of trees north of Elm off the railroad tracks.' He was questioned for the first time by counsel for the commission four and a half months after the assassination. The interview was a brief one; it lasted but a few minutes. The counsel did not ask about the smoke, and Miller was dismissed before he could mention the crucial observation contained in his affidavit" (Lane 1966, 40). This is another example of the Warren Commission investigators not caring to learn the true facts of the case. Think about it: this was the murder of the president of the United States, not some terrorist in another country. Where was their integrity? Where was the search for the truth? Where is the justice for President Kennedy?

Lee Bowers

Lee Bowers was one of the best civilian witnesses, because he was behind the grassy knoll, up high in a railroad watch tower. He had also worked there for over ten years at the time and knew every nook and cranny of the parking area. He gave some interesting testimony about what he observed there in the railroad yard the day of the shooting, but as we will soon see, the Warren Commission was not willing to dig further for the truth.[47]

---

46 *What They Saw: James Simmons,* http://www.youtube.com/watch?v=_y6Elcp5FOw

47 Lee Bowers, http://www.youtube.com/watch?v=izqYhSV9AtY

THE TESTIMONY OF LEE E. BOWERS, JR. WAS TAKEN AT 2 P.M., ON APRIL 2, 1964, IN THE OFFICE OF THE US ATTORNEY, 301 POST OFFICE BUILDING, BRYAN AND ERVAY STREETS, DALLAS, TEXAS BY MR. JOSEPH A. BAIL, ASSISTANT COUNSEL OF THE PRESIDENT'S COMMISSION.

Mr. BALL: Did you notice any cars around there?

Mr. BOWERS: Yes; there were three cars that came in during the time from around noon until the time of the shooting.

Mr. BALL: Came in where?

Mr. BOWERS: They came into the vicinity of the tower, which was at the extension of Elm Street, which runs in front of the School Depository, and which there is no way out. It is not a through street to anywhere.

Mr. BALL: There is [sic] parking area behind the School Depository, between that building and your tower?

Mr. BOWERS: Two or three railroad tracks and a small amount of parking area for the employees.

Mr. BALL: And the first came along that you noticed about what time of day?

Mr. BOWERS: I do not recall the exact time, but I believe this was approximately 12:10, wouldn't be too far off.

Mr. BALL: And the car you noticed, when you noticed the car, where was it?

Mr. BOWERS: The car proceeded in front of the School Depository down across two or three tracks and circled the area in front of the tower, and to the west of the tower, and, as if he was searching for a way out, or was checking the area, and then proceeded back through the only way he could, the same outlet he came into.

Mr. BALL: The place where Elm dead ends?

Mr. BOWERS: That's right. Back in front of the School Depository was the only way he could get out. And I lost sight of him, I couldn't watch him.

Mr. BALL: What was the description of that car?

Mr. BOWERS: The first car was a 1959 Oldsmobile, blue and white station wagon with out-of-state license.

Mr. BALL: Do you know what state?

Mr. BOWERS: No, I do not. I would know it, I could identify it, I think, if I looked at a list.

Mr. BALL: And it had something else, some bumper stickers?

Mr. BOWERS: Had a bumper sticker, one of which was a Goldwater sticker, and the other of which was of some scenic location, I think.

Mr. BALL: And did you see another car?

Mr. BOWERS: Yes, some fifteen minutes or so after this, at approximately 12 o'clock, 20 to 12 [sic], I guess 12:20 would be close to it, little time differential there, but there was another car which was a 1957 black Ford, with one male in it that seemed to have a mike [sic] or telephone or something that gave the appearance of that at least.

Mr. BALL: How could you tell that?

Mr. BOWERS: He was holding something up to his mouth with one hand and he was driving with the other, and gave that appearance. He was very close to the tower. I could see him as he proceeded around the area.

Mr. BALL: What kind of license did that have?

Mr. BOWERS: Had a Texas license.

Mr. BALL: What did it do as it came into the area, from what street?

Mr. BOWERS: Came in from the extension of Elm Street in front of the School Depository.

Mr. BALL: Did you see it leave?

Mr. BOWERS: Yes; after three or four minutes cruising around the area it departed the same way. He did probe a little further into the area than the first car.

Mr. BALL: Did you see another car?

Mr. BOWERS: Third car which entered the area, which was some seven or nine minutes before the shooting, I believe was a 1961 or 1962 Chevrolet, four-door Impala, white, showed signs of being on the road. It was muddy up to the windows, bore a similar out-of-state license to the first car I observed, occupied also by one white male.

Mr. BALL: What did it do?

Mr. BOWERS: He spent a little more time in the area. He tried, he circled the area and probed one spot right at the tower in an attempt to get [sic] and was forced to back out some considerable distance, and slowly cruised down back toward the front of the School Depository Building.

Mr. BALL: Then did he leave?

Mr. BOWERS: The last I saw of him he was pausing just about in, just above the assassination site.

Mr. BALL: Did the car park or continue on or did you notice?

Mr. BOWERS: Whether it continued on at that very moment or whether it pulled up only a short distance, I couldn't tell. I was busy.

Mr. BALL: How long was this before the president's car passed there?

Mr. BOWERS: This last car? About eight minutes.[48]

By now, it may seem pretty clear that these vehicles and the men in them were part of the assassination team. Also, if the police closed off traffic after ten o'clock, how did these vehicles get in? Think about that for a second. Also, the man with a mic or telephone up to his mouth was obviously talking to someone; what about this witness Lee Bowers giving meticulous detail about these vehicles and their actions? This is a class "A" witness; a person who can remember that kind of detail is a godsend in any investigation. But the Warren Commission had little respect for his observations, such as the point which he later made that the second and third shots that he heard were right on top of each other. Bowers said when he brought this point to

---

[48] Warren Commission, Testimony of Lee Bowers, 1964.

their attention that they reminded him that he was not an expert on gunshots (Lane 1966).[49]

This very significant fact presented by Lee Bowers, suggesting that the second and third shots were too close together to have come from any one weapon, this was confirmed by the statements of Deputy Weitzman.

Mr. BALL: How many shots did you hear?

Mr. WEITZMAN: Three distinct shots.

Mr. BALL: How were they spaced?

Mr. WEITZMAN: First one, then the second two seemed to be simultaneously.[50]

Dallas's own Chief of Police Jessie Curry, who was riding in the motorcade, also stated he felt the shots were fired too close together to have come from the same weapon and it seemed pretty clear to him that there was more than one shooter that day.

Consistent with the chief's observations, Governor John Connally, who was an avid hunter and very familiar with weapons, also said that the rifle shots he heard were too close together to have come from a manual bolt-action rifle. According to Orlando Martin in his recent book, *JFK: Analysis of a Shooting*, "The amount of time separating the second and third shot was very minimal. Governor Connally, who had hunted before and was quite familiar with bolt-action rifles, later, declared that he was under the impression that someone was shooting with a semiautomatic rifle. The governor correctly assessed that the shots had come too close together to have been fired from a bolt-action rifle. In reality, the short time span between the reports of the shots happened because these two shots had come simultaneously from two different rifles" (Martin 2010, 66).

---

[49] Lane, M. (Producer) (1966). *Rush to Judgment* [VHS].

[50] Warren Commission, Testimony of Seymour Weitzman, 1964.

So now you have a police officer, a police chief, and many other excellent witnesses including a shooting victim, Governor Connally, who were very close to the murder scene and who were in different locations (one on the north side, one on the south side, one in front of the president, and one in the limousine), who all stated that they heard the same accounts of the shooting. This, in law enforcement, is what we call a confirmation of details, but the commission completely ignored them, once again staying on their predetermined path of the lone gunman. It should also be noted that these were not all of the witnesses who heard the shots in that order; you will see there were many others as well.

J. C. Price

This was another excellent witness who was brought to the world's attention by none other than Mark Lane, once again in *Rush to Judgment.* Price was a building superintendent whose building overlooked Dealey Plaza. On the afternoon of the assassination, he was sitting up on the roof of his building and had a bird's eye view of the shooting. He stated that he saw the shot from the grassy knoll area and said the shot came from behind the fence. He further stated that seconds after the shooting, he saw a man run from behind the fence where the shots were fired and head toward the Book Depository. He told Mark Lane that he never thought the shots came from the Book Depository and did not agree with the Warren Commission on their findings. The Warren Commission never called him in as a witness, even though he witnessed the entire shooting.[51]

Julia Ann Mercer

Julia Mercer was an interesting witness; on the morning of the president's murder, she was traveling west on Elm Street. She was driving in the far right lane when she was forced to switch over into the left lane because of an obstruction.

---

[51] JFK Assassination Witness J. C. Price Interviewed by Mark Lane, http://www.youtube.com/watch?v=iGCR2ZcKbnY

According to Mercer, a truck[52] was double parked on the road with its wheels halfway up the curb, forcing her to change lanes. Traffic was busy that morning, but she was able to get a very good look at the driver and the passenger of the truck. Mercer later identified the driver as Jack Ruby,[53] the soon-to-be-assassin who would shoot Oswald to death at the Dallas police station two days later.

According to Mark Lane, "Miss Mercer saw a heavyset, middle-aged man in a green jacket slouched over the wheel of the truck while the other man[54] reached over the tailgate and took out from the rear of the truck what appeared to be a gun case. The gun case was about eight inches wide at its broadest spot and tapered down to a width of about four inches or five inches. It was brown in color, had a handle, and was about three and a half to four feet long. The man then proceeded to walk away from the truck, and as he did, the small end of the case caught in the grass or sidewalk, and he reached down to free it. He then proceeded to walk across the grass and up the grassy hill which forms part of the overpass" (Lane 1966, 30).

Mercer was never called by the Warren Commission, which was ludicrous, because she had handpicked Jack Ruby out of a mug shot book at police headquarters the day of the assassination. Keep in mind that this was two days before Ruby even made the news for killing Oswald. But once again, the cover-up artists stepped in and altered

---

52 The truck was a green Ford pickup with Texas license tags. She stated to Mark Lane that painted on the driver's side were the words "Air Conditioning"; along the back of the truck were some tool boxes (Lane 1966).

53 Ruby apparently had a record on file with the police department; he had been arrested before on various charges.

54 Lane further stated Mercer was able to give a very detail description of this potential suspect, who was also identified by Lee Bowers, who spotted him from his location high up in the railroad tower. Mercer said it was a white male, who appeared to be in his late twenties or early thirties, and he was wearing a grey jacket and, brown pants. Lane further said that Miss Mercer stated that she could have identified both men if she saw them again (Lane 1966, 30).

Mercer's statement to the police by stating that she was unable to identify the driver of the truck that day. They were insinuating that she was an unreliable witness and therefore of no interest to the Warren Commission. Mercer later stated the signature that appears on the statement was forged and that she never signed anything that day; there was also a notary signature on the statement, but she insisted there was never a notary present that day.

It is so clear to any logical person that these men were somehow involved that day; the man with the gun case was the same person described by Lee Bowers who saw him behind the fence at the moment the president was killed. Jack Ruby has also been linked to the murder of the president in many ways. Ruby had something to do with the conspiracy, because Oswald knew him well, and they were seen together on many occasions prior to the assassination. The Warren Commission denied these facts, like they had so many others throughout the case. Their investigation was a complete sham. We will cover Jack Ruby in depth later.

Carolyn Walther

Carolyn Walther was another competent witness to the assassination of President Kennedy; she was down on the curb right below the Book Depository on Elm Street. She claims to have seen two men who were standing in one of the fourth or fifth story windows, and both of them had rifles. She said she used the height of the trees to determine how high up the window was in relation to the trees, and she claims, at the time, the trees down below were equal to the fourth or fifth floor level. Carolyn said that one man was wearing a white shirt and had light colored hair; he was in possession of a long rifle, while the other man was only visible to her from his shoulders to his waist; he was wearing a brown suit and had a much shorter rifle. The second man was aiming his rifle down toward the street. She stated he was using the windowsill as a rest for his arms and the rifle. This weapon, she said, was much shorter than the other man's rifle (Benson 1993, 470). Walther does provide some great detail and insinuates that these men were working together. They were also clearly not on the sixth floor (the so-called sniper's nest found by police) but a lower floor, which could explain a lot with respect to the rifle shots fired that day. You can see her statements on YouTube.[55]

Who were these men? Also, why wasn't her testimony ever used? That is a simple answer, because it did not follow the official version, which is why they used Howard Brennan's statements and not hers. He said he saw one person, not two, but these men were not in the sixth floor window, which was an even bigger problem for the commission, so they ignored it. But I can tell you this: her statements would have been used in Oswald's defense. That much is certain.

Bill and Gayle Newman

The Newmans had the best ground level position of the assassination; they can be seen in several films and pictures of the shooting. Bill, the more outspoken of the two, has told the world his story for decades. He states that he is certain that some of the shots that hit the president came from behind them and not from the Book Depository. He further stated that the head shot hit the president right in the temple area. They were perhaps as close to the limo as anyone else at the time of the shooting, and of course, they were never called by the Warren Commission (not a big surprise any longer, I'm sure).[56]

Mary Woodward

As an employee of the *Dallas Morning News,* Mary Woodward was standing on Elm Street, watching the motorcade go by. She had always claimed the shot that hit President Kennedy in the side of his head clearly came from the grassy knoll area (Turner 1991). She even reported this information prior to anyone else in the news media. She

---

[55] Carolyn Walther, http://www.youtube.com/watch?v=o_ZYa_nK-Gc

[56] Newman's testimony, http://www.youtube.com/watch?v=OgqZ8w5RtXg

had rushed over to her office to get her information out but was shocked to find out that her editor had altered her report. When she asked why they did this, she was told by her superiors that they did not want to rock the boat and therefore reported the official story: that the shots came from the Book Depository. Mary was outspoken about what she saw and maintained her story throughout the years. She can be seen in the third episode of *The Men Who Killed Kennedy: The Cover-Up.*

Dave Powers

Dave Powers, who was a presidential aide and also one of President Kennedy's best friends, was riding in the Secret Service follow-up car, only six feet behind the presidential limo. He was in a great position to observe the whole shooting and gave his testimony in an affidavit in May of 1964. I have condensed his statements to just the shooting incident.

I, David F. Powers, make the following affidavit concerning my knowledge of the events of November 21 and 22, 1963.

"At that time we were traveling very slowly, no more than twelve miles an hour. In accordance with my custom, I was very much concerned about our timing and at just about that point I looked at my watch and noted that it was almost exactly 12:30 p.m., which was the time we were due at the Trade Mart. I commented to Ken O'Donnell that it was 12:30 and we would only be about five minutes late when we arrived at the Trade Mart. Shortly thereafter the first shot went off, and it sounded to me as if it were a firecracker. I noticed then that the president moved quite far to his left after the shot from the extreme right-hand side where he had been sitting. There was a second shot and Governor Connally disappeared from sight and then there was a third shot which took off the

top of the president's head and had the sickening sound of a grapefruit splattering against the side of a wall. The total time between the first and third shots was about five or six seconds. My first impression was that the shots came from the right and overhead, but I also had a fleeting impression that the noise appeared to come from the front in the area of the triple overpass. This may have resulted from my feeling, when I looked forward toward the overpass, that we might have ridden into an ambush."[57]

When we read this statement by Dave Powers, we must remember that he was in the motorcade and very close to the attack. Of course, this is just his recollection, but he, like many of the other witnesses to this event, gave the same time span for the shots as five to six seconds, which of course is far too short of a time period for there to have been a lone shooter, (Also lets not forget the 1.6 second time frame between the first shot that hit the president in the throat, and the next one which struck the governor, that too was an impossibility for one shooter).

In further analysis of the possible shooter locations mentioned by Powers, we must reflect back on his observations. He stated, "My first impression was that the shots came from the right and overhead." The area he is mentioning is the grassy knoll that was to the right of the motorcade and higher than the street level. It was this perfect shooting position that Powers designates as the source of the rifle fire. You can see in the next picture that the knoll is much higher than the street level. Also, you have the fence line for cover, along with the trees and the bushes, which were used to conceal the shooters.

57 Warren Commission, Testimony of Dave Powers, 1964.

View from across Elm Street. Photo Credit: Author.

Also notice that Dave Powers used the term "ambush." He felt that they had driven into an ambush, and it seems that his statement was very much in line with the true facts. The president was killed by an ambush, one of the oldest military-style assaults. Everyone who has served in the military is familiar with the basic ambush tactic, and so were the assassins, apparently.

Looking down from the triple overpass. Photo Credit: Author

Arnold Rowland

He was one of the witnesses who saw activity in the School Book Depository that day. He stated that fifteen minutes before the president's motorcade arrived, he observed a dark-skinned man, possibly of Latin descent, standing in a window in the Book Depository with what appeared to be a rifle. This was the same window that was later identified as the shooter's nest. When Roland contacted the FBI to give them a full statement later that day, he was told that what he saw would have no bearing on the investigation. Other witnesses had observed the windows of the School Book Depository as well, and they attempted to give their statements to the police, but neither they nor the FBI appeared to be interested.

Tony Henderson

Tony Henderson was waiting for the motorcade to arrive when she observed two men of Latin descent standing in one of the easternmost windows of the sixth floor in the Book Depository. Boy, there sure seemed to be a lot of dark-skinned

Latin men hanging around inside a building that would later produce only one lone white male as a suspect.

Beverly Oliver

Some of the best witnesses were the people standing on the street and directly across from the motorcade. Beverly Oliver was one such witness; she said she observed a man shoot the president from behind the wooden fence on Elm Street. Miss Oliver gave some of the best eyewitness testimony of the president's wounds and of the activity inside the presidential limo. She stated she clearly saw the back of President Kennedy's head fall off after the fatal shot; she further said she will go to her grave believing that she saw the man who fired that fatal shot from behind the wall on the grassy knoll. Oliver said she was filming the incident with her 8mm camera, which is why she got such a graphic look at the president's head injuries. She claimed that an FBI agent called her the next day at her work and asked her for the tape she had made the day before. The agent told her he would return the tape in ten days, but that was the last time she ever saw the tape.

Maryanne Moorman

Standing next to Beverly Oliver that day in Dallas was a lady named Maryanne Moorman. She was also taking pictures of the motorcade as it was passing by. One picture she managed to take was of the fatal head shot, the instant it happened. In the background of this picture, there appears to be a man firing what could be a rifle at the president. This picture was also used by the media after the shooting and therefore would have been much harder to eliminate than the Beverly Oliver film. The FBI did review it and found it was of no use to their investigation and gave it back to Moorman. This was due to the less than adequate photo technologies of the 1960s, which compared to today's enhancements did not reveal the finer details of the photograph.

But the story does not end there; this picture surfaced again in the middle 1980s after Miss Moorman was contacted by photo analysts researching the case. The analysts had heard Beverly Oliver's story about the man shooting from the grassy knoll area and believed that Maryanne Moorman's picture might contain a photo of this individual. After almost a year of testing by three independent photo analysis firms, they were all able to confirm that the image of an individual now visible on the Mooreman photo could very well be one of the presidential assassins.[58] The photos were enlarged and are pretty amazing. What they show is a man wearing a police uniform, which is very much like a Dallas police officer's uniform of that era, and he is firing a weapon. Included in the photo is a puff of smoke, which was witnessed by Beverly Oliver and several of the railroad workers on the overpass coming out through the trees. This shooter was nicknamed the Badge Man, and it seems pretty clear that this was another possible shooter in front of the president's car. There is a slow motion video of the Orville Nix film circulating online, where you can now see a figure behind the wall where Badge Man was spotted. He is moving before and after the shooting; also notice the hail of blood and brain matter getting thrown back violently right after the head shot: a total impossibility if the shot had originated from behind.[59]

Jean Hill

Jean Hill is one of the most famous of the murder witnesses; she was standing just to the left of the presidential limo when the shots were fired.[60] She clearly saw a shot from the right side of the president's limo; she also took several pictures of the assassination, but all her pictures were confiscated from her by federal agents. Here is a segment from her book, *JFK: The Last Dissenting Witness,* which she coauthored with Bill

---

58 Badge Man, http://www.youtube.com/watch?v=xtOCJplSLf8

59 Nix film in slow motion, http://www.youtube.com/watch?v=XLERm5sKGSY

60 Jean Hill, http://www.youtube.com/watch?v=3g7lVON9kow

Sloan:[61] "On the other side of the street, at the top of a little green mound universally known today as the grassy knoll, Jean Hill had seen an incredible sight—one that no one else among the handful who shared her vantage point that day could see, because all the others were sprawled face down on the ground—and she was transfixed by it. It was the sight that was destined to haunt her for the rest of her life: A muzzle flash, a puff of smoke, and a shadowy figure of a man holding a rifle, barely visible above the wooden fence at the top of the knoll, still in the very act of murdering the president of the United States" (Sloan and Hill 1992, 23).

Was this the same person many of the witnesses saw as well, like Gordon Arnold and all the railroad workers on the overpass? It is simply amazing that with all these witnesses, the Warren Commission simply ignored them all. Jean also states that after the shooting, when she ran up the knoll and went behind the fence, she saw a police officer holding a rifle. Here is additional information from her book: "When she finally managed to reach the wooden barrier and ran behind it, she found herself in a parking lot area.[62] She looked back at the point from which she thought the shots had come and saw a single uniformed policeman whom she did not recognize. The policeman seemed to be guarding something. She noticed what looked like a rifle in the policeman's hand, and something far back in her mind told her to wonder why. None of the other officers she had seen was carrying a rifle. Why should this one be? And why should he be back here behind the fence" (Sloan and Hill 1992, 23). Jean's own internal instincts knew something strange was going on behind that fence, but her bizarre day was not over yet.

Within seconds of encountering the police officer with the rifle, two men calling themselves Secret Service agents

---

61 Sloan, B., and Hill, J. (1992). *JFK: The Last Dissenting Witness.* Gretna, LA: Pelican Publishing Co.

62 We must remember that these witnesses for the most part did not know much about Dealey Plaza, such as the fact that there was a parking lot behind the grassy knoll.

accosted her.[63] “Confused and breathless, Jean whirled away, her eyes frantically combing the plaza in search of either the man she now thought of as the shooter, or the other man she had seen running toward him. Then, without warning, she heard a movement behind her and felt a hand clamp down on her shoulder in a numbing, viselike grip. Secret Service, announced a low authoritative male voice. Where do you think you’re going? I’ve got to catch that man, Jean cried, struggling to free herself, I saw him shoot the president. You’re not going anywhere, the man snapped, you’re coming with me. We want to talk to you” (Sloan and Hill 1992, 26). Were these the same phony agents seen by so many Dallas police officers that day?

Jean’s nightmare continued, as another suspect came up and accosted her as well. This individual began digging around in her pockets and stole the pictures she had been taking of the motorcade. She never saw her pictures again; those photos would have provided a fantastic vantage point of the shooter behind the grassy knoll. Of course, she was lucky all she lost were her pictures. Afterwards, for several months, she was threatened by unknown callers, stressing the fact that she needed to keep her mouth shut about what she saw on November 22nd 1963.

Gordon Arnold

Further collaboration of a grassy knoll shooter came from Gordon Arnold; in November of 1963, Arnold was on leave from the Army and was traveling through Dallas. He had heard about a parade that was coming through downtown Dallas and wanted to get some pictures to send home. He found what he considered a good place to snap some shots by the grassy knoll. He made an attempt to come up behind the

63 We now know of course that the night before, at least one Secret Service agent on the presidential detail, who was partying all night in Fort Worth, reported the loss of his official credentials. We also know that these suspects also encountered two police officers behind the fence, confirming Jean’s story.

knoll but was met there by a man who displayed a badge and told Arnold that he was with the CIA. The man further told Arnold that this area was off limits and that he must leave the area behind the fence. Thinking this to be strange, but having no recourse, Arnold decided to walk around the front of the knoll and come in off the street.[64] [65]

The stairway leading to the grassy knoll. Photo Credit: Author

While he was focusing his 8mm camera, he observed the presidential limo turning from Houston onto Elm. When the motorcade was just about in front of him, he heard a loud shot ring out, which came right past his left ear. Arnold, knowing it was a gunshot, fell to the ground to protect himself. When the smoke cleared, he was approached by a man wearing a police uniform. He said the officer was not wearing a hat like most officers, and his hands were dirty. The man yelled at Arnold, "Were you taking pictures?" Arnold stated he was; the man then pulled his handgun and pointed it right in Arnold's face and demanded the film from

64 Gordon Arnold, http://www.youtube.com/watch?v=Vf3Y3uI6IHo

65 *The Men Who Killed Kennedy* excerpt, http://www.youtube.com/watch?v=PSQdnAcCbXI

his camera. Arnold, now in a complete state of shock and confusion, complied with the man's orders and gave him the film from the camera. This "officer" was also seen by the late Lee Bowers from his position in the railroad tower. As for Gordon Arnold, he left Dallas the next day for his new duty station but would always remember this stressful incident. How could he not?

There is still more startling information that was obtained from the Maryanne Moorman picture. This information confirms Gordon Arnold's story of the shot that came from behind him. After close analysis of the Moorman picture, two other men can be seen in the photo, one just to the left of the shooter location. This man is wearing an army uniform and holding a camera. It turns out to be none other than Gordon Arnold, who confirmed this after seeing the photo of himself.[66] It was now clear to Arnold that at least one of the president's killers was the man wearing the police uniform. As for the other man seen in the photo, it looks to many researchers to be a railroad worker, and in fact Arnold said he had seen this man as well behind the knoll, wearing a yellow worker's hat. This was obviously one of the spotters and points to the fact that this was indeed a well-planned assassination.

Ed Hoffman

Several others also saw this unidentified man in the worker's hat. One of them was Ed Hoffman, a deaf mute who was standing on the freeway overpass as the president's limo approached. He had stopped on the freeway once he realized it was the presidential motorcade coming toward him. He looked up as the motorcade was passing, and something caught his eye over along the fence line. He saw a cloud of smoke rising into the air. He then observed a man wearing dark clothing or a suit come out of the trees, carrying a rifle

---

66 There is a very emotional scene when the researchers show Arnold this picture; it can be seen in the Nigel Turner documentary, *The Men Who Killed Kennedy.*

and walking toward the railroad tracks.[67] This man in the suit met up with the man wearing the worker's hat and a railroad worker's outfit. The railroad worker received the rifle from the shooter, who then walked away in the opposite direction. The man in the hard hat then walked over to a railroad switch box, opened it, and pulled out a tool box. He broke the rifle down and placed it into the tool box. He was last seen by Hoffman walking toward the train station. Hoffman said he did make an attempt to drive to the station, but the men were long gone. He also said that he tried to give his story to the FBI and the Dallas police, but they were not interested.[68] After reading these gripping eyewitness accounts and the gravity of what they profess to have seen, how can anyone ignore them, considering the similarities between all of their statements?

The list of witnesses even includes a US Senator, Ralph Yarborough, who was in the vice president's car. For many years, he still recounted seeing Gordon Arnold jump to the ground after the rifle fire went over his head. He would later tell news reporters that Arnold, who was wearing his uniform, must have had some experience with live ammunition to move that quickly.

---

67 I have long wondered if there were two shooters behind the fence; Hoffman said the man he saw had a suit or dark clothing, and Arnold saw a person in a police uniform, who was also captured in a picture from across the street and seen by the late Lee Bowers as well. Considering the massive damage to the president's head, it is very possible he received two head shots, but of course, we will never be sure of this, because one of the rounds was a hollow point frangible-type bullet, which exploded and destroyed the president's head. But I am fairly certain two shots came from the grassy knoll area. One was the first shot that hit the president in the throat, and the other was the final and fatal head shot.

68 Hoffman's story can also be seen on the Nigel Turner documentary, *The Men Who Killed Kennedy,* or on YouTube by going to http://www.youtube.com/watch?v=veVqYo9I5gg

Carolyn Arnold

Carolyn is a very important witness, because she is someone who saw Lee Oswald in the lunchroom just before the assassination. She said at 12:15 p.m., she was absolutely certain she saw Oswald sitting alone in the lunchroom. She even knew which table he was sitting at and exactly what time it was, because it was the lunch hour. This timing is so important because, according to Arnold Rowland, it was at this exact time he saw a black or dark skinned man with a rifle leaning out of the sixth floor window. He said he thought it was presidential security. If this is true, then it could not have been Oswald in the window; the lone-gunman people just need to face the fact that Oswald was in that lunchroom. He was never in that sniper's nest, because too many people saw him before and after the shooting, including a police officer. He was in that lunchroom, *not* on the sixth floor shooting at the president.

Emmett Hudson

As groundskeeper for the Dealey Plaza area, Hudson was standing on the stairs that lead up behind the grassy knoll. His story is interesting because he claims that the second shot he heard hit the president in the right temple area. He told the following story to the Warren Commission (in his own words, of course, so please excuse the grammar): "Well, there was a young fellow, oh, I would judge his age in his late twenties. He said he had been looking for a place to park ... he finally [had] just taken a place over there in one of them parking lots, and he came on down there and said he worked over there on Industrial [Boulevard], and me and him both just sat down there on those steps. When the motorcade turned off Houston onto Elm, we got up and stood up, me and him both ... and so the first shot rang out and, of course, I didn't realize it was a shot. The motorcade had got further on down Elm. I happened to be looking right at him when that bullet hit him the second shot. It looked like it hit him somewhere along about the ... a little bit behind the ear and a little above the ear. This young fellow that was ... standing there with me ... he says, 'Lay down, mister, somebody is shooting the president.' He was already lying down one way on the sidewalk, so I just laid down over the ground and was resting my arm on the ground. When that third shot rang out ... you could tell that the shot was coming from above and kind of behind"(Benson 1993, 202).[69]

First, Hudson actually saw the bullet strike the president. Clearly, he said he was looking right at him and saw the bullet strike him in the temple area, right behind his ear, which indicates the shot came from the right front. He also said that the shot did come from behind him and above, which makes sense, because the grassy knoll and the fence line were directly behind him at the time. So we have another direct witness whose testimony was ignored by the authorities or was simply not believed. Plus he mentioned an additional shot fired after the head shot.

After this chapter, it is hard to believe the official story, but there is more. The next set of witnesses in chapter 4 are all law enforcement officers, and guess what? Their stories concur with the civilian witnesses as well.

---

69 Benson, M. (1993). *Who's Who in the JFK Assassination: An A-Z Encyclopedia*. New York: Carol Publishing Group.

Chapter 4

Law Enforcement Witnesses

"All truths are easy to understand once they are discovered; the point is to discover them."
—Galileo Galilei

Officer Joe M. Smith

Police officer Joe Smith was riding his motorcycle unit in the presidential motorcade the day of the assassination. After the president was shot and the motorcade sped off, Officer Smith dismounted his motorcycle and ran toward the grassy knoll, where he believed the shots had come from. He was not alone; about a hundred other people joined him, which is clearly visible in news footage that day. As he rounded the top of the knoll, he drew his pistol and confronted a man who was wearing a dark suit. The officer ordered the man to raise his hands, but the man produced a Secret Service badge and stated, "It's okay, I'm Secret Service." This mystery man then disappeared behind the knoll area. Officer Smith did not think much of the incident until he was told that there were no Secret Service agents in that area. As a matter of fact, all of the Secret Service agents were located in the presidential motorcade; at that time, they were all heading for the hospital. Even the Secret Service admits this fact and told the Warren Commission that all the agents were assigned to the motorcade and none were ever on the ground in Dealey Plaza.

Detective De De Hawkins

There were other Dallas police officers who encountered phony Secret Service agents, such as Detective De De Hawkins, who was investigating the rear of the School Book Depository when he encountered two men in business suits. He asked them what they were doing there, and they too produced official Secret Service badges and IDs. Who were these mystery men, and what were they doing at the murder scene?

Dallas Police Sergeant D. V. Harkness

Sergeant Harkness also encountered some fake Secret Service agents in the same location as Hawkins above, behind the Book Depository around 12:35, just after the shooting. He testified to the Warren Commission about his observations that day. When asked by Mr. Berlin, "Was anyone around in the back [of the Texas School Book Depository] when you got there?" Harkness stated, "There were some Secret Service agents there. I didn't get them identified. They told me they were Secret Service" (Corsi 2013, 69).[70]

Deputy Roger Craig

After the assassination, some very strange events began to occur and were observed by several witnesses. One of those witnesses was Deputy Sheriff Roger Craig. Craig said he observed a Latin male being detained by two Dallas police officers on Houston Street. He said he watched as the police officers released the man after talking with him for a few minutes. Shortly after that, Craig was entering the School Book Depository to begin a search of the building along with other officers, when he observed the same Latin male pull up in a Nash Rambler on the Houston Street side of Dealey Plaza. He then observed another man get into the passenger side of the car. This man, the man getting into the Rambler, Craig would later identify as Lee Harvey Oswald. Deputy Craig later observed Oswald while he was being interrogated by Captain Fritz of the Dallas Homicide Department.

According to Craig, Fritz told Oswald that someone had seen him leaving the building in a car, which Craig said upset Oswald very much.[71] Oswald then told Fritz to leave Mrs. Paine out of it, because that was her station wagon he was

---

70 Corsi, J. R. (2013). *Who Really Killed Kennedy?* New York: WND Books.

71 Lane, M. (Producer) (1987). *Two Men in Dallas.*

seen getting into and she had nothing to do with anything (Lane 1987).[72] But after the FBI became involved in the investigation, Fritz later told Craig that he could not have seen Oswald leaving with the Latin male because Oswald, according to the FBI and the Warren Commission, had already left the building prior to the search and caught a bus back home.[73]

Although Captain Fritz would later deny that Deputy Craig was ever in his office or that he had seen Oswald in there, pictures would later appear in the *Dallas News* of Deputy Roger Craig standing in Captain Fritz's office on the day of the assassination. Deputy Craig would later become a real thorn in the side of Captain Fritz's investigation when he began to criticize the Dallas police for covering up the material facts of the case.[74]

Deputy Roger Craig also became a star witness in the years that followed the death of President Kennedy. His stories appeared in print and also on videos such as Mark Lane's *Two Men in Dallas,* which is a riveting interview with Deputy Craig in the 1970s. Deputy Craig was also in the School Depository when the rifle was found. Yes, he was right there with Deputy Seymour Weitzman on the sixth floor when a German Mauser was located. Craig said he saw the word "Mauser" stamped right on the barrel, and Weitzman later testified to this fact, both verbally and in a sworn affidavit (Fiester 2012). According to Fiester, "Wiseman described the rifle with specific details, including the clip was locked on the underside of the receiver and the rear portion of the bolt was worn. Normally, once the last round

---

72 Interesting how Oswald filled in the blanks, because Fritz never said it was a station wagon; those were Oswald's words. If this is true, then Oswald may have left in this vehicle; if so, that sheds new light on some of these details surrounding the assassination. Please see the documentary, *Two Men in Dallas.*

73 Of course, keep in mind now that no one saw Oswald leave the depository, so no one can be certain of all his movements; therefore, it could be just as likely that Oswald did get that ride from the Latin male, as Craig described.

74 Roger Craig, http://www.youtube.com/watch?v=EtGz__wpDUI

of ammunition is chambered, the clip falls from a weapon. To describe the malfunctioning clip and other details of the rifle without actually handling it would be unlikely. Wiseman's contemporaneous statements directly conflict with later accounts of the rifle being collected by Day" (Fiester 2012, 41) (the reference is to Lieutenant Day of the Dallas police).

It was clear Craig knew too much, too much of the truth, and he also started to talk too much; he was even out helping other researchers. Finally, to make matters worse, he was writing his own manuscript for a book he was planning to publish.[75] Shortly after he began work on his book, there were several attempts on his life. His car was forced off the road and he was nearly killed. He was also shot at on several occasions, once being struck in the ear while he was walking across a street. A few years after these incidents, Craig was found shot to death; the murder weapon was reportedly a rifle. He suffered a gunshot wound to the chest, and the authorities ruled it a suicide. The story of Roger Craig is a real tragedy; he was a true American and an excellent police officer. His life only went downhill after he attempted to reveal the truth about the murder of President Kennedy; may he rest in peace.

Police Officer Bobby Hargis

Police Officer Bobby Hargis was riding to the left rear of the president's limo and gave some short but very powerful statements regarding his observations, once again clearly supporting the evidence of at least another shooter firing from in front of the vehicle.

---

[75] Craig, R. (1971). *When They Kill a President.* Self-published.

Here are his statements:

The testimony of Bobby W. Hargis was taken at 3:20 p.m., on April 8, 1964, in the office of the US Attorney, 301 Post Office Building, Bryan and Ervay Streets, Dallas, Texas, by Mr. Samuel A. Stern, assistant counsel of the President's Commission.

Mr. STERN: Will you describe what occurred or what you observed as the limousine turned into Elm Street?

Mr. HARGIS: Well, at the time that the limousine turned left on Elm, I was staying pretty well right up with the car. Sometimes on Elm we get right up next to it on account of the crowd, but the crowd was out down here at the triple underpass, so I was next to Mrs. Kennedy when I heard the first shot, and at that time the president bent over, and Governor Connally turned around. He was sitting directly in front of him, and [sic] a real shocked and surprised expression on his face.

According to this statement, the officer said clearly that the president was hit first and bent over; this was obviously the shot that hit him in the throat from the front. The officer further said that the governor was *not* hit yet, and Connally actually turned around in his seat, which can clearly be seen in the film of the assassination; this is very obvious in the film. You can see that the president was hit first, grabbing at his throat, thereby destroying the ridiculous and obscene theory of the magic bullet.[76]

Mr. STERN: Did something happen to you, personally, in connection with the shot you have just described?

Mr. HARGIS: You mean about the blood hitting—

Mr. STERN: Yes.

Mr. HARGIS: Yes; when President Kennedy straightened back up in the car, the bullet hit him in the head, the one that killed him, and it seemed like his head exploded, and I was splattered with blood and brain, and kind of bloody water. It wasn't really blood. And at that time the presidential car slowed down. I heard somebody say, "Get going."

Mr. STERN: Just a minute. Do you recall your impression at the time regarding the source of the shots?

Mr. HARGIS: Well, at the time it sounded like the shots were right next to me. There wasn't any way in the world I could tell where they were coming from, but at the time there was something in my head that said that they probably could have been coming from the railroad overpass, because I thought since I had got splattered, with blood— I was just a little back and left of— Just a little bit back and left of Mrs. Kennedy, but I didn't know. I had a feeling that it might have been from the

---

76 The governor and his wife made many statements confirming these facts. In 1992, they appeared on *The Larry King Show* (you can find it on YouTube). These two people, who were in the car, both stated the so-called magic bullet was simply a joke; they told Larry, "We were there, we know what we saw." Kennedy was hit first and the governor was hit a second later.

Texas Book Depository, and these two places were the primary places that he could have been shot from.[77]

(Warren Commission, Testimony of Bobby Hargis, 1964)

Here is an officer with nearly ten years of service who voiced his opinion on where he felt the shots came from. He stated the shot came from the front, clearly because of where the blood and brain matter went after the shot struck the president. You have to love the people who want us to believe the head shot came from behind; they want us to believe that the laws of physics failed to operate in Dealey Plaza.

Also, look at the last statement: after clearly stating that he thought the shots came from the front, he says that he had the feeling the shot might have come from the Book Depository? What is that? It is what we call an incoherent statement, or an alteration of his statement. I have read thousands of testimonies in my lifetime and can tell when statements are incoherent. This is one of those cases; that last sentence is not consistent with the rest of that statement, which may indicate once again that the commission altered his statement. He never thought of the Book Depository as a location of the shot, because he clearly says so in his next line of statements listed here:

Mr. STERN: You were clear that the sounds were sounds of shots?

Mr. HARGIS: Yes, sir. I knew they were shots.

Mr. STERN: All right, what did you do then? You say you parked your motorcycle?

---

77 Why he even mentions the Book Depository is strange, when he already stated that he was splattered with blood and debris, which came across the limo from right to left and to the rear; the Book Depository was way behind him. But let us not forget how many testimonies were altered by the Warren Commission in order to fulfill their objectives.

Mr. HARGIS: Yes, uh huh—

Mr. STERN: Where?

Mr. HARGIS: It was to the left-hand side of the street from, south side of Elm Street.

Mr. STERN: And then what did you [sic}—

Mr. HARGIS: I ran across the street looking over toward the railroad overpass, and I remembered seeing people scattering and running, and then I looked.

Mr. STERN: People on the overpass?

Mr. HARGIS: Yes, people that were there to see the president I guess. They were taking pictures and things. It was kind of a confused crowd. I don't know whether they were trying to hide or see what was happening or what, and then I looked over to the Texas School Book Depository Building, and no one that was standing at the base of the building was— seemed to be looking up at the building or anything like they knew where the shots were coming from so—

Mr. STERN: How about the people on the incline on the north side of Elm Street? Do you recall their behavior?

Mr. HARGIS: Yes; I remember a man holding a child fell to the ground and covered his child with his body, and people running everywhere, trying to get out of there, I guess, and they were about as confused as to where the shots were coming from as everyone else was.

(Warren Commission, Testimony of Bobby Hargis, 1964)

Consequently then, it seems very clear that Police Officer Hargis felt that the shots came from in front of him and not from behind the motorcade; he is just another in the long line of witnesses who said that some of the shots came from the fence line or grassy knoll area.

Deputy Seymour Weitzman

Deputy Constable Seymour Weitzman was on scene the day of the president's murder. Just after the attack, Weitzman took action by running in front of the crowds heading up the grassy knoll. He arrived at the top by scaling the fence. He was the first witness to make it up the knoll and encountered a railroad worker behind the fence. Weitzman told the commission, "I asked the yardman if he had seen or heard anything during the passing of the president. He said he thought he saw somebody throw something through the bush."[78]

Deputy Weitzman is actually one of the most important witnesses that the Warren Commission had available to them, so how did they use this valuable witness? They completely disregarded his statements. He was a law enforcement officer with a spotless career; what a gift in any investigation, but the commission ignored most of his information. He was interviewed by Joseph Ball, one of the counselors for the Warren Commission. Here is a short synopsis of the interview, which brought many other facts to light as well:

---

78 According to Mark Lane, "The commission would appear to have been informed about a most important eyewitness to the event: a railroad employee who thought the shots came from the area behind the fence and who thought he saw a man throw something into the bushes when the president's car had passed. However, just after Weitzman gave that information, commission counsel said, 'I think that's all,' and Weitzman was dismissed. He was not asked for the name or description of the employee. He was not asked if he looked into the bushes or if he found anything there. Nothing in the twenty-six volumes of evidence or in the report indicates that the commission or its investigators made any effort to locate or identify the railroad employee" (Lane 1966, 35).

THE TESTIMONY OF SEYMOUR WEITZMAN WAS TAKEN AT 2:15 P.M., ON APRIL 1, 1964, IN THE OFFICE OF THE US ATTORNEY, 301 POST OFFICE BUILDING, BRYAN AND ERVAY STREETS, DALLAS, TEXAS, BY MR. JOSEPH A. BALL, ASSISTANT COUNSEL OF THE PRESIDENT'S COMMISSION.

Mr. BALL: How many shots did you hear?

Mr. WEITZMAN: Three distinct shots.

Mr. BALL: How were they spaced?

Mr. WEITZMAN: First one, then the second two seemed to be simultaneously.

Mr. BALL: You mean the first and then there was a pause?

Mr. WEITZMAN: There was a little period in between the second and third shot.

Mr. BALL: What was the longest, between the first and second or the second and third shot; which had the longest time lapse in there?

Mr. WEITZMAN: Between the first and second shot.

What is so important about the above exchange is that Deputy Weitzman's statements totally concur with observations made by Lee Bowers and several other witnesses, who say they heard two of the shots come right on top of each other. So what comes to your mind at this point? How could Oswald (or any lone gunman) fire back-to-back shots in less than a split-second with a bolt-action rifle? Well, of course, they couldn't; the only rifle that shoots that quickly is a semiautomatic; this was not the rifle recovered by the Dallas police. So we have another simple fact that blows the whole case of the lone gunman out of the water. There were two shots—right on top of each other—this means a second gunman.

Mr. BALL: What did you notice in the railroad yards?

Mr. WEITZMAN: We noticed numerous kinds of footprints that did not make sense, because they were going different directions.

Mr. BALL: Were there other people there besides you?

Mr. WEITZMAN: Yes, sir; other officers, Secret Service as well, and somebody stated, there was something red in the street, and I went back over the wall and somebody brought me a piece of what he thought to be a firecracker, and it turned out to be, I believe, I wouldn't quote this, but I turned it over to one of the Secret Service men, and I told them it should go to the lab because it looked to me like human bone. I later found out it was supposedly a portion of the president's skull.

Mr. BALL: Which you picked up off the street?

Mr. WEITZMAN: Yes.

Mr. BALL: What part of the street did you pick this up?

Mr. WEITZMAN: As the president's car was going off, it would be on the left-hand side of the street. It would be the—

Mr. BALL: The left-hand side facing—

Mr. WEITZMAN: That would be the south side of the street.

Mr. BALL: It was on the south side of the street. Was it in the street?

Mr. WEITZMAN: It was in the street itself.

Mr. BALL: On the pavement?

Mr. WEITZMAN: Yes, sir.

Mr. BALL: Anywhere near the curb?

Mr. WEITZMAN: Approximately, oh, I would say eight to twelve inches from the curb, something like that.

(Warren Commission, Testimony of Seymour Weitzman 1964).

View of Dealey Park from Elm Street. Photo Credit: Author

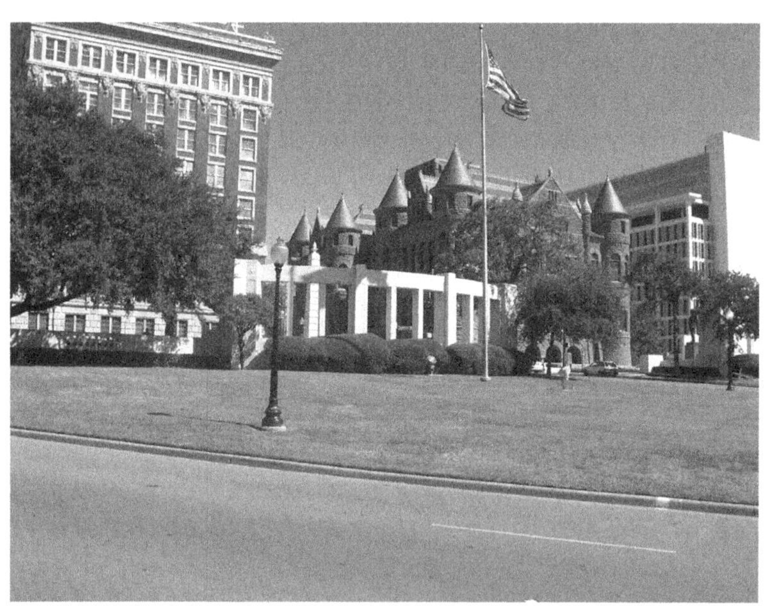

Well, first let's consider several facts here. For one, the deputy said that there were numerous footprints all over behind the fence right after the shooting. Whose were they? Why would there be footprints in the area of a probable shooter, because a shooter was seen in plain sight right in that location by at least three people, including Lee Bowers in the railroad tower. But the most incredible part of this testimony was this statement:

Mr. BALL: Were there other people there besides you?

Mr. WEITZMAN: Yes, sir; other officers, Secret Service as well.

This is stunning, considering that the agency itself states that there were no Secret Service personnel on the ground in Dallas or in Dealey Plaza. This fact was verified by several Secret Service commanding officers, one being Forest Sorrels, who was the special agent in charge in Dallas. He told several people, including the Warren Commission, that all the agents were riding in the motorcade. The Secret Service themselves stated that at no time were there any agents on the ground in Dealey Plaza, until Forest Sorrels returned from the hospital, much later in the afternoon. It should be noted that many others, as we have seen, also stated that they encountered imposter agents behind the fence, showing them official badges and IDs. So how could we not consider this to be vitally important information? Also, this statement was taken four and a half months after the murder, and the Warren Commission knew very well on November 22 that there were no agents on the ground in Dealey Plaza. So why did they not question the officer further? Why would they not be concerned about imposters identifying themselves as Secret Service agents at the scene of the assassination? Could it be they just did not care, or maybe they had their marching orders in hand from the Oval Office: to conclude that it was Oswald alone (the patsy) who killed President Kennedy.

Moreover, another very important aspect of the interview of Deputy Weitzman was that he stated that he turned over a piece of the president's head that he picked up from the street and gave it to the Secret Service. Weitzman stated that he found the piece of bone on the south curb, well behind where the limo was located, which would clearly indicate that the shot could not have come from the rear. If this were true, any brain and blood matter or skull fragments would have been found in front of the vehicle, having been blasted out in a forward direction, away from the so-called sniper's nest.

Next we come to the recovery of the rifle on the sixth floor of the Texas School Book Depository. It is widely known among assassination researchers that the first rifle found was not the so-called Oswald rifle, but it was in fact a German-made weapon, as stated here by Deputy Weitzman:

Mr. BALL: In the statement that you made to the Dallas Police Department that afternoon, you referred to the rifle as a 7.65 Mauser bolt action?

Mr. WEITZMAN: In a glance, that's what it looked like.

Mr. BALL: That's what it looked like? Did you say that or someone else say that?

Mr. WEITZMAN: No, I said that. I thought it was one.

Mr. BALL: Are you fairly familiar with rifles?

Mr. WEITZMAN: Fairly familiar, because I was in the sporting goods business awhile.

Mr. BALL: In this statement, it says Captain Fritz took charge of the rifle and ejected one live round from the chamber.

Mr. WEITZMAN: Yes, sir.

Mr. BALL: He did eject one live round?

Mr. WEITZMAN: Yes, sir; he did eject one live round, one live round, yes, sir. You said remove anything from the rifle; I was not considering that a shell.

Mr. BALL: I understand that. Now, in your statement to the Federal Bureau of Investigation, you gave a description of the rifle, how it looked.

Mr. WEITZMAN: I said it was a Mauser-type action, didn't I?

Mr. BALL: Mauser bolt action.

(Warren Commission, Testimony of Seymour Weitzman, 1964)

Okay, so was it a Mauser? It does appear so. We will also see that other police officers that day claimed that they saw the word "Mauser" stamped right on the barrel. I wonder what happened to the Mauser? By the way, a German Mauser is a highly accurate weapon, just the opposite of that old World War II Italian Mannlicher-Carcano, which was a horrible weapon the Italians called the "humane weapon." This is because they claim you could not hit anything with it. So then, is this the rifle that the presidential assassin chose to use to commit the crime of the century? Not to mention he paid only a few dollars for it, and the scope was misaligned as well (the scope, by the way, was worth around $2.00).[79] Also consider that Oswald could have walked into any gun store in Texas at that time and purchased a really nice weapon without even giving his name. This was legal at that time. He could have purchased a Remington or a Browning semiautomatic. Why would an assassin, especially one the Warren Commission said was so well trained, use an old, outdated bolt-action rifle when so many other quality weapons were available?

79 It should be noted that Oswald never did admit to owning this rifle; he did admit to owning a pistol, but not the rifle. He also claimed, and many researchers agree, that the backyard photos had been faked.

Another very interesting observation made by Deputy Weitzman was that the weapon was found with a round still in the chamber. This would mean that the shooter, after seeing his final shot blow off the best part of the president's head, took the time to eject that shell with the bolt and push it forward to install another live round, which was found in the chamber. Well, I have to say, that is simply not believable. The shooter had to have known he would never get off another shot at that point, with the car speeding away. This indicates to me that the weapon was planted at the scene; this rifle may not have even been used that day at all. No one in their right mind would have ejected and reloaded another round at that point; he would have taken off as fast as possible and made his escape. Also, the empty shell casings were also found too close together on the floor.[80] Anyone who has ever fired such a weapon knows that when those shells are ejected, they go just about anywhere they want, and certainly not lined up in a straight line.

As a final consideration, how was it possible for Oswald to have been on the sixth floor, considering the fact he was seen in the lunchroom at the time of the shooting by several people?[81] Oswald was a patsy, just like he stated to the press; why in the world would he use the word "patsy"? That's a pretty strange word to use in that situation; of course, he was insinuating that he had been set up by someone. He would be the only political assassin I can remember who would not admit wholeheartedly that he had committed the shooting. Political assassins almost always admit to their deeds; that's because they are fanatical to their causes. Why would they conceal their acts? They are usually proud of themselves for having committed their crimes; besides, Oswald had no motive. I have studied and taught criminology for years, and

---

80 Roger Craig witnessed this before the shells were moved and photographed.

81 I agree with many researchers that if any rounds were fired from the Book Depository and hit their intended target, they could have also come from the west side of the building, not the east side of the building, or possibly below the sixth floor; in my opinion, that sniper's nest was staged. Oswald was never there, and that is certain in my mind, but it seems the Oswald rifle was there and was possibly used in the assassination.

most experts in my field agree: almost all suspects have a motive for their crime (unless they are mentally ill). If you can think of a motive for Oswald, let me know (and I don't want to hear that he was some idiot just trying to make a name for himself by killing the president, or that he was some loser who was making up for his inadequacies in life). Ridiculous, simply ridiculous, I mean a real motive.

Agent George Hickey

Agent Hickey was riding in the follow-up car behind the presidential limo; he was the agent seen standing up in the car with the AR-15 rifle. He told the Warren Commission that he heard two of the shots, which came right on top of each other, much like other witnesses. Here is his statement: "I stood up and looked to my right and rear in an attempt to identify it. Nothing caught my attention except people shouting and cheering ... [When Kennedy] was almost sitting erect, I heard two more reports, which I thought were shots and appeared to me completely different in sound [82] than the first report and were in rapid succession. [83] There seemed to be practically no time element between them ... the last shot seemed to hit his head and cause a noise at the point of impact, which made him fall forward and to his left"[84] (Benson 1993, 183).

---

[82] This was because these shots came from in front of the vehicle and from a different location than the first shot he heard. This is the same sound heard by Holland, the railroad supervisor, who clearly noted the difference between the sounds of the shots he said came from behind, and the shot he heard from the grassy knoll.

[83] Once again, we have another witness who heard two shots right on top of each other, and this one was a law enforcement officer who was at ground level right behind the limo; clearly this is another solid witness.

[84] Wow, how much more evidence do we need? First, he hears shots in rapid fire, and then he sees the president hit by this rapid fire of bullets.

Agent Clint Hill

Of course, most people know that Agent Hill was the Secret Service agent who is seen running to the president's limo as it began to speed away. The point I want to bring out here is his initial statement to authorities on what he had seen that day; clearly Agent Hill had possibly the best look at President Kennedy's wounds, more so than any other law enforcement officer that day.

In referring to previous research, Jesse Ventura, Dick Russell, and David Wayne, in their recent book, *They Killed Our President* (2013), provided Hill's initial statement to authorities: "The right rear portion of his head was missing. It was lying in the rear seat of the car. His brain was exposed. There was blood and bits of brain all over the entire rear portion of the car. Mrs. Kennedy was completely covered in blood. There was so much blood you could not tell if there had been any other wound or not, except for the large gaping wound in the right rear portion of the head (Ventura, Russell, and Wayne 2013, 8).

So there you have it. Agent Hill stated clearly that the rear of the president's head was missing; it had fallen off into the back seat, blown out by that shot from the grassy knoll. Remember, the Warren Commission wanted us to believe that the wound to the rear of the president's head was fired by Oswald and left only a very small entrance wound. But based on Hill's testimony above, we see that the destruction described by the agent could not have been made by an old fully jacketed military round fired from the rear; it could not have happened that way. If there was a head shot from the rear, it would have left a much smaller hole in the rear of the president's head. The problem in determining if there was a second head shot to the rear of the head is the shot from the right side obliterated the rear of the president's head, thereby eliminating any evidence of this other potential wound. Also consider that there are so many fraudulent autopsy photos and x-rays out there, that it is difficult to trust the majority of them or to use them to determine if any evidence existed for a second head shot.

Agent Glenn Bennett

Agent Glenn Bennett was also riding in the follow-up car behind the president. Like many of the agents, he saw something opposite of the official story; many have never heard of him or read his statement. He told the Warren Commission, "I looked at the back of the president. I heard another firecracker noise and saw the shot hit the president about four inches down from the right shoulder" (Benson 1993, 37). It should be noted that where the agent saw the bullet strike the president is exactly where we find the hole on his shirt and suit coat that he was wearing that day. The fictitious story that the shot came through his throat from behind is disproven based on the evidence and the overwhelming eyewitness statements.[85]

Robert Bouck

Bouck was a government employee of the Protective Research Section of the Treasury Department who reportedly signed a receipt that stated, "One receipt from the FBI for a missile removed during the examination of the body" (Benson 1993, 47). This is incredible information, because it backs up the statements made by FBI Special Agents Francis O'Neil and James Sibert, who were both there during the president's autopsy. They claim that a bullet was, in fact, removed from the body. That bullet has never been seen again. It was never in the Warren Report; this is why Robert Bouck is

---

[85] The late President Ford, who served on the Warren Commission, really did the investigation a total injustice by pushing this wound up several inches in order to support the magic bullet. Here is a YouTube video of FBI Agent James Sibert making a statement about Ford's obstruction of justice: http://www.youtube.com/watch?v=GDNZBfPkbPk

such a powerful witness, having signed that receipt for the projectile, which is now MIA.[86]

Agent Paul Landis

Landis was another Secret Service agent who was in the follow-up car and believed that the shots were coming from in front of the motorcade. Landis told the Warren Commission that he felt that the shots were coming from the right front, and he was certain that the head shot did come from the right-hand side of the road.

Agent Roy Kellerman

Kellerman, Special Agent in Charge of the White House detail, was riding in the limo in the front seat. He is another very important law enforcement witness, because according to his eyewitness statement, he said he heard the president cry out, "My God, I am hit," and this was long before Governor John Connally was even shot. This is a critical point indeed, because it proves there were at least two gunmen. Also a point brought out by Benson (1993);[87] according to some investigators the president was most likely hit by a ricochet (or, in my opinion, received the wound to his back first before he was hit in the throat; this is obvious because the shot that hit him in the throat, entering near his neck tie, would have prevented him from speaking at that point).

According to Ventura, Russell, and Wayne (2013), Agent Kellerman told the Warren Commission that he felt they had driven into an ambush and were taking fire from all sides. (This sounds like Dave Powers's testimony; he too referred to driving into an ambush.) The authors go on to point out that

---

86 Why is it missing? Well, it seems obvious that the bullet would not have forensically matched the Oswald rifle, so it had to disappear; it's as simple as that.

87 Benson, M. (1993). *Who's Who in the JFK Assassination: An A-Z Encyclopedia*. New York: Carol Publishing Group.

Kellerman would not be intimidated by the commission; he stated, "There had to be more than three shots, gentlemen" (Ventura, Russell, and Wayne 2013, 37).

Agent Francis O'Neil

Agent O'Neil was one of two FBI officials who were present during the president's autopsy. O'Neil made some critical notes during the procedure; he believed there appeared to have been surgery to the head prior to the president's autopsy. David Lifton, in his book and documentary, *Best Evidence,* made some incredible statements regarding this fact. Also, O'Neil made note that there was a missile—a bullet—removed from the president's body. This missile has never been located and could prove not only that there was a second shooter but many other facts as well, which is why I am sure it remains missing. Think about this: if it had been from the Oswald rifle, it would have shown up in the Warren Report to bolster their case. Am I correct?

Agent James Sibert

Sibert was the second FBI agent at the autopsy of the president, as mentioned above; it was these agents who observed what they considered to be surgery to the president's skull and also the removal of a bullet from the body of the president.[88] Their detailed report stands as one of the only "unaltered" pieces of evidence we have pertaining to that botched, inept, and pitiful autopsy.

Agent Vincent Drain

FBI Agent Vincent Drain was a very important witness in this case. Agent Drain was responsible for transporting

---

88 Keep in mind that when the president left Parkland, he still had his brain, most of it, but as Paul O'Connor stated, when they started the autopsy, 90 percent of his brain was missing; this can be verified because it was removed during the surgery to the head reported by the FBI agents in their report of the autopsy.

the rifle that was recovered by the Dallas police to FBI headquarters in Washington, but there is more to his story (of course). Henry Hurt, the author of *Reasonable Doubt*, interviewed Agent Drain and Lieutenant Day regarding a fingerprint found on the rifle. Most researchers believe that there were no prints found on that rifle, and the facts point to this conclusion. With regards to that fingerprint, though, Lieutenant Day stated that before Drain departed for Washington, he told the agent that he had found a print on the rifle [89] and showed Drain where it was located. According to Hurt, Drain flatly disputes this, claiming that Day never showed him any such print. He said, "I just don't believe there was ever a print." He noted that there was increasing pressure on the Dallas police to build a case against Oswald. Asked by Hurt to explain what might have happened, Drain stated, "All I can figure is that it [Oswald's print] was some sort of cushion, because they were getting a lot of heat by Sunday night; you could take the print off of Oswald's card and put it on the rifle. Something like that happened" (Hurt 1985, 109).[90] It should further be noted that the FBI sent the rifle back to Dallas, advising that they could not find any fingerprints on it.[91] Further, according to Fiester (2012), the print was not even on the surface but was buried underneath the stock of the rifle; the FBI report on Day's location of the print is extremely detailed, and Day explains in this report that he pretty much tore the rifle down to get to it, having removed the wooden stock to find it. Meaning, of course, this was a very old print, located on the bottom part of the barrel and was not part of the prints located the day of the assassination (Fiester 2012, 31).

These are just a handful of the witnesses and the leads that the Warren Commission and the FBI failed to follow up

---

89 If this truly was the case, then why in the world were they asking the FBI to search for a print, if they already had located one? This makes no sense at all, like most of the evidence in this investigation presented by the Warren Commission.

90 Hurt, H. (1985). *Reasonable Doubt: An Investigation into the Assassination of John F. Kennedy*. New York: Henry Holt.

91 Oswald's rifle, http://www.youtube.com/watch?v=P2W_-ID8RMI

on. Almost none of the information you just read had any bearing on their investigation, and the few items that were used were altered to fit the lone gunman firing from behind. Think about the mysterious Latin men who were seen all around the Book Depository windows by eyewitnesses, including Deputy Roger Craig. Also, what about the men who were seen behind the fence on the grassy knoll? They were observed by Gordon Arnold, Ed Hoffman, Lee Bowers, Jean Hill, Maryanne Moorman, Beverly Oliver, and more. Of the hundreds of witnesses that day, only a very small portion were ever questioned by investigators. It was clear from the start that the Warren Commission, the Dallas police, the Secret Service, and the FBI did not want the truth to surface in this case; even the testimony of police officers was ignored, and they were told not to worry about what they had seen. The investigation was a complete sham; we lost our president to a major conspiracy that day in Dallas, and America has never been the same. As Jesse Ventura always says, "Wake up."

Chapter 5

The Magic Bullet Theory

"Facts do not cease to exist because they are ignored."
—Aldous Huxley

The job of the Warren Commission was made clear to them from the very start: they were to conclude that one man, Lee Harvey Oswald, had fired three shots from behind the president's car, killing him in the process. What they were forced to come up with to make this all fit together was perhaps the biggest lie ever concocted, up to that time.[92]

The magic-bullet or single-bullet theory states that one bullet caused seven wounds to President Kennedy and Governor Connally, breaking through two dense bones, and came out nearly perfect (or pristine, which is the term used by many to describe it). The bullet actually had very little lead missing from it (around two grams) and was reported not to have had any blood or tissue attached to it; this is strange in itself. Arlen Specter, the long-serving senator from Pennsylvania, was an attorney for the Warren Commission and came up with the magic-bullet theory. The path of the bullet proposed by Specter was simply ludicrous and is still considered a joke by most ballistic experts and medical examiners, including Cyril Harrison Wecht, a world-renowned forensic pathologist who has studied the assassination for decades. [93]

---

92 I say "up until that time," because if you study the 911 Commission report, as Jim Marrs did, you may believe that is an even bigger lie … at least in his opinion, but we won't go there now. Marrs, J. (2006). *The terror conspiracy: deception, 9/11, and the loss of liberty.* New York, NY: Disinformation

93 Dr. Wecht was one of nine forensic pathologists who served on a panel for the House Select Committee on Assassinations in the late 1970s which reopened the assassinations of JFK and MLK.

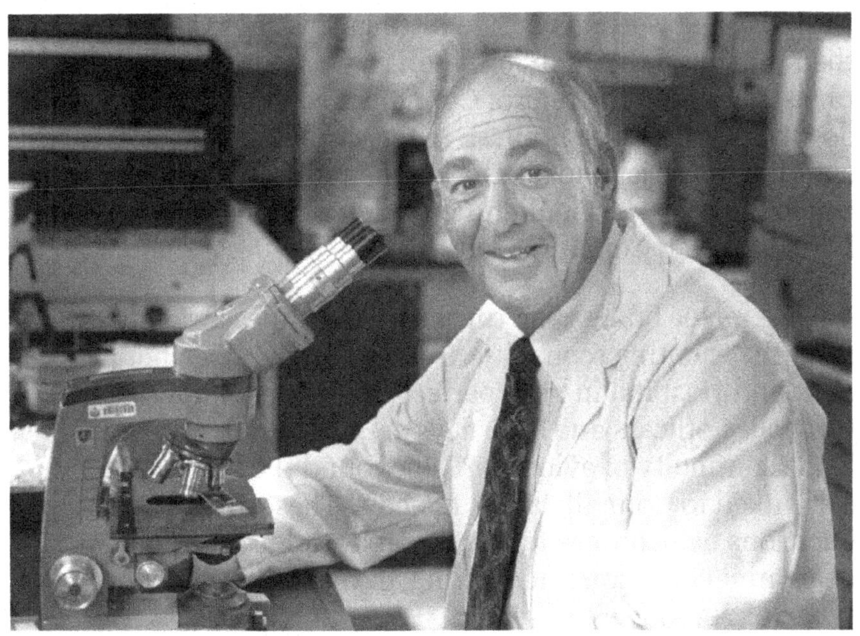

Dr. Wecht became an expert on this case when he was brought in on the House Select Committee on Assassinations in the late 70's, a powerful critic of the Warren Commission's *lone gunman* theory he penned his own book in the 90's titled *Cause of Death*. In this book Dr. Wecht brings out his logical, medical, and expert opinions regarding the Commission's findings and what he really believes occurred, and did not occur, that dark day in Dallas. Based on hard forensic evidence, and the physical sciences, which were lacking in the official WC report, Dr. Wecht makes the case that the magic bullet theory, which is the cornerstone of the lone gunmen scenario, was simply impossible. He was asked by the Select Committee "Is it your opinion that this bullet could not have caused all the wounds to President Kennedy and Governor Connally? He then replied to the Committee in his testimony , "Based upon the findings in this case, it is my opinion that no bullet could have caused all these wounds" (Wecht 1993 p. 45)

Here is the theory set forth by Specter: the bullet entered the president's back on a downward trajectory and then changed direction, exiting through his throat. Then the bullet paused for 1.6 seconds before hitting Governor Connally and then turning right, then left, then right again. After all these turns, it entered the rear of Connally's right armpit and went downward through his chest. Afterward, it took a right turn, entering his wrist and shattering the radius bone before it exited his wrist. The bullet then made a dramatic U-turn and buried itself in Connally's left thigh.

The magic bullet then turned up five miles away from the shooting scene; it was found on the stretcher at Parkland Hospital in near perfect condition. I know what you police officers and attorneys are all thinking: Where is the continuity of evidence? Who found the bullet? How is it linked to Connally and Kennedy? These are all good questions, which were totally ignored. Not to mention its near-mint condition after hitting all those bones at a probable speed of 2,500 feet per second.[94]

Now what I just described is not a script from a science fiction movie, it is the actual conclusion set forth by Specter and the Warren Commission regarding the wounds to President Kennedy and Governor Connally. There are so many holes in this theory that it is hard to believe any logical person would consider it; it was simply ridiculous. But what most people do not know is that in 1964, there were dissenters on the Warren Commission. For one, Senator Richard Russell, who was reportedly hesitant about even signing his name to the report. He wanted to include a footnote recording his dissent in the final version of the report but was overruled by Earl Warren. Senator Russell actually thought there may have been a conspiracy to cover

---

94 Warren Report p. 10–11. Also, let's take into account that even if they could prove that the bullet came from the so-called Oswald rifle, it does not prove that it was in fact the murder weapon. My opinion is that this weapon could have been fired prior to the assassination and the bullets retrieved. This could be why it was in perfect condition (or it could have come from the president's back wound, which had no exit point).

up the facts. He later stated publicly, "We have not been told the truth about Oswald by federal agencies."[95]

The other dissenter in the Warren Commission was Congressman Hale Boggs. Boggs, who had publicly voiced his doubts about the single-bullet theory, accused the FBI of tapping his telephone and publicly denounced the bureau's "Gestapo tactics." Congressman Boggs would later disappear while on a flight through Alaska; he was never seen again.

There is very clear and hard evidence available to tear apart the single-bullet theory, and over the years, many researchers have disproven it. Some of this evidence involves the bullet fragments that were removed from Governor Connally. The fragments removed from his body and those that can be seen through his x-rays clearly outweigh the missing lead from the pristine bullet found on the stretcher at Parkland Hospital (and not by a little: by a lot).

Dr. Milton Helpern, the former chief medical examiner of New York City, made the following statements regarding the magic bullet:

> *The original pristine weight of this bullet before it was fired was approximately 160–161 grains. The weight of the bullet recovered on the stretcher in Parkland Hospital was reported by the Warren Commission at 158.6. This bullet wasn't distorted in any way. I cannot accept the premise that this bullet thrashed around in all that bony tissue and lost only 1.4 to 2.1 grams of its original weight. I cannot believe either that this bullet is going to emerge miraculously unscathed, without any deformity, and with its lands and groves intact.... You must remember that next to bone, the skin offers greater resistance to a bullet in its course through the body than other kinds of tissue.... This single bullet theory asks us to believe that this bullet went through seven layers of skin, tough, elastic, resistant*

---

95 By the way, Russell was not a liberal, not at all. He was the leader of the opposition party trying to prevent the growth of the Civil Rights movement; he died in 1971.

skin. In addition this bullet passed through other layers of soft tissue and then shattered bones. I just can't believe that this bullet had the force to do what the commission has demanded of it, and I don't think the commission has really stopped to think out carefully what it has asked of this bullet (Benson 1993, 179).

This point is very relevant and has been echoed by many other forensic experts over the years. Yes, the bullet found could be traced back to the rifle found on the sixth floor, but was that projectile fired on November 22,1963? We will never know. It could have been fired weeks earlier and retrieved, just to set up Oswald in the future by planting it at the hospital. Actually, one of the government's own pathologists, Dr. Pierre Finck, made this comment regarding the single bullet theory: "It was impossible for the reason that there are more grains of metal still in Governor Connally's wrist than there are missing from that bullet. That bullet could not have done it" (Benson 1993, 137).

Aubrey Bell, who was an emergency room nurse supervisor at Parkland Hospital, said she held and observed the bullet fragments taken from Governor Connally's body. She stated, "The smallest was the size of the striking end of a match, and the largest was at least twice that big. I have seen the picture of the magic pristine bullet, and I can't see how it could be the bullet from which the fragments that I saw came" (Benson 1993, 34).

Perhaps the strangest point about the single bullet theory was the location of the president's rear entry wounds. Some of the actual autopsy photos did make their way into official hands; it was impossible for the conspirators to eliminate or alter all of them. So the commission had to deal with some of the actual evidence in the case; one such piece of evidence was the location of the president's back wound. Dr. J. Thornton Boswell's drawing of the president's back wound clearly shows the location of the entry wound to be down toward the center of his back, between the shoulder blades. This wound location would have made it impossible for the bullet to have entered there and then exited through the president's throat, not to mention that there was no exit wound located for this shot, (See Figure-1 page 19). There is no way that even Arlen Specter, the creator of the magic-bullet theory, could have concocted that trajectory. Despite this, he made up a great story, as history shows.[96] According to James Fetzer, "It would fall to Arlen Specter, then a junior counsel to the commission, to refine what would become the official account of the death of JFK, based upon three shots with two hits and one miss. He proved quite adept at doing this" (Fetzer 2009).

One of the very few defenses mustered by Specter was that prior to the shot, the president's head must have been tucked down into his chest, while he was bent over. This, he states, accounts for the exit wound in his throat. I can hardly believe that any responsible person would believe this evaluation; all you need to do is watch the film of the assassination and the president's movements to see that this theory is pure fiction.

I have examined this film many times over, as so many researchers have done, and when the film is run in very slow motion, you do not need the great Arlen Specter to explain what happened.[97] It very clearly shows the president's head

---

96 On the afternoon and evening of the assassination, radio and television reported two wounds to the body: one to the throat and the other to the right temple. This last wound caused a massive blowout to the back of the head. Those who watched "JFK: As It Happened" (1988; NBC footage from November 22, 1963), as broadcast over A&E, observed Chet Huntley report that he had a wound to the throat and that his death was "a simple matter" of a bullet right through the head. It was later added that it "entered his right temple," attributing that finding to Admiral George Burkley, the president's personal physician. Later, Frank McGee said the shots had been fired from above and behind; he remarked, "This is incongruous. How can the man have been shot from in front and from behind?" (Fetzer 2009).

97 Once again go to http://www.youtube.com/watch?v=eqzJQE8LYrQ to watch the assassination.

being struck from the front.[98] It also shows the back of the president's head completely exploding just after the moment of impact. This is the same part of his head that the official autopsy reports and x-rays show was still completely intact, but not all of the photos were hocused; we still have some actual photos, thanks to a little fate.

Further analysis of the film points to the solid conclusion that President Kennedy and Governor Connally were both struck by different bullets. If you watch the film of the assassination, you can see that the president was hit almost two seconds before the governor; he is seen grasping at his throat while the governor is totally unaffected by the gunfire at this point. It is not until the governor turns around that he is struck; this was not only confirmed by the film but the governor himself; his wife Nellie proclaimed, until her death, that there was no magic bullet.

A few points before we proceed. It should be noted once again that many researchers, such as David Lifton, believe that the president's body had been manipulated prior to its arrival at Bethesda Hospital. Bullets had been removed and wounds had been distorted (such as the throat wound, which had a small entrance hole at Parkland but was completely torn open before it arrived at Bethesda). This was the same wound that was used by the Parkland doctors to insert a tracheal tube.[99] This wound was totally distorted by the time it reached the autopsy, more than likely because they needed to remove the projectile that did not exit the president's body. If this bullet was located, it would have been obvious to everyone that it came from a different rifle than the Oswald rifle, thereby proving a conspiracy.

---

[98] I have actually shown this film to many of my students during my teaching career, and I get the same results: the shot clearly came from the front; it is a simple matter of common sense and observation (with very little physics indeed).

[99] Remember Dr. Crenshaw's description: "The incision Dr. Perry had made in his throat at Parkland for the tracheotomy had been enlarged and mangled, as if someone had conducted another procedure. It looked to be the work of a butcher."

To confirm my theory, here is a segment from Volume III of *Inside the Assassination Records Review Board,* written by Douglas P. Horne, the chief analyst for military records during the investigation, which concerns an article written by Dr. Charles Crenshaw in 1998:

> The wound which I saw after Dr. Perry concluded his work looked nothing like what I saw [referring to the bootleg autopsy photos] in the photographs taken at Bethesda. Dr. Perry had made a very small and neat transverse incision. I took it to be about one to one and one half inches in length. It was certainly not the length I saw in the autopsy photos. The gaping nature of the wound was also inconsistent with what I saw. When the body left Parkland, there was no gaping, bloody defect in the front of the throat, just a small bullet hole and the thin line of Perry's incision.... "The author once again refers to the article by Dr. Crenshaw" Photographs of President Kennedy's throat show a defect more than twice as long as the tracheostomy incision I remember and more than twice the length these doctors, my colleagues in the trauma room one, had earlier estimated in interviews with author David Lifton. In a televised interview with ABC News for the show *20/20* aired in April 1992, Crenshaw expressed his opinion that the original tracheostomy incision had been tampered with, enlarged prior to the time the autopsy photographs showing the incisions were taken (Horne 2012, 3:671).[100]

As I mentioned above, the bullet that made this entrance wound in the throat was never found in the body, even after extensive x-rays were taken, per FBI agents at the autopsy. Also, there was absolutely, positively no exit wound for the bullet, so I ask then, where did the bullet go? In my opinion, right into the hands of the Secret Service[101] and the conspirators prior to the autopsy, and then it disappeared, of course. Because of these reasons, how could anyone in their right mind not conclude

---

100 Horne, D. (2009). *Inside the Assassination Records Review Board.*

101 Sadly, we must include the Secret Service in this, because they were in complete control of the body at this point, period. No one came near the body without their knowledge.

that a conspiracy had taken place? Whenever my students ask me about the Kennedy murder, it is easy to find grounds for a conspiracy. You don't have to look very far at all.

I have tried to offer my understanding and my reasoning about the murder of JFK. My goal in this book is to provide enough information for the average reader to conclude that the original investigation and the investigation in the 1970s were simply deceptive at the least; there is ample evidence that we have been lied to throughout the last five decades and we are still being lied to today. Bill O'Reilly's new book is a prime example.

A case in point is that many of our leaders have supported the official lone gunman theory and continue to support that theory. One such leader was the first President Bush, who was also the CIA director in the late 1970s, appointed by Gerald Ford (as a member of the Warren Commission, Ford had been caught illegally passing information to the FBI during the investigation). Ford passionately supported the lone gunman theory, right up until his death, even though information had come out over the decades that blew holes in the official story. This is the same Gerald Ford who was never elected president by the people. He also exonerated Richard M. Nixon, our most famous political criminal, by issuing him a presidential pardon after he dishonored us with his role in the Watergate scandal.[102]

---

[102] Chapter 12 discusses the deathbed confession of E. Howard Hunt, a prominent CIA operative who was also a Watergate burglar assigned by Richard Nixon to break into the Democratic headquarters, for what reason we still do not know. There is great speculation on that subject, which we will save for another time.

Chapter 6

The Autopsy Cover-Up

"A lie can travel halfway around the world while the truth is still putting on its shoes."
—Mark Twain

Among the many excellent researchers who have studied the Kennedy assassination is David Lifton, whose ground-breaking book, *Best Evidence,* completely broke open the JFK conspiracy with regards to the medical evidence. His best-selling book, published in 1980, shed new light on the discrepancies between the official autopsy report and statements made by the medical staff at Parkland Hospital. According to Lifton, the hospital staff and the autopsy staff had to have been looking at two different bodies. The autopsy doctors stated that the president's head had a small hole in the upper right rear, which appeared to be an entrance wound.[103] The larger hole they reported was located in the right front part of the president's head. This area, they claimed, was where the bullet exited and did most of the damage. When compared to the statements made by the hospital staff at Parkland, the discrepancies become very apparent (Callahan 1993, 130).[104]

Dr. Charles A. Crenshaw, whose testimony to the Warren Commission was covered earlier, was the first attending physician to work on the wounded president, and he gave graphic details of what he observed. He stated, "I noticed

---

103 Of course, this flies in the face of the statements by Paul O'Connor, who was the medical technician that day during the official autopsy, and also Gerald Custer, who was the official government x-ray technician who took the entire set of autopsy x-rays of the president. Both men stated that the president was not only missing 90 percent of his brain, he had a hole the size of a softball in the rear of his head.

104 Callahan, B. (1993). *Who Shot JFK? A Guide to the Major Conspiracy Theories.* New York: Simon & Schuster.

that the entire right hemisphere of his brain was missing, beginning at the hairline and extending all the way behind his right ear. Pieces of the skull that hadn't been blown away were hanging by blood-matted hair. Part of his brain, the cerebellum, was dangling from the back of his head by a single strand of tissue, looking like a piece of dark gray blood-soaked sponge that would easily fit in the palm of my hand"[105] (Crenshaw 1992, 86–87).[106]

Dr. Robert McClelland, another attending physician, gave a similar description of the president's wounds: "The wound was in the right back part of the head; very large.... A portion of the cerebellum fell out on the table as we were doing the tracheotomy."[107] Dr. Ronald James gave this statement regarding his observations: "My impression was there was a wound in this area of the head." He was referring to a fraudulent autopsy photo, which showed the back of the head still intact. When shown the set of x-rays used by the Warren Commission, Dr. James said, "There was no damage to the face that was visible.... These x-rays are incompatible with the actual wounds"[108] (Warren Commission Report 1964).

There were witnesses at the Naval Hospital who can confirm the statements of the Parkland Hospital Staff. Paul O'Connor, who assisted in the autopsy of President Kennedy, was ordered not to talk about what he had seen for the rest of

---

105 Crenshaw, C. (1992). *JFK: Conspiracy of Silence*. New York: Penguin Books.

106 Dr. Crenshaw, http://www.youtube.com/watch?v=Z1SUz2bgAVs and http://www.youtube.com/watch?v=XyEHZFZQh54

107 This is very important to the investigation, as the cerebellum is in the very rear of the head, the section that many of the fraudulent autopsy photos clearly showed was still intact; in those forged photos, even the president's hair was still in place. They were absolute forgeries, and testimony such as this proves that point without any doubt. There was no hair left in the rear of his head because much of this area was missing, having been blown out in Dallas.

108 This is another critical point, because the fraudulent x-rays showed that the facial area had been shattered, which was clearly not the case; Dr. James knew this and stated so for the record.

his career in the Navy.[109] He and other enlisted Navy personal in the autopsy room, such as Jerrol Custer, the x-ray tech, were threatened with court martials if they ever spoke out about what they had observed.[110] Shortly after his retirement from the US Navy, Paul O'Connor spoke to David Lifton, and what he said was pretty incredible.

> O'Connor stated that the wounds he observed were very consistent with those seen by Dr. Crenshaw and Dr. McClelland at Parkland. The back of the head was completely blown away, and he is sure of this fact because one of his tasks during the autopsy was to remove the president's brain for further examination. O'Connor further stated that he could not even find the president's brain; it was missing. He was interviewed by David Lifton regarding his handling of the president's body and Lifton asked, *"But when you say he didn't have any brains in there, did you have to go through the medical procedure to remove the brain?"* "No sir, replied O'Connor, "there wasn't anything to remove." *"What do you mean by that," I asked?* "The cranium was empty," he replied. *"The cranium was empty?" I asked flatly; not quite a question. If O'Connor was right, there was no question but that the body was altered prior to its receipt at Bethesda"* (Lifton 1980, 602).[111]

---

109 Paul O'Connor, http://www.youtube.com/watch?v=mKZILDdQwAI

110 According to interviews conducted by the Assassination Records Review Board (ARRB), the autopsy was a scene of complete chaos; they point to the fact that the Secret Service collected evidence that later disappeared, such as photos, x-rays, and slides taken of the president's brain (Horne 2009). Whether the president's brain ever made it into the actual autopsy is still a mystery. O'Conner says he never saw it, and Dr. Humes says he gave it to the Secret Service. This is exactly the kind of chaos described by many who were there. For more information, see Douglas Horne's book, *Inside the Assassination Records Review Board: The U.S. Government's Final Attempt to Reconcile the Conflicting Medical Evidence in the Assassination of JFK* (2009).

111 Lifton, D. S. (1980). *Best Evidence.* New York: McMillan Publishing Co.

According to O'Connor, the brain had been removed, by whom we may never know. In any investigation, investigators often do not get all the facts at once; there are always holes. In this case, however, we have another material fact: the brain was missing and may never have arrived with the president's body. That is clearly an obstruction of justice, and those who were in control of the president's body should have been held responsible and questioned regarding the alteration of President Kennedy's body. Also, two Secret Service agents, William Greer and Roy Kellerman, were both present at the autopsy, and according to Vincent Palamara's book *Survivor's Guilt*, they were implicit in withholding evidence at that time; he states, "Greer and Kellerman were the only two agents to remain with the president throughout the autopsy, and Greer never left. The president's clothing, vital in any autopsy, especially one involving gunshot wounds, was withheld by Greer. In addition, vital images on a roll of 120 film were destroyed by a Secret Service agent that night; it appears strongly that Greer was the culprit in this illegal destruction of evidence. Palamara further points that one of the medical doctors, Dr. John Lattimer stated, "This had been done deliberately by one of the agents present" (Palamara 2013, 199).[112]

O'Connor further told David Lifton that even the autopsy doctors, Boswell and Humes, were "aghast" at the fact that the brain was missing. In his book *Best Evidence,* Lifton continued to ask this vital witness more questions regarding his observations of the president's body that day at the hospital.

> "Lifton went on to tell... *"I was determined to get the most precise information possible about his recollections. I wanted to understand how he reconciled what he had seen that night with certain facts about the autopsy which was in the public record. One was the brain." Lifton went on to tell O'Connor that the Supplementary*

112 Palamara, V. M. (2013). *Survivor's Guilt: The Secret Service and the Failure to Protect President Kennedy.* Waterville, OR: Trine Day LLC.

Autopsy Report stated that there was a brain. He asked O'Connor, "Where did that brain come from?" O'Connor replied, "I don't know, that's another thing. I've heard about that too, and that's very puzzling, because there was no brain with the body, near the body, or in the casket, or anything that I know of" (Lifton 1980, 603).

So Lifton continued to press O'Connor regarding other aspects of the autopsy. He asked about the president's skullcap and other pieces of bone, which was also in the report, and O'Connor stated they were also missing and the hole in the skull was so large that the autopsy doctors later filled the giant eight- by four-inch hole in the rear of the head with plaster of Paris. He stated, "Well, there was just a great massive hole in the skull. That was the only thing that was there. There was no round definition showing that the bullet had entered. It was just a great big blown-out piece of skull" (Lifton 1980, 603).

O' Connor also reported other strange occurrences that happened that night. He said the autopsy room was packed with people, some in uniforms, and others in suits; dozens and dozens of military personnel and civilians were present in the room. He said the doctors working on the body were being controlled by some of the men in the room and had orders barked at them along with verbal commands not to probe or to get too detailed about the descriptions of the wounds. It was clear to O'Connor that a proper autopsy was not going to occur that night, but then we still have the bizarre events involving the presidential casket.

David Lifton also interviewed O'Connor regarding the casket that the president's body was in when he arrived at Bethesda Hospital. O'Connor told Lifton (and later, author William Matson Law for his 2004 book, *In the Eye of History: Disclosures in the JFK Assassination Medical Evidence*) that the president arrived in a cheap gray shipping casket, like the ones used during the Vietnam War.

O' Connor stated:

"Then I found out that the casket I saw come into our morgue in Bethesda wasn't the same coffin that he was put in at Parkland to ship to Bethesda. He was put into a bronze, ornate casket at Parkland that came from the O'Neal Funeral Home. Aubrey Rike[113] *was an ambulance driver for the O'Neal Funeral Home. Rike told me they put him in a bed liner. Now a bed liner is something that goes over a bed; it's a plastic covering that keeps bodily fluids from bleeding into the mattress. It's not a body bag. A body bag is a bag that a body is put into and zipped from the head to the toe. He was wrapped in sheets around his chest and his torso, and when we received him, he was not in a bed liner. He was in a body bag, nothing wrapped around his torso. It was an unclothed body; the only thing on his body was a bloody sheet around his head. So that was another thing that was extremely disturbing to hear about.* When William Law asked Paul O'Connor what he thought about the fact that the president's casket had been changed, O' Connor replied that *"somebody somewhere high up in government—it had to be the government—was concealing evidence, vital evidence, from the American public about what actually transpired between Parkland and Bethesda."* (Spartacus Educational Publishers, 2012) [114]

This information is completely contrary to the witnesses at Parkland Hospital, who stated that the president had been put in a very expensive bronze casket. As told by Paul O'Connor, funeral home employee Aubrey Rike stated that he not only had driven the bronze casket to the hospital, he also helped place the president's body inside that casket. According to Rike, "They told us to go into the trauma room and prepare the president to be moved.... It was an expensive

---

113 Aubrey Rike also wrote his own book, called *At the Door of Memory: Aubrey Rike and the Assassination of President Kennedy.* Southlake: JFK Lancer Productions & Publications, Inc.

114 On a final note: after leaving the military, Paul O'Connor became a law enforcement officer and served as a deputy sheriff and a police officer; he retired in Florida. O'Connor has never changed his story and can be seen on video giving his statements to Lifton in the video version of *Best Evidence.*

bronze-colored type, it was a bronze casket. One of the most expensive we had in stock" (Livingstone 1993, 737).[115]

Aubrey Rike went on to explain the process that was used to place the president in the casket: "It had a white satin lining inside the casket. We wrapped him in one of the sheets and placed him in the casket" (Livingstone 1993, 737). Others also described the expensive bronze casket as it was verified by Aubrey Rike. It can also be seen in several news reels on the day of the assassination, both in Dallas and while the casket was being removed from *Air Force One*. So where did the cheap gray shipping casket come from that arrived at Bethesda Hospital? That is a good question, and when and where did President Kennedy's body get transferred to this cheaper casket?

There is even more evidence involving the gray casket; another eyewitness saw both of the caskets arrive at Bethesda Hospital. According to Dennis David, who was chief of the day at Bethesda Naval Hospital the day of the assassination, he saw two different caskets that day in Maryland. He said two vehicles arrived at the hospital that night, separated by approximately forty-seven minutes. Both of these vehicles were said to be carrying the remains of President Kennedy. At approximately 6:30 the evening of the assassination, a black Cadillac ambulance or hearse arrived at the hospital, carrying the president's body. According to two interns who helped unload the contents, the president's body was in a rubber body bag, which had been placed inside a simple gray metal shipping casket.

At 7:15 p.m., the official naval ambulance, also said to be carrying the president's remains, arrived at the hospital. The president's wife Jacqueline and Attorney General Robert Kennedy arrived with this ambulance. The president was said to be inside the $10,000 bronze casket, which the hospital staff offloaded for what appeared to be a second time. Another witness to the second casket arriving was

---

115 Livingston, H. E. (1993). *Killing the Truth*. New York: Carroll & Graf Publishers.

Jerrol F. Custer,[116] a naval x-ray technician who took all the x-rays of the president's body. Custer, who remembered the event clearly, said that while he was walking with an aide and a military security officer by his side, carrying the x-rays he had just taken, he saw Mrs. Kennedy arrive in the front lobby of the hospital, along with the bronze casket.[117] As the president's widow walked through the lobby of the hospital, Custer looked at her in astonishment. In his hands were the x-rays of the president's wounds, which he had taken in the autopsy wing of the hospital. His apron was still covered in the blood from the dead president when he saw Mrs. Kennedy in the lobby.[118]

So what, if anything, was in that second casket? The casket weighed 1,000 pounds by itself, so there was no way for anyone carrying it to notice the missing 180-pound body of JFK. It would clearly seem that somewhere between Dallas and Maryland, the president's body was removed from its original casket, his gunshot wounds were altered, his brain was stolen, and he was then placed into a body bag, which was then placed in the cheap shipping casket; this was the one that arrived well ahead of the motorcade. To believe anything other than this requires one to make illogical conclusions due to the number of witnesses to this event, but in addition, there is even more evidence to this disturbing story.

---

116 Custer gave graphic statements to David Lifton regarding the wounds that he saw the day of the autopsy. Custer also said the president's brain was completely gone. He said he could fit both of his hands into the wound in the president's head. He was shocked by how massive the wound was. You can see his statements in Lifton's video, *Best Evidence*; I recommend this video if you can get your hands on it. Lifton does a great job of bringing out the facts of the autopsy and the movement of the president's body.

117 Custer's statements, http://www.youtube.com/watch?v=VE13gEWgmQo

118 We have seen already that the main goal of the Warren Commission, established by LBJ, a potential coconspirator, was to come to the conclusion that Oswald was the lone shooter, period. This was despite what needed to be done, including altering the wounds on the president's body and removing as much valuable evidence as possible.

Another witness who observed the expensive bronze casket was Dr. Charles Crenshaw, who was the last person to see the president's body before the casket was sealed. He gives the following account in his book, *JFK: Conspiracy of Silence*:

I observed a bronze casket being wheeled toward Trauma Room One by two male employees from O'Neal Funeral Home. I opened the door, allowing them to enter, then followed them in. I was the only doctor in the room. All of the tubes had been removed from the president, his body had been cleaned, and he had been wrapped in two white sheets. The casket was opened, and two nurses placed a plastic mattress covering over the white velvet lining to keep any blood that might still seep from the wounds from staining the material. (Crenshaw 1992, 110).

Most likely, the bronze casket mentioned by Dr. Crenshaw, which was taken off the plane in public view, was empty; the president's body had already been removed from it in Dallas before *Air Force One* took off from Love Field. There is also very strong evidence, such as radio transmissions from Air Force One, which confirms that the agents in charge on board ordered a helicopter to be waiting on arrival in Maryland. It appears then that the president's body was removed from the opposite side of the plane while on the tarmac, and possibly air lifted to another location prior to being brought to Bethesda Hospital, (Many investigators feel the body was taken to Walter Reed Army Hospital where it was altered prior to the autopsy).

Dr. Charles Crenshaw's story is far from over; I have included another quote from his book so you can hear his story in his own words. Here is the second part of his statement:

It wasn't until years later when I saw the autopsy pictures of John Kennedy taken at Bethesda Naval Hospital that I realized there was something rotten in America in 1963. The doctors there had recorded the condition of John F. Kennedy's cranium and stated that it had substantially changed during a period of six hours and over a distance of 1,500 miles. Great effort had been made to reconstruct the back of the president's head, and the incision Dr. Perry had made in his throat at Parkland for the tracheotomy had been enlarged and mangled, as if someone had conducted another procedure. It looked to be the work of a butcher. No doubt someone had gone to a great deal of trouble to show a different story than we had seen at Parkland. (Crenshaw 1992, 110–111)

Dr. Crenshaw's words clearly speak for themselves; here is the testimony of an intelligent, well-educated and respected physician who had over thirty years of experience with gunshot wounds. He knows what he saw that day in Dallas, and he had examined the president's body for nearly an hour, longer than anyone else that day. Over the years he had stated many times over for the record that he had observed two frontal entry wounds, one that entered the president's throat and the other which entered the right temporal area. Until his death Dr. Crenshaw continued to profess the absurdity of the magic bullet theory which he believed was simply a fictional story put out to support the lone gunmen scenario. So who should we believe? Medical doctors and medical personal who were eyewitnesses, or the Warren Commission and the government; the choice is yours of course, but I know what side I line up on.

To reiterate, we know that the casket that was seen being unloaded from *Air Force One* was empty. It seems that the coconspirators had removed the president's body from the casket, possibly while Mrs. Kennedy was in the front of the plane, watching Johnson taking the oath of office; this was prior to takeoff in Dallas. I am certain that the body was then hastily examined there, and it was determined that there was too much evidence that the president had been hit from the front, confirming the Dallas doctors' statements to the press.[119] Then the president's body was placed in a body

---

119 Many researchers also believe that there was a postmortem manipulation of the body, because bullets were removed along with the president's brain.

bag and slipped into a cheap gray shipping casket, no doubt obtained in the Dallas area. If you're wondering how in the world the Secret Service would have allowed this, well, that is a simple matter. The true conspirators could have told the Secret Service agents anything they wanted, because they were in complete control. They might have said that they needed to take these precautions in order to protect the president's body. The agents, having already seen (and some would say allowed) the president to get murdered in the streets of Dallas, most likely complied.

The conspirators had to act, and act quickly; fortunately for them, they were in complete control of the situation, both on *Air Force One* and at Bethesda, a military hospital. So there it is: the president was removed from the original casket and possibly examined on the plane prior to the autopsy; the body was then placed in a body bag, which arrived at the rear of the hospital in an unmarked hearse, not in the motorcade taken by Mrs. Kennedy.

So then we do have strong evidence that the president's body was altered in order to try and eliminate any evidence of shooters firing from in front of the motorcade, but what about any post-mortem alterations? In referring to a book review found in the April 2010 edition of *JFK: Deep Politics Quarterly,* Ventura, Russell, and Wayne (2013) make these assertions regarding the alterations of the president's wounds: "At this point, Dr. Humes performed clandestine surgery on the head to enlarge the head wound to create evidence of a temporal/parietal exit and an incision was made to remove evidence of a right forehead entry. The scalp and the skull were manipulated to conceal the size and location of the occipital blowout, and a wound was created to simulate a small entrance wound on the back of the head" (Ventura, Russell, and Wayne 2013, 175).

We next return again to the recollections of Dennis David, who was the chief of the day at Bethesda Hospital when the president's body arrived for the autopsy. His story is absolutely staggering, and once again, thanks to David Lifton, we have a true account of what occurred that day. Dennis David's statements completely confirm the experiences of Paul O'Connor and truly give us a picture of what occurred after *Air Force One* arrived in Maryland. Here is more detailed information regarding his recollections, [he made some powerful statements to Lifton] *"Now the casket, the first one, what we call the first casket, that went to the back door, did that come in after the Kennedy's arrived?"* [David], "No it came before." *"It came in before?"* [Asked Lifton] "It came in before," [repeated David] "It came in a black Cadillac ambulance without any markings, and there was no escort with it. When it arrived ... there was just two attendants in the front, and there were six or seven men ... I didn't see credentials ... I assumed they were Secret Service, who were in the back with the casket.... They opened it up, they got out, and they along with some of the sailors that we had down there, unloaded the casket, and they took it into the morgue proper." [Lifton] *"From the black Cadillac ambulance?"* [David] "Right" (Lifton 1980, 575).

You could spend an entire chapter alone just on what Dennis David saw that day, but one final point must be made: how did Dennis David know that the official ambulance in the motorcade was in fact empty? Because, of course, he had already seen the body arrive. He stated to Lifton, "I was in the office and was standing there looking toward Wisconsin Avenue, when the motorcade with the Navy ambulance in the lead came in the front gate. This was like fifteen or twenty, thirty minutes after the black ambulance had arrived." Lifton asked, *"You're telling me that you actually witnessed this up on the second floor?"* [David], "Up on the second floor. Yes, looking out a window ... in the office." [Lifton], *"I see, so you actually witnessed the arrival with the motorcycles and the whole business?"* [David], "Yes. Up there." [Lifton], *"Did you watch Jackie get out of the ambulance with Robert Kennedy?"* [David], "I was standing right on the second floor balcony when Mrs. Kennedy came through the door of the front entrance of the Naval Medical Center" (Lifton 1980, 576).

Therefore, we are certain now, based on eyewitnesses, that the first black ambulance truly contained the body of the president, and Mrs. Kennedy was sitting next to an empty casket in the official motorcade, along with her brother-in-law, Robert Kennedy. What a tragic lie we have been told, and what a tragic end to such a powerful American president. Read *Best Evidence*; it is a thrilling and powerful book, simply ageless.

Chapter 7

Chief Jesse Curry:
The Man Who Knew Enough

"The truth is incontrovertible. Malice may attack it, ignorance may deride it, but in the end, there it is."
—Winston Churchill

As a former police officer, I am actually proud of Chief Jesse Curry, who was the chief of police for the city of Dallas at the time of President Kennedy's murder. He appeared confused and a little disoriented on that incredible day, because he was himself a victim of misinformation from his own department, the FBI, and Dallas District Attorney Henry Wade. Also, his comments seemed to defend his department, which truly appeared to bumble the investigation from the start. However, after reading his book, *JFK Assassination File,* published in 1969, I began to truly respect him and see things from his perspective. In his book, which I will review later, he admits to many things that were kept out of the official reports. He saw and heard much valuable information during the aftermath, and he reports things in his book as they occurred. At the time he wrote his book, he believed that Lee Oswald was somehow involved. Despite this, he in no way believed he acted alone that day. He clearly believed through his own testimony that someone was firing from in front of the motorcade as well, and the FBI had covered up many of these facts. I will now cover several points from his book.

The Shooting at General Walker's House

General Edwin Walker was a former right wing radical who was living in Dallas. Just prior to the assassination, someone took a shot at him and nearly killed him; Oswald was later blamed for this shooting in the press. But according to Chief Curry, as well as the FBI, Oswald's rifle could not be linked to the Walker shooting. "The FBI report was inconclusive but indicated some unique similarities" (Curry 1969, 1).[120] Well, I have worked in law enforcement for many years and have been to court on several shooting cases; when the district attorney's office uses terms like "unique similarities," those are code words for a lack of substantial evidence. In other words, they were grasping at straws. They use terms like this to trick the jury into believing they have some solid evidence. The truth is that many projectiles will show similarities to each other, especially similar brands and calibers.

Now it is true, according to Curry, that Marina Oswald did state that her husband told her he did take a shot at the general, because he hated the general and what he stood for. She claims Oswald told her, "I hate his Fascist organization." But Marina's statements in court may not have been used against her husband, because you cannot be compelled to testify against your spouse if you choose not to. It is interesting to note that Marina was not a US citizen and could have been deported at any time. She spoke little English, as well, and was under tremendous pressure; years later, she stated that she complied because she feared she would be sent back to Russia. Let's consider: even if Oswald took a shot at Walker, it does not mean he shot the president. One has nothing to do with the other, when you consider Walker and Kennedy were polar opposites. If he did shoot at Walker, where was the FBI? After all, Special Agent James Hosty was supposed to be watching him. He had been to his house at least twice, which we know of. But the bottom line is Oswald had absolutely no motive to kill the president. Kennedy was trying to sign a peace treaty with the Soviets and refused to go along with the CIA's plans to invade Cuba. He even fired all of the rabid anticommunist sacred cows who were running the agency, like Dulles and Cabell. Why would Oswald want him dead?[121]

---

120 Curry, J. (1969). *JFK Assassination File.* Dallas: American Poster and Printing Co.

121 Not to mention the fact that the Warren Commission painted Oswald as a leftist; if he believed Kennedy had similar viewpoints, it would make no sense that he would want to kill him.

Where was his motive to commit this crime? If he did try to kill Walker, why would he try to kill JFK, who supported the absolute opposite views of General Walker and his radical right wing group? It would not be feasible to imagine that Oswald would hate both a radical right wing group and President Kennedy as well. On a further note, General Walker hated JFK. The General Walker Group planned a massive protest along the motorcade route the day of the president's visit. Oswald hated Walker because of his fascist views but then turned around and killed the president? This makes no sense. Killers need motives, even deranged killers, but Oswald was not deranged. In fact, he was very sane. When questioned by reporters, he stated, *"No sir, I didn't kill anyone. I'm just a patsy. I don't know what dispatches you people have been given, but I emphatically deny these charges."* Does that sound like the ramblings of a deranged individual? Not at all. Oswald spoke at least two languages; he was educated and a former marine with intelligence training; the man was actually pretty smart, by all accounts.

Security in Dealey Plaza

Chief Curry admits that security was extremely light in Dealey Plaza. He said that there was no security in front of the Texas School Book Depository, which had several open windows. He also observed that there were only two officers on the railroad overpass that he could see. So why was security so light in that area? This was the chosen site of the ambush, as Dave Powers pointed out, an absolutely perfect site for an ambush. It should be noted that most researchers feel Chief Curry was an honorable man and had nothing to do with the poor planning or the cover-up of the murder; he also had little to do with the parade route, which was chosen by the Secret Service and Dallas Mayor Earl Cabal's office.

The Sequence of Shots

Considering once again that it took 2.5 seconds just to cycle the Oswald bolt-action rifle, let's read Chief Curry's comments concerning his observations that day: "For a brief moment I almost started to relax. I made the left turn west and proceeded at a speed of approximately eight to ten mph toward the triple underpass. I did see a few unauthorized people on the overpass and wondered how they had gotten up there. About halfway between Houston and the triple underpass I heard a sharp crack. Someone in the car said, is that a firecracker? *Two other sharp reports came almost directly after the first.* All of the reports were fired *fairly close together*, but perhaps there was a longer pause between the first and second reports than between the second and the third" (Curry 1969, 30). Once again, over and over, the witnesses stated that two shots *came too close together to have been fired from the same weapon.* Here, the chief also confirms this fact; there were at least two shooters.

Evidence of a Frontal Shot

The evidence of at least two shots from the front of the president's vehicle is simply overwhelming. Here is another excerpt from the chief's book, describing his observations and interactions with the doctors at Parkland Hospital just after the shooting: "As Dr. Perry took charge he sized up the situation. A small neat wound was in the throat. The back of the head was massively damaged and blood from the wound covered the floor and the aluminum hospital cart.... Dr. Perry examined the throat wound and assessed it as the entrance wound. He was no amateur at assessing wounds. By his later testimony he stated he had previously treated from 150 to 200 gunshot wounds. The doctors were so absorbed by the treatment of the massive head wound that his other wounds, the lower back and upper neck, were never noticed since he was lying on his back.... Dr. Perry insisted that the president was shot from the front—entering at the throat and exiting out of the back of the head.[122] Immediate speculation began about shots coming from in front of the motorcade from the grassy knoll or the triple underpass" (Curry 1969, 34).

---

[122] Dr. Perry may not have had all the facts, but he was certain that the president was shot from the front, period.

The Autopsy

The president's autopsy was ridiculous, a misguided travesty of justice; Chief Curry agreed, and so did many journalists as well, who pointed out that the removal of the president's body from Dallas was a crime; it was a way to return to safe ground with the best evidence in any murder investigation: the body. On January 14, 1967, he wrote in the *Saturday Evening Post,* "If the law had been observed, there might have been no controversy, and the Bethesda doctors, the FBI and the Secret Service would have escaped the heavy responsibility they now bear. Sadly and ironically the report of the autopsy performed on the murdered Oswald in Dallas is a model of clarity and precision alongside the sloppy, ambiguous and incomplete record of the autopsy President Kennedy received. The president's body remains the object of obscene speculation, and the country suffers needless, disruptive controversy. As matters stand, no single element of the Warren Commission's version of the assassination is more suspect than the official account of the president's autopsy" (Curry 1969, 39). There were certainly a lot of reasons to remove the body from the Texas authorities, but none better than the excellent work that would have been done by Dr. Rose in Dallas. We would have seen clearly the true facts right from the start, and the conspirators simply could not allow that to happen. Their cover-up would have been over before it started.

Nitrate Test

Chief Curry wrote, "Oswald's face did not reveal any nitrates from having fired a rifle, thus offering no proof that Oswald had recently fired a rifle" (Curry 1969, 86). The initial statements regarding Oswald's nitrate test, given publicly on all the networks by the Dallas Police Department and District Attorney Henry Wade, were grossly incorrect.

No Magic Bullet

Chief Curry does a great job of describing what he saw in the Zapruder film. He had seen the film several times before it was viewed by the public or even the Jim Garrison jury in 1968. He states with certainty that the president and Governor Connally were hit with separate bullets. He said Kennedy was clearly hit first, between frames 206 and 225. He also says that there was no shot from the sixth floor window until frame number 210. He states, "After emerging from behind the sign Kennedy's face is distorted. His left hand clutches his lapel, and his right is rising toward his throat. By frame 230 Kennedy had hunched forward with both hands at his throat. This is about 1.3 seconds since Kennedy had disappeared from view behind the sign. Kennedy was then profoundly affected by the first shot, *but Governor Connally was still clutching his hat in the air completely unaffected by the shot.* By Governor Connelly's own testimony he had heard the first shot and had mentally wondered what was wrong before he was shot. The first shot would have already reached the car in that case because bullets travel faster than sound. Both the governor and Mrs. Connally are sure that it was the second shot entering the car that struck him. The Zapruder film tends to collaborate this testimony" (Curry 1969, 102).

So the theory of a magic bullet is not feasible. Sorry, Mr. Specter, Mr. Johnson, Mr. Bush, Mr. Ford, Mr. Hoover, and anyone else who insisted that the magic bullet was real. They were hit with separate bullets, but don't just believe me, the former police Chief, Governor Connally, and the Parkland doctors; watch the film and look at all the other evidence out there, which also proves the magic bullet theory to be totally incorrect.

Eyewitness Statement from Officer J. M. Smith

Officer J. M. Smith states in his eyewitness account, "I was standing in the middle of Elm Street from the southeast curb of Elm and Houston Street at the time of the shooting. I heard the shots and thought they were coming from the bushes or the overpass." Curry adds, "*This statement is similar to those of other officers who thought the shots were coming from the direction of the underpass*" (Curry 1969, 105).

Chief Curry was an excellent police officer and investigator, with a massive amount of investigatory training; he even went through the FBI's National Police Academy. As an inspector for the Dallas Police Department, he was in charge of all training and research. He was a solid, well-rounded police officer, and I would say the information in his book is very credible and well thought out indeed.

Chapter 8

Where Was the Secret Service?

"In an age of universal deceit, telling the truth is a revolutionary act."
—George Orwell

Many researchers have asked where the president's protection was during his trip to Dallas. The official number of Secret Service agents working on the trip through Texas was somewhere around twenty total, but this number also included agents who had gone on ahead and were not with the vehicles when he traveled through the streets of Dallas. It should be noted that back in 1963, the Secret Service did not concern itself with all of the details and responsibilities it has today, such as securing all the manhole covers and providing roof top surveillance along a motorcade route. They simply did not have the agents to fully infiltrate the areas to be visited by the president prior to his arrival. That being said, the Secret Service would rely on crack military units or Army Intelligence units to back them up, thereby adding another solid layer of protection for the president. But these teams were never used in Dallas, as confirmed by the late Colonel L. Fletcher Prouty, who worked in Army Intelligence in 1963. He stated in his book *JFK, the CIA, Vietnam, and the Plot to Assassinate John F. Kennedy*[123] that there was minimal if any protection for the president in Dallas; according to his research, the Army Intelligence unit normally assigned to protect the president in major cities had been called off by someone in high places, possibly the Pentagon.

During President Kennedy's visit to Dallas, there were several other breeches of security involving his protection, including a party the night prior to the assassination. There were several eyewitnesses who observed the majority of

---

123 Prouty, L. F. (1992). *JFK, the CIA, Vietnam, and the Plot to Assassinate John F. Kennedy*. New York: Carol Publishing Co.

the president's Secret Service detail at a local nightclub, getting drunk. The entourage had gone to the Press Club for drinks and later moved on to the Cellar, an all-night beatnik club. The nightclub, which had no liquor license, had a reputation for giving away free drinks to local politicians and police officers. According to Robert Groden, "In Fort Worth the night before the visit to Dallas, the majority of the president's Secret Service agents had a boisterous party that lasted into the early hours of November 22nd. The party was held at a local nightclub, the Cellar, which was owned by Pat Kirkwood, a friend of another local nightclub owner, Jack Ruby. Back at his hotel, the president's protection was provided by only two unarmed Fort Worth firemen during his stay" (Groden 1993, 9).[124]

As mentioned by Groden, the owner of the Fort Worth club, Pat Kirkwood, was a close acquaintance of Jack Ruby, the man who would later shoot Oswald on national television. Kirkwood's father was also a partner in a Fort Worth gambling establishment. He was a close friend of Ruby as well and of Lewis McWillie, another local man who had a colorful background; many would call him a thug. According to released FBI documents, McWillie was a murderer and was employed by Florida Mafia chieftain Santos Trafficante; he was also a key figure in the CIA's plot to kill Cuban President Fidel Castro.

---

[124] This point has been buried very deeply; the Secret Service had many issues, even in 1963. After the 2012 scandal in Colombia, many in Congress said that the Secret Service appeared to have a culture of corruption and foul escapades. There is talk at this printing of other scandals waiting to surface.

The agents stayed at the club until approximately 3:30 a.m.;[125] four of these agents would be in the follow-up car behind the president at the time of the assassination. At the Cellar, another three agents assigned to guard the president's hotel suite had left their posts to take a coffee break with their friends. As pointed out by Groden, they left two Forth Worth firemen in charge of the president's protection at the hotel.[126] These agents were later heard making jokes about the fact that the president was being guarded by two firemen who had no weapons.

It should be noted that Secret Service regulations prohibit the use of intoxicating liquor of any kind while on a protection detail.[127] Their regulations provide further that violation of this provision is cause for removal from the service; none of the agents involved in these incidents in Fort Worth were ever disciplined, even after their deplorable performance the day of the assassination. Despite this, when the security breach happened on the part of the president's agents, the vice president's detail, which was fully rested, responded to the gunfire with split-second timing. Immediately after the first shot, LBJ's personal agent shouted, "Get down!" while forcing the vice president out of the line of fire.

---

125 This information was verified and stated as fact by the director of the Secret Service during sworn Warren Commission testimony in 1964 taken by Earl Warren. Warren appeared disgusted by the behavior of the agents, going as far as to question their abilities and their complete lack of action the day of the assassination; the director was forced to agree that the all-night party and lack of sleep did affect the actions of his agents that day in Dallas (Warren Commission Testimony, April 1964).

126 These are the kind of ridiculous facts that most Americans have never heard about, but this information has been out there for years.

127 The US government has revealed details of serious allegations against Secret Service agents and officers since 2004. This includes claims of involvement with prostitutes, leaking sensitive information, publishing pornography, sexual assault, illegal wiretaps, improper use of weapons, and drunken behavior. It was not clear how many of the accusations were confirmed to be true.

The next breach of security occurred during the motorcade route through downtown Dallas. It was common procedure during that era for agents to ride on the bumper of the presidential limousine when they were traveling at slower speeds. Typically, these lower speeds would be less than forty miles per hour, but certainly less than ten miles per hour. While riding in a presidential motorcade, it was the direct responsibility of those agents in the follow-up car to protect the president at all costs; this was their primary mission. A secondary mission was to protect the first lady as well, but her personal agent, Clint Hill, performed his duties in an excellent manner that day. If you watch a video of the motorcade going through the streets of Dallas, you will see a very attentive Agent Hill going on and off the rear bumper of the limousine, especially during slower speeds and when the crowds increased in size. No such protection was ever provided to the president. Not one time did any agent ever get on the bumper behind the president, not even when the crowds overflowed into the streets in large numbers. Not to mention the fact that there were hundreds of open windows all along the parade route, with many people hanging out of them along with crowds that were twenty deep. Still, no agent is ever close enough to the president to protect him when the shots strafed the presidential car.

When the president's limo rounded the corner of Houston onto Elm, it slowed to eight miles per hour. Now consider the fact that there were dozens of open windows in the Book Depository straight ahead, as well as several possible shooting locations where an assassin may have been hiding on that turn, including block walls, a picket fence, trees, and bushes, not to mention the railroad overpass. Then we have the Secret Service agent and driver, William Greer, who brings the limo almost to a complete stop while they are under fire, receiving multiple gunshots into the car. Why in the world would these normally protective agents have acted this way? Why would the agents to the rear of the limo have stayed on the follow-up car even after the gunfire started? Wasn't their job to protect the president at all costs? I ask you to consider this lack of response as either total incompetence on their part or a planned event. Keep in mind that the president was shot and killed from multiple locations just after that turn onto Elm. Had the agents been doing their job, watching the windows and staying close to him, we might have had a wounded president but not a dead one.[128]

Perhaps the worst breach of security that occurred in Dallas was the fact that the parade route was changed at the last moment.[129] The original route would have all but eliminated the chance of any accurate rifle fire hitting the president's car as it moved toward the Stemmons Freeway, rather than the route they chose, which turned onto Houston and then onto Elm, where he was ambushed. The Secret Service agents should have known that this change would have put the president's life in jeopardy. The route was made even more dangerous considering the very slow speeds that were needed to negotiate that area with such a large limousine. The slow turns through Dealey Plaza, the opportunity for triangulated gunfire, the dozens of open windows throughout the area, along with the great sniper locations available, all worked to the killer's advantage.[130]

---

128 Sadly, it was the last shot that was fatal; the agents had several seconds in order to protect his life, but they failed.

129 It should be noted that Mayor Earl Cabell was the brother of Charles Cabell, who had been recently fired by President Kennedy. Charles Cabell was one of the assistant directors of the CIA, which the president was trying to reorganize after the Bay of Pigs disaster. There were rumors that the mayor had a say in the motorcade route being altered the day before the assassination.

130 Dave Powers, the presidential aide riding in the follow-up car, stated, "We might have driven right into an ambush" (Marrs 1989, p. 9).

Just take a look at this picture of Dealey Plaza; what a perfect place for an ambush. Photo Credit: Author.

On a final note about the president's security, I mentioned earlier that the Secret Service protection did not entail as much responsibility as it does today. It would have been impossible for the handful of agents to cover the entire parade route in Dallas (or any other major city, for that matter). So, as I have mentioned, the Secret Service had the authority to call in extra protection. In Texas, that would have been the 315th Field Detachment of the 112th Military Intelligence Group out of Fort Sam Houston (Prouty 1992, 292–293). This information was provided by the late L. Fletcher Prouty in his best-selling book, *JFK, the CIA, Vietnam, and the Plot to Assassinate John F. Kennedy.* Prouty, during the Kennedy administration, served as the chief of special operations for the Joint Chiefs of Staff. He was directly in charge of the global system designed to provide military support for the clandestine activities of the CIA and Army Intelligence.[131]

---

131 Fletcher Prouty, http://www.youtube.com/watch?v=PuRTDKowt0o

This highly polished military unit that Colonel Prouty describes in his book had been used on many occasions when the presidential motorcade had to traverse through a city lined with crowds and tall buildings. It was the job of this detail to take up positions around the parade route in order to protect the president from potential acts of violence, such as the ambush that occurred in Dallas. Prouty states, "According to the Secret Service's own guidelines, when a presidential motorcade can be kept at forty miles per hour or faster, it is not necessary to provide additional protection along the way. However, when the motorcade must travel at slower speeds, it is essential that there be protection personal on the ground, in buildings, and on top of buildings in order to provide needed surveillance" (Prouty 1992, 293).[132] He also commented on the choice of the parade route chosen by the Secret Service agent in charge of the Dallas area, saying that it was dangerous and put the president's life at risk, and that the parade route chosen was totally against Secret Service protocol.[133] In considering the choice of the parade route, which led the president right into an ambush, Prouty makes these final observations: "The conclusion that has been made is that it was part of the plot devised by the murderers; they had to create an ideal ambush site, and the Elm Street corner was it. Furthermore, no matter what route was selected for the presidential motorcade, the Secret Service and its trained military augmentation should have provided airtight protection all the way. This they did not even attempt to do, and this serous omission tends to provide strong evidence of the work of the conspirators. Someone on the inside was able to call off these normal precautions" (Prouty 1992, 293). It was even noted by researchers that agents at the Fort Worth office of the Secret Service were told they were not needed in Dallas.[134]

---

132 Fletcher Prouty, http://www.youtube.com/watch?v=Zy5H9gc61ls

133 Prouty further said that the route was chosen by the Secret Service and the Dallas Police Department.

134 Keep in mind that there were thousands of threats against the president at this time and most coming from the southern states and particularly the Dallas area of Texas.

According to Prouty, three days before the Texas trip, the Army commander in charge of the intelligence unit to be used in Dallas received a call from his superior officer, advising him that his detail would not be needed in Dallas and telling him to stand down. He advised the commander that another Army unit would cover that city. He further stated that his information had come from the head of the Secret Service. The commander, after he realized that something was not right, contacted Colonel Prouty and advised him what had occurred after the fact. Colonel Prouty then realized what had taken place in Dallas. He was a highly trained intelligence officer with several years of CIA and Army Intelligence training. He then understood the depth of this crime and knew that it must have been ordered by someone very high up in the chain of command. At this point, he decided to remain silent regarding his knowledge in order to protect himself and his family. This information was the motivation for his book.

So why was the assistance of this skilled and experienced Army unit refused? Who knew ahead of time the plan that was in place? Who then was responsible for this act of pure treason? This may remain a mystery, just as many other aspects of this case, but one fact regarding this breech in security cannot be denied. The Secret Service detail should have known that there was a lack of protection and surveillance in the streets that day, as evident by the lack of police officers and all those open windows, especially in Dealey Plaza. According to the Warren Commission Report, no buildings on the parade route were ever checked (this included the Texas School Book Depository). The report points out, "The Secret Service did not arrange for a prior inspection of the buildings along the motorcade route, either by the police or by custodians of the buildings, since it was not the usual practice of the Secret Service to do so" (Warren Commission 1964, 195). This statement is totally inaccurate, according to the statements made by witnesses such as Prouty. He stated that the Secret Service, through the use of supplemented Army Intelligence units, did check buildings and roof tops. The Warren Report also stated that according to the Dallas police, only three uniformed officers were posted by the Secret Service at Elm and Houston Streets, which was the site of all the gunfire; why? (Warren Commission 1964, 195).

The agent in charge while in Dallas was Forrest Sorrels. Agent Sorrels should have been held to answer for the many blunders that his agents committed during the Dallas trip and, of course, the murder of the president.[135] When asked by the Warren Commission why the parade route had been changed, Agent Sorrels stated, "The Elm Street route through Dealey Plaza was the most direct one to the Trade Mart" (Warren Commission 1964, 195). This, of course, was totally incorrect. Even the Warren Report conflicts with the agent's own statement. The report states, "There were far safer routes via freeways directly to the Trade Mart, but these routes would not have been in accordance with the White House staff instructions given to the Secret Service for a desirable motorcade route" (Warren Commission 1964, 195). It should be noted here as well that the White House staff was not (nor has it ever been) in charge of the president's security. The route chosen by Sorrels and the Secret Service ended in the death of President Kennedy.

As mentioned in the Warren Report, had the motorcade proceeded straight forward down Main Street, they could have used the freeway to get to the Trade Mart. Not only would this have saved time, but the speed of the motorcade would have added to the protection of the president as well as avoided the ambush in Dealey Plaza. As Prouty pointed out, clearly something was wrong here. It seemed that the protection of the president came in last place in Dallas. It also seems that Agent Sorrels was not telling the truth regarding the parade route.

---

135 It should be noted that in the video version of *Rush to Judgment*, Mark Lane interviewed witness Orval Nix, who was very good friends with Agent Sorrels. He stated that Sorrels always believed that some of the shots he heard and witnessed came from behind the fence on the grassy knoll area (Lane 1967).

In viewing a picture of Dealey Plaza, it is hard to believe that any intelligent person would have believed his statements.

Full shot of Dealey Plaza. Photo Credit: Author.

The final (and possibly the most incredible) aspect of this botched trip was the fact that the FBI had been warned of an assassination attempt in Dallas. There were also assassination attempts in Chicago, where suspects were arrested with weapons,[136] as well as in Miami, where they apparently took those threats seriously enough that the president did not ride in a motorcade in Miami; so what happened in Dallas? It could be that Dallas was controlled at that time by many cohorts that hated the president, including the underground network that Ruby belonged to, the corrupt Dallas Police Department, the Dallas mayor (who was certainly no Kennedy fan), LBJ (who was also no fan of Kennedy and feared that he would be off the presidential

136 Watch this video clip from ABC News to hear the whole story of the Chicago assassination attempt: http://www.youtube.com/watch?v=NBKcJAwwKrQ

ticket in 1964), and the Mafia, who almost certainly used Ruby to silence Oswald.

Abraham Bolden

Before moving on, I must include a section on the statements and testimony of former Secret Service Agent Abraham Bolden, who was the first African American agent assigned to the presidential detail. For further details, you can read his book, *The Echo from Dealey Plaza.* This book includes many details on how the Secret Service set him up for trying to tell the truth about the murder of President Kennedy; they had him arrested and removed from his position. In addition to all this valuable insight concerning his personal experiences, he also talks at length regarding the facts concerning the threats made against President Kennedy in Chicago, Miami, and Dallas, as well as the detailed ineptness of the presidential detail while in Texas.

In describing all the threats that were happening during 1963, Bolden states, "The way I saw it, there were at least three factions in America actively trying to get at Kennedy. First, the organized Cuban émigré population based in Miami resented him for his ineffectiveness against Castro, and specifically for the complete fiasco at the Bay of Pigs. Second, Mafia bosses across the country wanted Kennedy out of the way, believing that with JFK gone, Bobby's relentless pursuit of organized crime and corruption would end.[137] The last group was the least organized but perhaps the most numerous: the right wingers[138] and racists who couldn't abide his liberalism and intellectualism and who were outraged

---

137 And they were 100 percent correct on that point. See the PBS documentary, *JFK, Hoffa, and the Mob* (1993). This documentary explains the inside story of how the Mafia contributed their assistance to the murder of JFK. Remember, Dallas was controlled by the Mafia, especially what I call the Texas Syndicate. There were a lot of happy mobsters in this country the day the president was killed—a lot.

138 The right wingers he is referring to include the Texas oil tycoons and political party members like LBJ, Bobby Baker, Clint Murchison, and their henchmen like Malcolm Wallace.

by his unequivocal commitment to equal rights for all Americans" (Bolden 2008, 72–73).[139]

In his book, Bolden explains a few of the active and very viable threats he observed for himself in Chicago. It is for this reason that the president's trip to the city was cancelled, as was his visit to the annual army-navy game at Soldier Field. As Bolden explains, the initial reaction of the Secret Service was to ignore these threats, which very much upset him. He told Agent in Charge Martineau he did not have enough agents to investigate all the threats to the president. He actually overheard a phone call in which Martineau stated to someone, "All of our agents are tied up at the moment," and they didn't have any agents to send over there. When he hung up, Martineau explained that the call had been from the Chicago office of the FBI, which had information concerning the president's upcoming trip. A woman who owned a rooming house on the city's North Side had gone into one of the rooms to do some housekeeping and had discovered two rifles equipped with telescopic sights. She rented the room to two men she believed to be Hispanic, and she had also seen two white men going in and out of the room (Bolden 2008, 55–56). The agency finally investigated the incident but totally botched the case. This allowed the possible suspects, who had emptied their room, to escape while they were under surveillance. These suspects, according to Bolden, were never seen again, and there were no further attempts to find out who they were. Could these men have been some of the shooters in Dealey Plaza on November 22?[140]

It should also be noted that Bolden made the point that just a few days before the Dallas trip, the Secret Service had received further threats against the president's life by

---

139 Bolden, A. (2008). *The Echo from Dealey Plaza.* New York: Three Rivers Press.

140 I know this sounds amazing. Here are some potential killers with weapons, and they ended the investigation when they lost them? What about fingerprints in the room? What, if anything, did they leave behind? What about their vehicle? Did it have a license plate? These agents would have clearly flunked out of the LA Police Academy.

anti-Castro Cubans. Then we have the information, which was sent to all the FBI offices in the country, warning about a right wing group attempting to assassinate the president on his trip to Dallas, which apparently no one in the Secret Service took seriously either. This threat was also verified by a former FBI agent, who brought this point up on Oprah Winfrey's talk show in the 1990s. He still had a copy of the warning that went out to all of the officers just days before the murder of the president.[141]

Bolden goes on to explain that the lack of concern for the president that he felt was rampant in the agency. He said that "*the women and booze mentality of the presidential detail was putting the president at risk*" (Bolden 2008, 73). He felt that the suspects were exploiting these weaknesses in the president's protection. I mentioned earlier that the presidential protection detail was at a late-night party the night before the assassination, and Bolden confirms this as a fact many times over in his book. He also gives a solid explanation to how the conspirators managed to get their hands on official Secret Service badges and credentials. He states, "I firmly believed that the officer who confronted the unknown suspect behind the picket fence immediately after the assassination was indeed shown an authentic Secret Service commission book, the book that had been lost by, or taken from, an alcohol-impaired agent the night before. Further, I was convinced that the Secret Service leadership acted to conceal or at least obfuscate this fact by providing new commission books for all the agents in the service.

---

141 Many people believe that warning came from Oswald, although there is no evidence of this. I believe that it very well may have been him. Although this is speculation, it makes sense that it could have been him. After all, he did go into the Dallas FBI office before the assassination and left a note. Agent Hosty never gave a clear description of what the note really said, he did testify that he was ordered to destroy the note by his superior officer, which he did once Ruby killed Oswald. I have always wondered what that note really said, because as Jim Garrison once said, if the note was a real threat against Hosty, the FBI, or the Dallas police, they would have kept it because it would make the case of the lone nut even stronger ... correct?

The service has, of course, publicly denied this" (Bolden 2008, 73).

It is so important in any police investigation to have witnesses on the inside; Abraham Bolden is our inside man in the Secret Service. It is clear that the agents who lost the president were upset, but they did not do their job, and even witnesses inside the motorcade felt that way. One was Senator Yarborough, who was riding in the vice president's car; he said that the Secret Service agents in the following car appeared to react very slowly, if at all. He stated that he observed them from behind, and except for Clint Hill, none of them made any attempt to save the president. Also, according to the senator, there was ample time to do so. In the documentary, *The Men Who Killed Kennedy*, he makes these claims, as well as other points, including this detail: the cars were going under the triple overpass before any of the agents responded at all (Turner 1988).[142] Bolden lends information that would support what the senator had witnessed. He claims, "One of the younger agents riding on the car behind the presidential limousine heard what sounded like a rifle shot. He started to jump from the running board to assist the president, just as Agent Clint Hill had run to protect the first lady. But the young agent was called back to the follow-up car by a more senior agent, just as the third and fatal shot tore into the back of the president's skull" (Bolden 2008, 52).

Finally, Bolden adds further information with regard to the missing Secret Service badges: "I was there when all the Secret Service's identification books were secretly replaced by the Bureau of Printing and Engraving. In my own opinion, the replacement gives credibility to the whispered rumor that an agent had lost his identification or had it stolen from him" (Bolden 2008, 105). Bolden firmly believes that the conspirators managed to get the ID from a drunken agent in the Cellar the night before the assassination. This is further confirmation that the imposter the Dallas police encountered

142 Their reaction time was pitiful; no doubt the effects of all their partying the night before and their overuse of alcohol.

behind the grassy knoll was in fact using a stolen Secret Service ID. But of course, the Warren Commission and the FBI could have cared less about this information, which is why there has never been (or ever will be) any investigation done in order to disclose who these phony agents were. This simply adds more fuel to the fire that there was a massive cover-up in Dallas.

Chapter 9

So What about Lee Oswald

"The truly educated man is that rare individual who can separate reality from illusion."
—Unknown

There is so much evidence proving that Lee Oswald had nothing to do with the murder of President Kennedy that entire books have been written on this subject. I will attempt here to condense, as much as possible, the information on Lee Harvey Oswald's involvement with the intelligence community as well as the Kennedy assassination.

At seventeen years of age, Oswald joined the US Marine Corps. While in the marines, he was stationed in Japan at a U-2 spy plane station. He was also given Russian language classes; this can all be verified through his military records. He received a hardship discharge when his mother became ill (or at least that was the official cover story). He defected to the Soviet Union in 1959.[143] While in Russia, Oswald was treated like a dignitary; according to Jack Swike, the author of *The Missing Chapter*: "Oswald got 770 rubles per month, and his diary claimed that his income was equal to that of the plant manager's where he worked in Minsk. Oswald was also furnished with a nice apartment with two balconies that overlooked a river" (Swike 2008, 13).[144]

When he returned to the United States in 1962, he brought with him his Russian-born wife, Marina Prusakova;

---

143 Was this the real Oswald? J. Edgar Hoover reported around this time that someone may be using Oswald's birth certificate; that's interesting, to say the least. Ventura, J., and D. Russell (2010). *American Conspiracies*. New York: Skyhorse Publishing.

144 Also according to Swike, Oswald was the only person whom he found that earned a stipend while in Russia.

they settled in the Dallas area and had two daughters.[145] In the summer of 1963, Lee moved to New Orleans, where he had grown up, and renewed his acquaintance with a man named David Ferrie. Ferrie was Oswald's commander in the Civil Air Patrol when Oswald was a teenager. Ferrie was also a soldier of fortune who was a proclaimed anti-Castro patriot. He had been involved in the Bay of Pigs disaster and hated President Kennedy for not supporting the invasion with air support.[146] Ferrie also had many links to the American Mafia and was good friends with Santo Trafficante and other powerful Mafia bosses, his favorite being Carlos Marcello of New Orleans.[147]

During his time in New Orleans, Oswald began to involve himself with other acquaintances of David Ferrie. One of these individuals was Guy Banister, a retired FBI agent who once headed the Chicago FBI office. Banister was now a private investigator and had an office in New Orleans. This office had the same address that was on Oswald's Fair Play for Cuba Committee flyers that he handed out on Canal Street in New Orleans. These flyers were also found in a garage at a home used by Oswald. It was the home of Ruth Paine, a family friend. The Fair Play for Cuba Committee, although an actual organization, was used by Oswald to make him

---

145 I will save speculation on what Oswald was doing in Russia; many feel he was a spy for the Office of Naval Intelligence, others think he was a decoy for other spies in Russia at that time. Either could be true, but one fact is certain: no one went to Russia at that time just for fun and games. He was there for a reason, you can bet on that.

146 We actually know now that Kennedy did not call off the air support, as most people thought; the whole Bay of Pigs disaster was a total screw-up by the CIA. Clearly, because he was president, Kennedy shouldered the blame publicly, which was clearly taking the high road, a far cry from our current president (Obama), who will not own up to anything.

147 On an interesting note, David Ferrie was murdered on February 22, 1967; this was the same day that one of Ferrie's CIA operatives, Eladio del Valle, was hacked to death and shot through the heart. Ferrie had told Jim Garrison just prior to his death that there was a death warrant out for him because Garrison had named him in his investigation (Belzer and Wayne 2013, 167–168).

appear as a procommunist, which was part of his cover in the CIA.[148] It should also be noted that Jack Ruby, who appeared in the Dallas police station during a press conference with Lee Oswald, corrected the news reporters when one of them misspoke the name of the Fair Play for Cuba Committee. It is interesting how Ruby, whom many claim did not know Oswald, knew the exact name of that organization. The reason is because he was involved in the assassination and knew Lee Oswald very well. Not to mention that Ruby knew almost every officer on the Dallas Police Department, which is one reason he had easy access to the police station in order to kill Oswald.[149]

When you really dig in and study the movements of Oswald during the summer of 1963 in New Orleans, it becomes very clear that he was being sheep dipped to look like a hotheaded communist. It is not known if Oswald went back to New Orleans on his own, or if he was sent there on some bogus mission by his handlers.[150] Oswald did have a good friend in New Orleans, perhaps his only good friend, Ron Lewis, who would later write his own book on their relationship: *Flashback: The Untold Story of Lee Harvey Oswald* (Lewis 1993).[151] Lewis claims that he and Oswald worked for Guy Banister and that Oswald knew Jack Ruby very well; they were both involved in arms transportation pertaining to Banister's business. He said that he and Oswald both received their money from the same paymaster;

---

148 Although the Fair Play for Cuba Committee really did exist and was based in New York at the time, Oswald was the only member in the New Orleans chapter.

149 More who knew Jack Ruby, http://www.youtube.com/watch?v=DUK3GNl2_Uo

150 Being "sheep dipped" is an old term that simply means that Oswald was being groomed to look like he was pro-Communist, when he was actually working for the government at the time. This is one reason the CIA has never wanted to release all their files on Oswald and why Army Intelligence and the Office of Naval Intelligence destroyed all their files on Oswald many years ago.

151 Lewis, R. (1993). *Flashback: The Untold Story of Lee Harvey Oswald.* Roseburg, OR: Lewcon Publishing.

Clay Shaw who was directly involved in the New Orleans operation, run out of Banister's office on Camp Street.[152]

Also of importance, regarding the Camp Street location, is the fact that E. Howard Hunt, the CIA spy, had an office there as well. He was running one of his spoof agencies out of the same office as Oswald and Banister. It should be no surprise then that Hunt was involved in all of this. He admitted on his deathbed to being involved in the plot to murder President Kennedy, which he called "the big event."[153] Also, remember that Hunt was one of the Watergate burglars and was sent to prison for it.[154]

As mentioned above, Guy Banister was a former FBI operative who at one time was in charge of the Chicago FBI office. The big question was, did he still have ties to the FBI? He certainly had ties to the CIA and was running several anti-Castro operations right out of his New Orleans office.[155] There were other FBI agents involved in Oswald's life at this time; James Hosty, a former Dallas FBI agent, told the House Select Committee in 1978 that he was assigned to keep tabs on Oswald while he was in Dallas.[156] If Oswald had been a real assassin, then Hosty's abilities would appear to be right in line with the Secret Service on the day of the assassination. Hosty admitted to having several contacts with Oswald in the summer of 1963, and witnesses at the FBI office

---

152 Banister's operation, http://www.youtube.com/watch?v=U-ObQc7es_c

153 Hunt interview, http://www.youtube.com/watch?v=PsBiVJsgzmI

154 It is not surprising to me that Nixon used Hunt, his old CIA pal, to pull off the Watergate burglary; when you watch Hunt's deathbed confession, you will see why Nixon used him: he was a fixer, a real plumber, and great organizer.

155 It should be pointed out that Banister was operating these agencies in the heart of downtown New Orleans, right across the street from the Secret Service, the Office of Naval Intelligence, and other federal agencies. Also, consider this point: if Oswald was such a solid communist, what was he doing hanging out in such a location? He should have feared for his life in that part of town. I think my point is obvious here.

156 Turner, N. (Producer) (1991). *The Men Who Killed Kennedy: The Witnesses* [DVD].

said they had seen Oswald in there on occasions (Turner 1991). As an example, several days before the assassination, Oswald walked right into the FBI headquarters in Dallas and delivered a note to Agent Hosty.[157] After all, this assassination was what the Dallas police and the Warren Commission called a "well-planned and -thought-out execution of the president" (really?).[158] Finally, when Oswald was arrested on the afternoon of November 22nd, he had Hosty's telephone number in his pocket.[159]

Hosty later appeared on several talk shows and media outlets, giving interviews regarding his contacts with Oswald. In one documentary, he told the interviewer the above story, that Oswald had in fact come to his office only a few days before the assassination and left him a note. According to Hosty, the note was a threat by Oswald. Unfortunately, what it really said may be lost to history; we have heard several versions of this note over the years. The clerk who received the note said Oswald made threats to the Dallas police and to

---

157 Now is this really something a killer would do right before the assassination? Walk right into the FBI office located in the city where he was planning this murder, just days before the event, and put his face on video? I ask again, does this make any sense?

158 I ask you to really think about the importance of this point: the FBI and Hosty admitted this under oath, and there was videotape of Oswald walking into the Dallas FBI headquarters on that date. Many researchers believe that Oswald, acting as an informant, was actually bringing Hosty a warning about the assassination attempt in Dallas, and further that Oswald had infiltrated a right wing attempt on the president's life; this would make sense, seeing that warnings did go out to all FBI offices in the United States around this time.

159 Oswald also had in his wallet David Ferrie's library card from the New Orleans Public Library, so how did the Warren Commission explain that? They didn't; it never made it in the report, as far as I can tell. The FBI announced several times that they could not find a link between Ferrie and Oswald; what do you call the library card? They also said they could not find a link between Ruby and Oswald, and we now know that was a complete joke as well.

the FBI, stating he was going to blow up their buildings if he was not left alone.

After Oswald was killed by Jack Ruby, two days after the murder of the president, Hosty was ordered by the special agent in charge of the Dallas office to destroy the note. According to Hosty's testimony to the Select Committee on Assassinations in 1978, his supervisor, Special Agent Gordon Shanklin, told him to "destroy that God damned thing, I never want to see it again." Hosty then ripped up the note and flushed it down the toilet, according to his own testimony. Hosty was once asked how he could destroy such a valuable piece of evidence, and he stated that it was not evidence, because Oswald was dead, and it was perfectly legitimate for him to destroy the note at that time. He did state that he wished at times he had kept the note, because for many years after the president's assassination, he had felt as if he was the FBI's scapegoat. He believed they were trying to conceal the fact that their agency had contact with Oswald just prior to the assassination and apparently did nothing to control or stop him (considering the official version that Oswald acted alone), a fact that the Warren Commission was not properly informed of during their investigation.

To reiterate, many investigators feel that the note delivered to Hosty was a warning to the FBI regarding the assassination, and lends to the credence that Oswald had been working as an informant of the FBI. We do encounter this viewpoint throughout many aspects of the investigation. But there is solid and factual evidence pointing to this conclusion that Oswald did work for the FBI. During the Warren Commission's investigation, Lee Rankin, their chief counsel, received information that Oswald was in fact working for the FBI at the time of the president's assassination. This information was so incredible and overwhelming that it was never included in the official report, but there are actual transcripts of the conversations held between Rankin, Boggs, and Dulles regarding this volatile information; it is so powerful I have included it here for you to read. You will be amazed.

Lee Rankin: If that was true and it ever came out and could be established, you would have people think that there was a conspiracy to accomplish this assassination that nothing the commission did or anyone could dissipate.

Hale Boggs: You are so right.

Allen Dulles: Oh, terrible.

Boggs: The implications of this are fantastic. Don't you think so?

Rankin: Now it is something that will be very difficult to prove out. I am confident that the FBI will never admit it, and I presume their records will never show it.

Dulles: Why would it be in their interest to say he is clearly the only guilty one?

Rankin: They would like to have us fold and quit.

Boggs: This closes the case, you see?

Rankin: They found their man. There is nothing more to do. The commission supports their conclusion, and we can go on home, and that is the end of it.

Boggs: I don't even like to see this being taken down.

Dulles: Yes, I think this record should be destroyed.[160]

This is truly stunning information; after reading this, how can anyone ever take anything the commission reported as true facts? They were in the business of concealing

---

160 MPI Media Group. (2006). *The Murder of JFK: A Revisionist History* [DVD].

information from the public; I hope this proves that point to any of you who were still holdouts. We were lied to, let's face that fact.

So it should now seem pretty clear that Lee Oswald was being monitored and controlled very tightly by government agencies, while all the time being sheep dipped and paraded as a communist. After all, they could not have picked a better scapegoat than Oswald. Oswald defected to the Soviet Union (supposedly) and, in the eyes of the public, had denounced his citizenship[161] and lived in a communist country for three years. Some researchers believe that Oswald needed to be sheep dipped because, after his return to America, he had taken up residence in the white Russian community in Dallas, who were all rabid anticommunists. One of Oswald's best friends and cohorts was a man named George de Mohrenschildt, who was a shadowy, exiled Russian count who lived outside of Dallas. He liked Oswald very much; they both had many mutual interests such as literature, Russian life, and Russian culture.[162] It should also be noted that de Mohrenschildt's wife Jeanne was good friends with Jacqueline Kennedy and her family.

To further add to the mystery surrounding George de Mohrenschildt and his relationship to Lee Oswald, there are other aspects to his life that must be noted. For one, it seems certain that he was somehow affiliated with the CIA. According to Benson (1993), "de Mohrenschildt was involved in CIA training for the Bay of Pigs invasion in Guatemala. At the time of JFK's death, he lived in Haiti where he was representing the interests of Dallas oil billionaire Clint Murchison" (Benson 1993, 110). Murchison was also a very good friend of LBJ's and was at his home the night

---

161 According to official records, this is not true; he never truly gave up his US citizenship, which is why he was allowed back in the United States.

162 Please keep in mind that Oswald was not the loser that the Warren Commission made him out to be. He was very intellectual; he spoke at least two languages, was well educated in the Marine Corps, and was an expert on Russian history.

before the assassination.[163] De Mohrenschildt was himself heavily involved in the oil business. This connection led to a relationship during that time with George H. W. Bush, the former president of the United States, who was also involved with the CIA at that time, even though he has refused to admit this.

According to many researchers, including Russell Brown, the author of *The Immaculate Deception* (1991), former President Bush had a much longer career with the CIA than he admitted to, and that is how he met George de Mohrenschildt. "Bush claims he never worked for the CIA until he was appointed director by President Ford in 1976. Of course, Bush has a company duty to deny being in the CIA. The CIA is a secret organization. No one ever admits to being a member." Brown further points out, "The truth is that Bush had been a top CIA agent since before the 1961 invasion of Cuba, working with Felix Rodriguez and other anti-Castro Cubans. Bush may deny his work for the CIA in 1959, but there are records in the files of Rodriguez and others involved in the Bay of Pigs invasion of Cuba that expose Bush's role" (Brown 1991, 31).[164]

Also, Russ Baker, the author of *Family of Secrets,* has a lot to say about the relationship between George H. W. Bush and George de Mohrenschildt. Bush says that he met de Mohrenschildt through a nephew who was a college student during the early 1960s, but it is clear that they knew each other very well and that de Mohrenschildt still had a lot to say about Lee Oswald and the CIA. According to a historical letter, which Baker supplies in his book, de Mohrenschildt

---

[163] Several books have been written on the subject of LBJ's involvement in the assassination of JFK; most of them provide very strong motives and clear evidence that Johnson was somehow involved in the murder or cover-up. Some of these books are reviewed later. You should also watch the final episode of the *The Men Who Killed Kennedy*. You need to see all of the episodes, but the last three have powerful information in them regarding the cover-up. Get them and watch them; you will not be disappointed.

[164] Bowen, R. S. (1991). *The Immaculate Deception.* Carson City, NV: American West Publishers.

was pretty much begging the elder Bush, who was director of the CIA in the 1970s, for help with an urgent matter. Because of the importance of this letter, I have included an excerpt here, stated in de Mohrenschildt's own words: "Maybe you will be able to bring a solution into the hopeless situation I find myself in. My wife and I find ourselves surrounded by some vigilantes; our phone is bugged; and we are being followed everywhere. Either FBI is involved in this or they do not want to accept my complaints. We are driven to insanity by the situation.... I tried to write, stupidly and unsuccessfully, about Lee H. Oswald and must have angered a lot of people.... Could you do something to remove this net around us? This will be my last request for help, and I will not annoy you any more" (Baker 2009, 67).

This letter was written in 1977, just a few months before de Mohrenschildt was found shot to death in Miami; the cause of death was not ruled a homicide, but there is a lot of reasonable doubt in this case. De Mohrenschildt was found with a single 20 gauge shotgun blast to his head, and there was a shotgun supposedly found lying close to his body. Shotgun suicides are very rare indeed. In my years investigating deaths in Los Angeles, I never saw one, but they do happen from time to time. This one was rather convenient, though, occurring right after the House Select Committee on Assassinations (HSCA) had subpoenaed him to testify about the assassination and his relationship with Lee Harvey Oswald. De Mohrenschildt had testified to the Warren Commission in 1963, but since that time, he had made other statements retracting this testimony. Actually, as mentioned, de Mohrenschildt was in the process of writing a book, and the information contained in his manuscript may have implemented some of his old CIA buddies. What this may have signaled to the powers still in control was that de Mohrenschildt had developed a case of loose lips and was not willing to play ball with them anymore. Perhaps they thought it was time for him to leave the scene, permanently.[165] He was

[165] This is a lengthy subject, but for more information, read Russ Baker's book, *Family of Secrets*.

bringing up claims that the CIA had something to do with the murder of the president and that the FBI was covering up the facts.[166] According to Benson, de Mohrenschildt, later commenting on his book, stated, "That's when disaster struck. You see, in that book I played devil's advocate. Without directly implicating myself as an accomplice in the JFK assassination, I still mentioned a number of names, particularly of the FBI and CIA officials who apparently may not be exposed under any circumstances. I was drugged surreptitiously. As a result I was committed to a mental hospital" (Benson 1993, 110). Benson goes on to remark, "On the day he agreed to an interview with the HSCA, he was found dead of a gunshot wound through his mouth" (1993, 110–111).[167]

Well, after that lengthy synopsis regarding George de Mohrenschildt, we come to another colorful figure, the convicted assassin of Lee Harvey Oswald, Mr. Jack Ruby. It has been established that Oswald knew Ruby and knew him well. Of course, the Warren Commission said they found no connection between them. For one, it was established by Mark Lane in 1966 that Lee Oswald had been seen in Jack Ruby's Carousel Club on several occasions; he was identified by several individuals, including former employees at the club (Lane 1966).

One of these employees was Beverly Oliver, who had worked for Ruby for quite some time; she stated she saw Oswald in the club with Ruby on many occasions. She also said she saw David Ferrie in the club with Oswald and Ruby. This is the same Beverly Oliver who had her pictures confiscated the day of the assassination. She states in an episode of *The Men Who Killed Kennedy* that Jack Ruby introduced her to Lee Oswald one night at the club while they were all sitting together. She has sworn to this encounter for many decades, never wavering, and is certain beyond any

166 There is some solid information posted in the *Reading Eagle*, Friday, April 1, 1977.

167 George de Mohrenschildt's death, http://www.youtube.com/watch?v=l95ENklkmHc

doubt that the person she met in Ruby's club that night was Lee Harvey Oswald (Turner 1991).

It appears then that Oliver is stating the truth regarding her observations, but there were other witnesses who saw Jack Ruby and Lee Oswald together prior to the assassination of President Kennedy. I have listed a few here, but there were more.[168]

- Esther Ann Mash, an employee at Jack Ruby's nightclub, witnessed Oswald in the club with Ruby.
- Dallas attorney Carroll Jarnigan was in the club and saw Lee Oswald in there with Ruby.
- Madeline Brown, a frequent visitor to the Carousel Club and mistress to LBJ, saw Lee Oswald in the club with Jack Ruby in the fall of 1963.
- Numerous Carousel Club performers, including Jada, a club favorite, who later disappeared.
- Another employee of the Carousel Club, Billy Willis, said he saw a man in the club who looked very much like Oswald.

If we then establish the fact that Ruby and Oswald knew each other, it makes sense that there was a clear look of recognition on Oswald's face when Ruby spoke up at one of the press conferences with Oswald in the Dallas police station (and when Ruby approached him in the basement of the jail with a gun in his hand in order to execute him). If you watch the video, Oswald looked right at Ruby with a puzzled look as he approached. I don't think he would have assumed that Ruby would have killed his old CIA buddy.[169]

But Ruby was clearly following orders; he was on a mission to keep Oswald from talking, and talk he would have later that day in a press conference scheduled at the county

---

168 A little research shows there were others who saw Ruby and Oswald together. The Warren Commission simply did not care to find the truth, of course, because that would mean they would have had to do their job and really investigate.

169 Oswald's murder, http://www.youtube.com/watch?v=DUK3GNl2_Uo

jail, with over 150 reporters from around the world. It is obvious that Ruby had stalked Oswald for two days around the police station, just waiting for his moment to strike.[170] After he was convicted, Ruby tried to tell us what his motives truly were, once he realized that the plotters were wrong and he would go to the electric chair for the murder of Oswald. Many researchers feel that Ruby had believed that he would come off as a hero for murdering Oswald and thereby receive a light sentence.[171]

There is further evidence of Ruby's involvement, such as a picture taken around the School Book Depository right after the assassination by a news crew. Some have claimed it was not him, but it is clearly Ruby (unless he had a twin). As confirmation, a witness who worked in the Book Depository saw Ruby milling around in front of the building, acting like he was a police officer trying to get statements from witnesses. Then we have the contact made with Seth Kantor, a local newsman who had known Ruby for several years. Kantor confirms that he saw Ruby at Parkland Hospital in the hallway of the emergency room area. His testimony was absolutely clear and precise, and he has always been certain that it was Jack Ruby he had a conversation with that day in

---

170 I really don't think Ruby wanted to complete the mission, which is why he did not shoot Oswald on sight the day before. He apparently had his weapon with him. Why else would someone need to pack a gun in a police station? Also, if you read Robert Blakey's book, he also felt that Ruby was stalking Oswald (see *The Plot to Kill the President: Organized Crime Assassinated JFK*).

171 According to Billy Grammer, a former Dallas police officer, Ruby called the night before they were preparing to move Oswald out of the Dallas Police Department to the county jail and stated "If you move Oswald the way you are planning, we are going to kill him" (Benson 1993, 157). Grammer said at first he could not clearly identify the voice, but the next day, he was certain it was Ruby. It should be noted that Gordon Shaklin, head of the Dallas FBI office, said he received the same message from potentially the same caller, because he said the same thing to the FBI. Also notice that Ruby said, "We are going to kill him," not "I am going to kill him"; that is what we call a spontaneous statement in law enforcement; many times people don't really think before they speak.

the hospital. How could he have been mistaken? It was clear he wasn't, but the Warren Commission completely changed his testimony, stating that Kantor was mistaken and really saw Ruby at the police station later that day.[172] Kantor refuted that change, saying it was ridiculous, and he was forever upset that the Warren Commission perjured his testimony.[173]

To back up Kantor's observations that day, and to add another interesting fact about Ruby's appearance at Parkland, there was another witness not well known to the public who also testified before the Warren Commission that she also saw Ruby at the hospital on November 22nd. Wilma Tice was certain that she saw Jack Ruby at Parkland Hospital and told her story to the Commission. Because this information was made public she received several death threats and reported some of them to the Dallas Police who have records on file regarding these threats. One such report which I located was taken on July 22, 1964 in which she reported that a phone caller told her she needs to keep her mouth such about seeing Ruby at the hospital or else. Later that day she found that someone had attempted to lock her in her own home by boarding up the doors and windows from the outside and she called the police. Because of these threats the Dallas Police kept a close watch on her and her residence for several months in 1964.

So what was Ruby doing at the hospital anyway? Many researchers believe that he was the one who planted the pristine bullet on a stretcher in the hallway. This remains a possibility, but there is no real evidence pointing to this fact.[174]

---

172 Seth Kantor, http://www.youtube.com/watch?v=EgDXFqIjAO0

173 The Warren Commission gave no weight to Kantor's story, stating that he was mistaken and had actually seen Ruby at the police station later in the day. How insulting was that? Really, he was a newsman; I am sure he had his facts straight. There are two words that speak to these actions by the Warren Commission: cover-up.

174 There is much more intriguing information on this subject in the next chapter.

Finally, what did Ruby have to say about his murder of Oswald? And what was he going to tell Earl Warren and the other commission members if he had been granted permission to go to Washington with them? We will never know, because his attempt to do so fell on deaf ears. Once again, they were not interested in the truth or Ruby's true motives. Ruby did speak to the public a few times; he once said, "I was used as a scapegoat ... but if I am eliminated, there won't be any way of knowing the true facts of this case. Right now I am the only one that can bring out the truth."[175] Ruby said this to the Warren Commission members when they visited him in the county jail. But there was a press conference long after his trial in which he clearly stated that he was a pawn in a conspiracy. When asked by the news media about the depths of this conspiracy, Ruby said it came from very high up in the government. He said that the conspirators had so much to gain by putting him in that position that they would never let the true facts of the case come out. This sounds eerily reminiscent of what Oswald told reporters at the Dallas police station: "I am just a patsy; no sir, I did not kill anyone.... I don't know what dispatches you people have been given, but I emphatically deny these charges." Oswald and Ruby were two pawns in a giant chess game that ended in the murder of our president, and the cover-up continues to this day (just think about Bill O'Reilly's new whitewash book as an example).

Was Oswald Even in the Window?

In investigating the question of whether Oswald was in the sniper's nest at all, we must first turn to the witnesses who saw him before and after the shooting. We have Police Officer Baker and the building manager, who spotted him in the lunchroom within eighty seconds after the shooting. According to the officer, Oswald was not out of breath and

---

175 Ruby asked the commission members over and over again to take him to Washington because it was not safe for him to talk in Dallas, but they refused. It was obvious that Ruby knew if he talked in Dallas, he would have written his own death warrant.

was drinking a Coke in the lunchroom. Interestingly, the Warren Commission left out the fact that Baker said Oswald was drinking a Coke; I guess it made it sound way too casual and added to the uncertainty that he was in that window only seconds earlier. Then we have Carolyn Arnold, who clearly and unequivocally saw Oswald in the lunchroom at 12:15 p.m.,[176] and other employees who said they saw Lee even later, after Arnold had observed him, such as James Jarman, who said he saw Oswald as late as 12:20. Let's not forget Bonnie Ray Williams, who was eating his lunch in the exact window until 12:20 and did not see Oswald. If this had been a properly conducted investigation, we would have had answers to these important questions. Consider the fact that Arnold Rowland was certain he saw a man with a rifle in that sixth floor window just before the shooting. Rowland told the Warren Commission that he thought the man was a security person there to protect the president. Well, if Oswald was in the lunchroom at 12:15–12:20 or 12:25, depending on the witness, and the shooting went off at 12:30 with another man in the sniper's window, then Oswald could not have done the shooting. Another interesting side note is that the motorcade was actually a whole five minutes late, so why wasn't Oswald already in the window at 12:15, with the motorcade due in just ten minutes? Was it because the window was already occupied? Many researchers believe that Oswald was in the lunchroom because he was told to be there by his handlers. It makes sense to me, because then he would not be on the sixth floor, where he could have accidently run into the real assassins.

There are also other witnesses who were observing the sixth floor window; Thomas Dillard, chief photographer for the *Dallas Morning News,* was riding in the motorcade and captured a picture of the window just after the last round was fired. Robert Jackson, who was in his car, yelled out that he had seen a rifle sticking out of the window. According to Michael Benson (1993), Dillard's photo of the sniper's nest

176 The original time she stated was 12:25, but due to pressure from the Warren Commission, that time was changed to 12:15 (Turner 1991).

window immediately after the shooting clearly shows boxes and shadows in that window. Comparing this photo with the one taken thirty seconds later by James Powell gives us the impression that the boxes in the window had been rearranged after the shooting (Benson 1993, 112).

So what does this all mean? Well, if we consider all the facts surrounding the presence of Oswald in the building, we see that he was observed by a coworker in the lunchroom at 12:15 or 12:25 (Turner, 1991); the motorcade was scheduled to pass by at 12:25, which left him only ten minutes to get up to the sixth floor from the lunchroom,[177] load his weapon, arrange the boxes, get set to shoot, and fire his shots. Then, of course, he was seen by Officer Baker in the lunchroom (where he was last seen), no more than eighty seconds after the shooting. When you consider the fact that someone was seen milling around in that window just prior to the shooting, and of course in the window during the shooting, how can anyone in their right mind think it was Oswald? Really, go visit that building and see how large it is (even empty); the scenario set forth by the official version is totally and completely implausible, period. Oswald was innocent of that shooting. It's as simple as that; we don't need Columbo or Joe Friday to solve this case, just some basic police work.

177 Also, there was no elevator working that day, so most likely he would have had to use the stairs.

Chapter 10

The Real Case against Oswald

"The most dangerous thing is illusion."
—Ralph Waldo Emerson

Having been involved in hundreds (if not thousands) of prosecutions during my time on the LAPD, I feel that I have the right to my opinion: the case against Lee Oswald was not really a case at all, it was a pipe dream. The results of the Warren Commission investigation were simply not strong enough to have won a conviction in court based on the evidence and eyewitness reports. Also, due to Oswald's murder by Jack Ruby, the commission never did have to present their case in court. But I can assure you that even if District Attorney Wade was able to pull every crooked string possible, the case would not have ended in their favor. This of course is why Oswald had to be eliminated. In this chapter, I will cover some of the basic facts for you and let you, the jury, determine if you would have found him guilty within the spectrum of the law.

The Nitrate Tests

Through the use of the paraffin test, it was determined that there was no conclusive proof with any certainty that Lee Oswald had fired a rifle that day. Researcher Paul Chambers[178] does an excellent job of explaining the process and nature of a paraffin test: "Oswald was given a paraffin wax test of his hands and right cheek to determine if they showed the presence of nitrates. This test consisted of

[178] Chambers, G. P. (2012). *Head Shot: The Science behind the JFK Assassination.* New York: Prometheus Books. Chambers's book is an excellent read. He will give you many more details on ballistics and does a wonderful job of hammering Vincent Bugliosi's book, *Reclaiming History,* which is the Warren Commission simply rewritten. But please read *Head Shot* for some solid information.

pouring hot wax onto his hands and cheek and removing the wax cast after hardening. This process fixes nitrate compounds present on the skin into the wax." Chambers goes on to explain, "When a rifle is fired, these hot nitrate gasses blow back from the firing chamber onto the shooter's face even if the rifle's firing chamber were perfectly sealed" (Chambers 2012, 171).

Chambers concludes, "Oswald's paraffin test showed that no nitrates were present on his cheek, consistent with someone who had not fired a rifle" (Chambers 2012, 171). Although this evidence is conclusive that he could not have fired a rifle, there is also evidence that the paraffin tests on his hands were also negative. Mark Lane's book and movie, *Rush to Judgment,* claims that both tests were negative, using actual information from the Warren Commission's own investigation. I have verified this fact; the commission did not even consider the paraffin test results to be useful in the case against Oswald. Chambers further states, "Since the paraffin wax seeps down into the pores, it is a very sensitive test. Even washing one's face prior to the test will not remove all presence of nitrates" (Chambers 2012, 171). So the test was negative, even though we were told it was positive during press conferences held by District Attorney Wade hours after the shooting.

Oswald the Sharpshooter

Concerning Oswald's ability with a rifle, there have been claims that he was a crack shot, and the fact that he was a US Marine made him an expert with a rifle. Well, Oswald's Marine Corps records show this to be far from the truth. Although Oswald did qualify as a marksman in boot camp, this is pretty much less than average for the marines; actually, his later scores and abilities with a rifle placed him at the bottom of the scale in the Marine Corps. According to official records, he was just barely able to qualify in order to stay on active duty. In the marines, even if you don't carry a rifle for a living, you must still qualify with your rifle. If not, you will be disciplined and retrained or even discharged. Really, what good is a marine who can't shoot?

The Warren Commission credits Oswald with the shooting of the century. To take that shot, he would have had to hit a moving target through trees and thick foliage.[179] It was an impossible shot and, not only that, a horrible location for a real killer to have chosen, really. There were so many more probable shooting locations around Dealey Plaza and even from the Book Depository. But a fatal shot from the supposed sniper's location on the sixth floor would have simply been a miracle, if at all possible.[180] Moreover, there have been hundreds of attempts to duplicate this feat of marksmanship, and none have come close to succeeding; it is just simply not a doable head shot within the time allotted by the Warren Commission. Oh sure, you get these computer buffs who make it happen on the History Channel through the use of some sophisticated computer animation, but in a real life setting, with the president riding in an open car, crowds of people and police officers on the street below, and the immense pressure of such an event, not so doable. You would need to be calm enough and accurate enough to even attempt such a shot.

We must also consider that the weapon was a thirty-year-old, bolt-action, World War II rifle with a dysfunctional scope, which was terribly misaligned. The Warren Commission also said that only three shots were fired at the president; we now know this was incorrect. The true number

---

179 Not to mention that one of the first shots hit the president in the throat, a wound later determined by all the medical doctors at Parkland to be an entrance wound, an impossible wound to have been caused by a shot fired from that sixth floor window.

180 The FBI, the US Army, the Secret Service, and dozens of other shooting experts could not duplicate Oswald's shooting demonstration in Dallas. The reason being, it was impossible. It could not be done. Not from that angle, from that distance, and through similar obstacles, not to mention that piece of junk rifle, which was very old and fitted with a two-dollar scope, using thirty-five-year-old ammunition.

could have been as high as eight or nine shots.[181] But even using their number, which was three shots, Oswald would have had to fire those three shots in less than seven seconds, with an inaccurate, antiquated, bolt-action rifle, scoring two very accurate hits out of three.

Now you will read the story of a retired FBI agent who worked on the JFK assassination by following up actual leads; his name is Don Adams, and he adds a lot of great background information, which he obtained as an active agent in 1963. Adams said many leads were never followed up on because they led away from the lone assassin, Lee Oswald; he says the Warren Commission was a whitewash and that they covered up many existing facts.[182] When he saw the film of the assassination, he immediately knew the president was shot from the front; it was clear to this agent that at least some of the shots came from in front of the limo. The reason he never broke his silence is because he was ordered to keep his mouth shut. His superiors had been given their orders as well; the official story was, it was Oswald, and he acted alone. He also brings out a point that I have made many times myself: there was no way for Oswald (or anyone else, for that matter) to have fired three shots, scoring the two very accurate hits mentioned earlier, and to do so with a bolt-action rifle, which must be operated manually, in under seven seconds—simply no way. See his statements on YouTube.[183]

Even considering the fact that the rifle could have been resting on boxes for support, you cannot manipulate a bolt-action rifle accurately in that amount of time. Each round must be placed in the breech using a bolt, which must be operated by hand. Then, you must refocus your sights all over again after each shot, while making the proper adjustments

181 There is also speculation that silencers were used on some of the weapons, thereby eliminating many of the sounds of the rifle fire in the plaza.

182 Adams also brings up Joseph Milteer, a right wing radical who was caught in an undercover sting a week before the assassination, describing with absolute accuracy the plans to murder the president. For more information, see this YouTube video: http://www.youtube.com/watch?v=vPVJhQ558vo

183 Don Adams, http://www.youtube.com/watch?v=2GyRBGzLV74

for the movement of the vehicle, which includes the speed of the vehicle, the depth of the shot you intend to make, and any wind resistance.[184] Allowing for the fastest possible movements on Oswald's part to reload his weapon each time it was fired, you must deduct four seconds off the total of six and a half to seven seconds. This leaves us with a remainder of three seconds, maybe slightly more, which is the time that the Warren Commission and Specter said that Oswald got off three shots, two being highly accurate shots at a moving vehicle through heavy foliage. This is clearly impossible, and the fact that no expert since could ever duplicate this feat proves that point.

Many shooting experts have watched the film of the assassination and have agreed that when the president came out from behind the road sign, he had already been shot in the throat. You can watch it yourself and see. By that point alone, Oswald had no shot to take, *period*; he could not have even seen President Kennedy through the trees, which to this day still obstructs the view of the street.[185]

Another overlooked point concerns the fact that it would have been suicide for Oswald to have shot the president from his own work place; have you ever thought about how ridiculous that sounds? How could he get away, hide the weapon, not be seen leaving the building, and most of all not be seen by the dozens and dozens of his coworkers while preparing for the shooting? They all knew him; how is it none of them ever saw him with the rifle? The place was crawling with fifty or more employees all the time, and there was an entire team of floor repair workers in there that week to repair the floors; no one spotted him wandering around with

---

184 If it sounds like I know a little about shooting, I do; I was also a marine and went through the same training as Oswald. I was also on the LAPD shooting team and shot in the California Police Olympics and the World Police Olympics.

185 For several years now, the Sixth Floor Museum has had Plexiglas around the so-called sniper's nest so you cannot get into the window any longer.

his rifle.[186] Clearly the best location for any shooter would have been outside that building; the odds of being trapped in the building after a shooting were too great, and there were multiple well-concealed locations all around Dealey Plaza (such as the ones used by the real killers behind the grassy knoll).

It is also hard to forget that when Officer Baker of the Dallas Police Department entered the Book Depository, it was only seconds after the final shot was fired as the motorcade sped away. Baker testified and claimed to news reporters that he encountered Oswald in the lunchroom on the second floor, having his lunch. This is a certainty, because Oswald's boss was with him and identified Oswald on the spot. How in the world could he have been all the way up on the sixth floor one minute and in the lunchroom the next? If you visit this building today, you will see that it is old and antiquated; it had only one stairway on one side of the building. Oswald would have had to run all the way down the stairs after stashing the weapon on the opposite side of the building and then appear in the lunchroom only a minute or so after the shooting. It would have been close to impossible, but the Warren Commission said he did it. Once again, Oswald was correct when he stated, "I'm just a patsy."

Was There Another Oswald?

There are some researchers who have investigated the possibility that there was more than one Oswald; this is a very interesting concept, but I do not have the time to address it fully in this writing. Despite this, I will state the following facts:[187] On several occasions just prior to the murder of the president, a man claiming to be Oswald was seen around

186 This included Bonnie Ray Williams, an employee who actually ate lunch while sitting in that exact window; he left around 12:20. Williams then joined his friends on another floor of the building. You can see his lunch bag in the pictures taken by the Dallas police that day.

187 There are several good books out there that talk about the two Oswalds. By all means, if that interests you, do some research. I have listed some books in the reference section for you.

the Dallas area. One was seen at a local shooting range, making a spectacle of himself by shooting at other people's targets. Another possible look-alike was seen at a Dallas Ford dealership, making statements about the Soviet Union. Of course, all these men were described as being five foot seven or eight, and we know Oswald was nearly six feet tall, according to his Marine Corps records and his draft board records. We must also remember that one witness, Deputy Roger Craig, saw a man leaving the depository after the shooting, long after the real Oswald supposedly left the building, according to the official story, that is. Who were these men? Could one of them have shot the president or Officer Tippit?

In his latest book on the assassination, *They Killed Our President* (2013), Jesse Ventura and his fellow authors make some very interesting points regarding the possibility of a second Oswald. I have included a few of them here: They state, "Those mysterious anomalies in the history of Lee Harvey Oswald have made some researchers conclude that the only explanation that's visible is that U.S. intelligence had been 'running' two Oswalds as part of an operation. This theory is not as wild as it may first seem; in fact, quite to the contrary. When it comes to spies and covert operations, the employment of a double is a very useful technique" (Ventura, Russell, and Wayne 2013, 75). The authors go on to point out these major differences between the two historical Oswalds:

1. One spoke fluent Russian; the other did not.
2. One was five feet, nine inches tall; the other was five feet, eleven inches.
3. One had a tattoo of a dagger with a snake on his left forearm; the other did not.
4. One had a mastoidectomy scar on the left side of his neck; the other did not.
5. One had two scars on his left forearm; the other did not.
6. One still had all his permanent teeth; the other did not.
7. One still had his tonsils; the other did not.
8. One is buried in the grave of Lee Harvey Oswald; the other is not.

(Ventura, Russell, and Wayne 2013, 83)

This is all interesting information for sure, and I would highly recommend you explore all these possibilities. See my reference section for more excellent resources and for additional research ideas, and certainly read Jesse's new book; it's excellent.

Physical Evidence

When analyzing the physical evidence against Oswald, it is safe to say there was truly next to none available. Sure, he seems to have owned that ancient Italian rifle with a broken scope, which the Warren Commission claimed was found up on the six floor of the Book Depository. They also claim to have later found a palm print on the weapon, even though the Dallas crime lab never found one, and then it was sent off to the FBI lab in Washington for analysis. Their conclusion: no prints, but when the Dallas Police Department got the weapon back from the FBI, Lieutenant Day said that he found Oswald's palm print on the inside part of the weapon (which is really strange, considering the complete examination it had been put through not once but twice).[188]

An interesting story is told by the mortician who embalmed Oswald's body. His name was Paul Groody,[189] and he claims that the night before Oswald's funeral, he was awoken in the early morning hours by a knock at his door. He opened the door, and there were two plainclothes police officers, or Secret Service agents of some kind, who showed him their badges. The agents then asked to see Oswald's body; of course, Groody showed them where it was located and then left them alone. They later left, and he went back to bed. In the morning before the funeral, the mortician was startled when he found Oswald's body was a mess; he had ink on his hands and palms, and some of the ink had gotten onto the casket, which also required cleaning. Groody was not happy with what occurred but managed to clean up the mess before the funeral. Was

---

188 As stated, the FBI fingerprint experts found no such print on any part of the rifle.

189 Paul Groody, http://www.youtube.com/watch?v=P2W_-ID8RMI

this how they acquired Oswald's palm print on the rifle? Many researchers believe so, and even FBI Agent Drain, who worked on the so-called Oswald rifle, claims this was a great possibility, knowing the agency found no prints at all on that rifle.

So the fingerprint evidence was flimsy at best, most likely not even admissible in court; here is another excerpt from *They Killed Our President* regarding the fingerprint evidence: "As for the rest of the print evidence supposedly against Oswald, a partial palm print was found on the rifle, but it's also a convoluted piece of evidence. First off, the palm print wasn't on the outside portion of the rifle where a shooter, or anyone else, would actually touch it. It was only found after taking the rifle apart and was a partial print of someone's palm, which, they say, matched Oswald's palm" (Ventura, Russell, and Wayne 2013, 66).

There is another interesting story told by Groody, who happened to be the same mortician who helped dig up Oswald's body in 1981, when a court ordered the body exhumed to determine if it was actually Oswald. He claimed that someone had already dug up the body many years before. He said the coffin had been violated and the cement vault had been dropped and broken, which caused the casket and the body to deteriorate much faster than it should have. He stated that the head he found in the coffin in 1981 was not the same head he put in there, because there were no autopsy scars on that head; he especially noted the lack of a fisher scar, which would have indicated that the skull cap had been removed during the medical examination. More importantly, this autopsy scar required him to use mortician's wax to cover it up, so it was not something he would have easily forgotten. Groody claimed the story is the absolute truth and further claimed to have his own viewpoint on what happened. He claimed that someone had dug up the body and switched the heads so they would find the head of the real Lee Oswald if there was ever an exhumation ordered. You can see Paul Groody's fascinating statement in the documentary by Nigel Turner, *Men Who Killed Kennedy*.

Can I Get a Witness?

The only witness that the Warren Commission used to support Lee Oswald being in the sixth floor window was a man named Howard Brennan. Out of the one hundred or so witnesses they could have used, they selected Brennan, who claims to have seen a man in the sniper's window on the sixth floor just after the shooting. Although he could not identify that person, the Warren Commission claimed it was Oswald. It is even in the official record that Brennan could not pick Oswald out of a lineup only a few hours after his arrest. So consider the fact that out of all the witnesses mentioned in this book, and the dozens and dozens of others who were never called to testify or were never interviewed by the commission, they selected a man who was not even wearing his prescription eyeglasses that morning and who could not pick Oswald, their prime suspect, out of a lineup.

Also, as pointed out by Flip De Mey in his well-researched book, *Cold Case Kennedy*,[190] Brennan's statement did not fit the facts. Brennan said, "And I glanced up. And this man that I saw previous was aiming for his last shot. ... Well, as it appeared to me he was standing up and resting against the left window sill, with gun shouldered to his right shoulder, holding the gun with his left hand and taking positive aim and fired his last shot" (De Mey 2013, 341). Well, first off, the window was only open at the bottom, which is clearly seen in several photos that day, including the Dallas police crime scene photos. I'm not even sure the upper window could be opened, but that is irrelevant, because it wasn't. Let's face the facts on this: Brennan was simply a poor witness and very unreliable at best.

So then if no one saw Oswald in the window with the weapon during the time of the shooting, there was simply no smoking gun there for the Warren Commission to pin on Oswald. Also consider that Oswald failed the paraffin gun powder test, which meant he did not fire a rifle that day, and that a police officer, Marin Baker, saw him in the lunchroom

---

190 De Mey, F. (2013). *Cold Case Kennedy*. Tielt, Belgium: Lannoo.

just seconds after the shooting. This information would truly have hurt their case. Consequently, a solid defense team would have clearly been able to plant responsible doubt in the minds of any jury.

So how strong was the case against Oswald? Well, District Attorney Henry Wade could certainly have paraded in several witnesses to say that Oswald owned a rifle similar to the so-called murder weapon, but was it really the same rifle? I don't believe so, and here is some reasonable doubt for you. First, let's consider the pictures of Oswald in the backyard photos holding a rifle; this is not the same weapon found in the Book Depository. As a clear indication of this, you can see that the clamps that hold the sling are not in the same locations. This alone proves that the rifles were different, but there's more evidence that Oswald never even ordered that rifle; the order form for the rifle was clearly forged. In comparing Oswald's real handwriting to the order form and the envelope it was mailed in, there is no doubt at all that they do not match; they are not even close.[191]

In an effort to further examine the case against Oswald, we must consider the official investigation of the weapon purportedly used by Oswald and the probability of its effectiveness. After the assassination, the FBI put the so-called Oswald rifle through dozens of tests with their very best marksman. According to Bob Callahan, the author of *Who Killed JFK?*, FBI Agent Robert Frazier was initially assigned to test the rifle on November 27 to see if it was possible to copy Oswald's performance. Callahan noted in his book, "During the course of the morning Frazier and two other FBI agents, Charles Killion and Courtland Cunningham, all tested the gun for accuracy. Each agent fired three shots with the Manlicher. All nine shots were high and to the right. And keep in mind that the agents had been aiming at a stationary target only fifteen feet away. The time it took them to make these shots was very important. None of the men were able to get off all three shots in the time

191 Lee Harvey Oswald, http://www.youtube.com/watch?v=dn-Gmrlpbh0

it had taken to hit Kennedy" (Callahan 1993, 34). It should also be noted that the Warren Commission never found one sharpshooter in either the FBI or the US Army Special Forces who were able to duplicate what they said Oswald had pulled off.[192] This fact, as I have said all along, made it impossible for Oswald—a menial shot at best—to have committed this crime.

The Magic Bullet as Evidence

As I mentioned previously, there was no continuity or chain of evidence with regards to the pristine or magic bullet; as a matter of fact, the Warren Commission could not even confirm which stretcher the bullet was actually found on;[193] there is confirmation regarding this from one of the FBI agents present at the autopsy, who said the bullet might have come from Kennedy's stretcher and not Connally's. James Sibert stated he was told by FBI Agent Charles Killion from the FBI Headquarters Firearms Laboratory that the bullet was found at Parkland Hospital on a stretcher along with a stethoscope and a pair of rubber gloves. The bullet was reported to be a 6.5 millimeter rifle projectile with a copper alloy full jacket.

---

192 I actually met one of the Special Forces members, an army colonel, who test fired the Oswald rifle. I could not get him to give me permission to use his name in my book, so I won't; of course, he was still a little funny about ever having been involved in that case. I am certain he knew more information than he was telling me, but he did tell me off the record that the rifle was a piece of "shit," quote; it was old and had some rust on it. The bolt would stick all the time, and the scope was totally worthless; there you have it.

193 The person who found the bullet has always maintained that the magic bullet was not found on the governor's gurney, and then we have the Secret Service agent who brought the bullet to the FBI lab, who said it was found on Kennedy's stretcher. Also, there are conflicting stories about other bullets handed over to authorities that day, including one nurse who said she found a bullet on Governor Connally's gurney in the operating room. This bullet was turned over to a Texas Highway Patrolman, who to this day remembers the entire incident with great detail. So where did that bullet go? They destroyed it, I'm sure, because it came from another weapon other than the Oswald rifle.

The reason that the agent even contacted FBI headquarters during the autopsy was to inform them he had a missing bullet. This was because the doctors had located a wound in the president's back that had no exit point. The wound, according to the doctors and the agents, was approximately five to seven inches below the shoulders and two inches deep; therefore, the agent assumed the bullet that caused this wound was now missing. Sibert was then told by Agent Killion that the bullet he was referring to had been located; Secret Service Agent Richard Johnson had received a bullet that was found at Parkland Hospital on or near to the president's stretcher and this must have been the missing bullet from the president's back wound (Dankbaar 2012).[194]

Sibert's official FBI report on file states as follows:

> Inasmuch as no complete bullet of any size could be located in the brain area and likewise no bullet could be located in the back or any other area of the body as determined by total body x-rays and inspection revealing there was no point of exit, the individuals performing the autopsy were at a loss to explain why they could find no bullets (Dankbaar 2012).

How about that? There it is, folks; if someone tells you there is no evidence of a cover-up in this case, bring them right to this page and let them deal with the truth, plain and simple: there was no exit for the back wound, so it could not have gone through Connally, period, end of story. And it appears to any logical conclusion that the stretcher bullet very likely came from the president's stretcher, as stated by the FBI and the Secret Service. Also, let's not forget the little fact that nether the Parkland doctors nor the Bethesda doctors found any other wound to the rear of President Kennedy's neck or back, thereby totally and completely eliminating any entrance for the magic bullet to have gone through the president.[195]

---

194 Dankbaar, D. (Producer) (2012). *Confessions from the Grassy Knoll: The Shocking Truth* [DVD].

195 The throat wound was clearly, then, without question, an entrance wound.

So let's face the reality that this bullet would have been pretty much useless as evidence in a case against Oswald (or anyone else, for that matter), because there was no chain of evidence to track its original source.

We cannot complete this discussion without bringing up a very important witness to the assassination of President Kennedy. This man was another shooting victim that day. James Tague was standing in the wrong place on November 22nd. Tague could have been severely injured, but as fate would have it, he received only a minor wound to his face. It turns out that Tague would have a much larger role to play in this event. He was hit that day by a ricochet shot, which forced the Warren Commission and Arlen Specter to come up with that most ridiculous and bizarre scenario, the magic bullet theory. This theory came to be because Tague's injury meant only one bullet caused all the wounds to the president and the governor, because remember now, there could only be three shots. Of course, we have also seen in this chapter that even two shots in seven seconds would have been impossible. Here is a segment from James Tague's book, *Truth Withheld: A Survivor's Story*: "That Oswald fired off three shots in five and a half seconds with the rifle found in the School Book Depository is hogwash. The Warren Commission could not find one ace marksman to duplicate that feat" (Tague 2003, 187),[196] a point I have already made crystal clear.

To recap then:

(1) Oswald was in the lunchroom when the shooting went down; this was verified by multiple witnesses. He was never seen on the sixth floor or in the stairway.
(2) It was impossible to pull off the shooting from that window with his weapon, which is evident by the fact that many true rifle experts have tried and failed.
(3) There is concrete and verifiable evidence that JFK was also shot from the front, and that the bullet which

---

196 Tague, J. T. (2003). *Truth Withheld: A Survivor's Story.* Dallas: Excel Digital Press.

caused his back wound never exited his body; so no magic bullet there.

(4) Oswald failed the paraffin tests.

(5) No one saw him do it, and therefore, no one ever conclusively identified Oswald as the killer of President Kennedy.

(6) The magic bullet would have been thrown out of court (or used in Oswald's defense).

(7) Lee Oswald could not have known that the motorcade would pass by his building because of the last-minute changes made to the parade route. Even Dallas Police Chief Curry did not know the actual route until the day before.[197]

The case against Oswald was so weak that many attorneys, including Judge Jim Garrison, came to the same conclusion: that Oswald would have walked.[198] This is why it was so important that they framed Oswald as a lone nut and a crazy communist with a desire for murder. Because of this, it was a priority that he be killed before they could hold a trial (or, for that matter, before he could talk to the world about his situation); Oswald was simply innocent and the true facts would have been proven in court. They knew that if this case ever went to court, the evidence they had would not have held up under close scrutiny. Also, as previously mentioned, the fact that the president's body was flown out of the jurisdiction of the local and state authorities, and then autopsied in another state, would have totally destroyed any continuity of evidence with regards to the body. Therefore, any evidence extracted from that body would have been inadmissible in Texas state court.

---

197 Palamara, V. M. (2013). *Survivor's Guilt: The Secret Service and the Failure to Protect President Kennedy*. Waterville, OR: Trine Day LLC. (p. 105).

198 According to Lamar Waldron, Gerald Posner, author of *Case Closed,* later admitted, "I've always believed that had Mark Lane represented Oswald, he would have won an acquittal" (Waldron 2013, 17–18).

Chapter 11

Means, Motive, and Opportunity

"We can easily forgive a child who is afraid of the dark. The real tragedy of life is when men are afraid of the light."
—Plato

No book can be large enough to cover all of the theories, facts, and assumptions that revolve around the murder of President Kennedy.[199] As a good investigator, it is important to evaluate your potential suspects by this formula: means, motive, and opportunity. Many times you have two of these elements present, but one is missing. As an example you may have a suspect who wants to murder the president and has a deep rooted hatred for him, maybe based on some psychotic abnormality; he might also have the means, such as he owns several weapons, or let's say he was an explosive expert in the military, but because of the extreme protection surrounding the president (not, of course, in the case of President Kennedy's trip to Dallas in 1963), the suspect is unable to acquire the opportunity to carry out his deed.

In the case of Lee Harvey Oswald, the Warren Commission never did establish any real motive for the murder of President Kennedy; of course, they said that Oswald was a communist, but at the time of his death, Kennedy was attempting to establish a relationship with the Soviet Union and was actually accused by the right wingers of being soft on Communism. So why in the world would a true communist desire to kill a man who had a solid understanding of world issues and who was trying to bring

[199] Of course, there have been many books written on this subject; some can take weeks to read in your spare time. I have tried here to provide a very readable and fast-paced book that gets right to the points on every subject. I truly hope I have been successful.

about a better working relationship with other world leaders? Good question, right? I ask again, where was the motive?

It should be further noted that Oswald never once admitted to the murder; he clearly stated that he was a patsy and committed no acts of violence against anyone. Doesn't it seem a little strange that he would choose the word "patsy"? If he was a raving political killer, he would be the first one that I have ever heard of who did not brag about his deed or admit to it publicly; political assassins are almost always proud of the crimes they have committed and gladly admit to them; the killers of both President Lincoln and President McKinley are two good examples.

Of course the Warren Commission and their supporters pointed out that Oswald had the means (the rifle), but what about the opportunity? It is an established fact that Oswald did not acquire his position stacking books at the Book Depository on his own; according to researchers and the Warren Commission, two people helped secure his new job there. One was George de Mohrenschildt, whom we have seen was a very mysterious figure with links to other key figures in Texas and the CIA, including George H. W. Bush, and the other was Ruth Paine, a friend of the Oswalds. Marina Oswald and the children were actually living with Paine in the Dallas suburb of Irving during the time of the assassination. Oswald never received the position at the Book Depository on his own; it was provided for him.

So that leads us to look into who might have had the triple crown—means, motive, and opportunity—in the murder of JFK. When my students find out I am well researched with regards to the Kennedy assassination, the number one question that comes up, of course, is who killed JFK. With fifty years now having passed, the answer to that question is not an easy one; most people who have researched the case for themselves are not able to connect all the dots, so to speak. After decades of study, you can become an expert on who *didn't* do it before you can answer the question of who did do it. It is similar to investigating a case of arson: the main focus of an arson investigation is not so much how it happened, but how it did not happen. That's right, arson investigations really go in reverse of the typical criminal investigation; once the investigator is able to eliminate all other causes of the fire, it then becomes clear that it was an intentional act. I have looked at the murder of President Kennedy in much the same fashion; having a background in criminal investigations and forensics, as well as a solid understanding of history and political science, this has allowed me to see the assassination from a multilayered perspective.

One of the first things you learn when you are working as an officer in the giant concrete reality of Los Angeles is to keep things as simple as possible. Doing this helps a good investigator stay on course. Many times out there in the field, you realize that the answer to the riddle can be as plain as the nose on your face; of course, that is not always the case, but the goal is to look at the simple and easy things first before you dig into the more complicated details of an investigation. Unless you have been asleep through the first few chapters of this book, I believe you now know that we have, at the minimum, been misled in this case. As an example, how could dozens of witnesses have been completely ignored when they stated they saw at least one shooter behind the fence line above the grassy knoll? Not to mention the video confirmation depicting the president's body movements after the final head shot, which confirms the location of at least one shooter firing from in front of the motorcade. Keep in mind that some of these witnesses included law enforcement officers as well, trained individuals who investigated crimes for a living, law men like Deputy Seymour Weitzman, Deputy Roger Craig, Dallas Police Chief Jesse Curry, and Police Officer Bobby Hargis, who were all on duty that day and who all took action in an attempt to apprehend the murderers of the president.

All of these factors point toward conspiracy; it only takes two for a conspiracy, but rest assured, there were more than two suspects involved in the crime of the century. So let us consider the real probable suspects in this case. I won't bore you with the ridiculous and the farfetched, like the KGB, the Cubans, or the communists; let's go right to the heart of the matter, what I call the big three: the CIA, the Mafia, and the Texas connection. All of these groups are vital to understanding the murder of President Kennedy, because they all had the means, the motive, and the opportunity, especially if they were all interconnected, and we will see just how connected they were.

When we begin a solid examination of the who-done-it in this case, one good question to contemplate is, what two organizations have been responsible for a vast number of murders, both in the United States and throughout the world? Okay, I know this is not *Jeopardy* ... the answer: the Central Intelligence Agency and organized crime. According to both President Kennedy and Lyndon Johnson, the CIA had been operating a Murder, Incorporated around the globe.[200] There is also solid evidence that Kennedy was attempting to control the operations of the CIA and bring them back to what they were created for: to gather intelligence, not to take down dictators, overthrow regimes, and plan murders and assassinations. According to L. Fletcher Prouty (1992), "President Kennedy was seriously upset by the failure of the CIA and the Joint Chiefs of Staff to provide him with adequate information and support prior to his approval of the brigade landing at the Bay of Pigs. He was also upset by the results of the total breakdown of the CIA leadership during the operation that followed the landing" (Prouty 1992, 155).

President Kennedy clearly saw that the CIA was becoming a shadow government in the United States, and he was determined after the Bay of Pigs fiasco to bring them under control. The CIA was not too happy about this, to say the least; the president was challenging not only their supremacy but also their very existence, stating to his advisors that he wanted to "shatter the agency into a thousand pieces." Prouty further points out that the president was concerned enough about his

200 The Central Intelligence Agency was responsible for the overthrows of several governments, including Guatemala, Chile, and Iran.

problems with the CIA to discuss them with Supreme Court Justice William O. Douglas; according to Douglas, Kennedy had some major concerns that he relayed to him. Douglas stated, "This episode seared him. He had experienced the extreme power that these groups had, these various insidious influences of the CIA and the Pentagon, on civilian policy, and I think it raised in his own mind the specter: Can Jack Kennedy, president of the United States, ever be strong enough to really rule these two powerful agencies? I think it had a profound effect ...it shook him up" (Prouty 1992).

The president's concerns were clear; after taking over the presidency from the Eisenhower administration, there was no doubt of who had been running the country: the CIA and the Pentagon. During the Eisenhower presidency, the CIA and the Mafia, under the watchful eye of then Vice President Richard Nixon, were working together on special assignments, mostly in Cuba; this combination of the CIA and the Mafia would one day prove fatal to President Kennedy. Many researchers feel that Kennedy would have attempted to pull the plug on the CIA in his second term, and his brother Bobby was all over organized crime, bringing indictments on an unheard-of scale, with further investigations to come. Never in the history of American criminal justice had anyone taken on both of these deadly customers in such away. Several books have been written on the role of the CIA in the murder of the president, but certainly Fletcher Prouty's book, *JFK: The CIA, Vietnam, and the Plot to Assassinate John F. Kennedy* (1992)[201] is one of the best reference books pertaining to this subject. Prouty states, "Kennedy set out to prove he was strong enough, and he might have done so had he had a second term in office. Instead, he was first overwhelmed and then murdered" (Prouty 1992, 155).[202]

201 Prouty, L. F. (1992). *JFK, the CIA, Vietnam, and the Plot to Assassinate John F. Kennedy*. New York: Carol Publishing Co.

202 Weberman and Canfield's book *Coup d'État in America: The CIA and the Assassination of John F. Kennedy,* is another excellent book on the CIA's involvement in the president's murder, although a little out of date, it proved to be a crystal ball of sorts as new revelations continue to emerge during its writing.

But regardless of who had more to gain by the president's death, many people believe that the Mafia had the most to lose if Kennedy won a second term; although I believe the Mafia was involved in the murder, the real masterminds of the operation were CIA operatives such as E. Howard Hunt, Frank Sturgis, and David Morales (and, of course, the Texas connection, which for sure involved the local Mafia). As an example, Jack Ruby was certainly operating on orders when he killed Oswald; the Mafia was able to deploy some of its influence and assets at key moments, as suggested by Walt Brown (1995) in his book, *Treachery in Dallas*. Ruby used his police connections to gain access to headquarters and silence Oswald.[203] Brown further points to these important issues regarding Ruby's assignment: "If made to appear a spontaneous act, as suggested by Ruby's presence at Western Union at 11:17 a.m., or four minutes before the shooting of Oswald, it would then tend to mitigate the charge of with malice aforethought, and Ruby would be charged with manslaughter, which carried a maximum five-year sentence, and with preprogrammed judicial errors in the trial, he would get a new trial and ultimately serve a couple of years, for which he would be well paid, and would reenter society with celebrity status. He bought it at the time of its telling, and with stride" (Brown 1995, 328–329).

Finally, I must include a short segment about the final investigation conducted by the FBI on Carlos Marcello; this was in the 1980s, while he was incarcerated at Texarkana Federal Prison in Texas. During this time, Marcello shared a cell with an FBI informant named Jack Van Laningham, who befriended Marcello and developed a relationship with him. Hundreds of hours of their conversations were recorded by the FBI, and what they reveal is startling, including information on the Kennedy assassination. Marcello pretty much admitted being involved with the murder, which I am sure he was to some extent, because that was his area of control. He told Van Laningham that Kennedy was a thorn

---

[203] Brown, W. (1995). *Treachery in Dallas*. New York: Carroll & Graf Publishers.

in his shoe and needed to be eliminated, and Ruby was his go-to man in Dallas and was ordered to kill Oswald. He said that Ruby was in his pocket because Ruby had been stealing money from Marcello over the years, so instead of having Ruby killed, he waited for his time to use him. According to Van Laningham, only a very few of the recordings have ever been released by the FBI; hundreds of hours remain under lock and key. Other statements made by Marcello regarding the assassination were not recorded, because the conversations took place outside of their cell. Van Laningham was given a series of polygraphs regarding this and other information he provided to the FBI; he passed, and the FBI agent in charge, Thomas Kimmel, said he believed that his informant was being truthful with the agency.[204]

But there is no way the Mafia or Marcello could have altered the motorcade to have it proceed right through the kill zone, nor did they have the power to control the autopsy in Bethesda, or get the FBI to cover up several aspects of the investigation, or get Gerard Ford of the Warren Commission to pass information to J. Edgar Hoover in order to thwart any efforts toward solving the case. This type of control just reeks of CIA (and even White House) manipulation. There have been several books written on LBJ's involvement in the assassination and cover-up; there is no doubt that he played some kind of role and certainly was one of the masterminds of the cover-up by giving so much power and authority to the Warren Commission. We have seen, of course, the Warren Commission was completely controlled by LBJ and his neighbor and good friend, J. Edgar Hoover of the FBI. According to several sources, LBJ was certainly capable of assassination and murder; just watch the final episode of *The Men Who Killed Kennedy*: *The Guilty Men* or read Brown's *Treachery in Dallas,* which may be the best book ever written on the Texas syndicate and LBJ's involvement in the murder of JFK.

---

204 Fischer, E. (Producer) (2010). *Did the Mob Kill JFK?* [Television episode, air date 2/10/2014, Military Channel].

But you should form your own conclusions, as I have done over the decades; my only desire in this text is to pass on some useful information and you can be the judge and jury. After all, this research is ongoing; it is alive, active, and collective. But it does bother me that there are still books coming out, like *Killing Kennedy*, which is just regurgitation of old and useless information that has been disproven over and over again. I recently heard that there are plans to release a National Geographic special on O'Reilly's new book; I am simply stunned. Why don't we just go back to proving that the earth is flat? I guess being a TV personality makes you an expert on any subject you decide to write about. Welcome to America.

Chapter 12

Potential Players

"That men do not learn very much from the lessons of history is the most important of all the lessons that history has to teach."
—Aldous Leonard Huxley

This chapter discusses the role of some famous intelligence operatives in American history, including E. Howard Hunt, who Victor Marchetti (a former CIA managing official) once stated had a "substantial" roll in the JFK assassination (Benson, 1993, p. 280), and Frank Sturgis, an infamous CIA operative. These very colorful figures were involved in the famous Watergate break-in, as well as the JFK assassination; this is according to their own words and deathbed testimonies. This chapter also addresses the facts concerning other important figures such as Jack Ruby, Lyndon Johnson, Richard Nixon, Sam Giancana, and other potential plotters.

E. Howard Hunt and Richard Nixon

Hunt became a CIA man way back in 1949 and was promoted to chief of the CIA office in Mexico City in the 1950s. He was involved in many overthrows and became an expert on covert operations. In 1963, he operated what appears to have been a CIA substation at 544 Camp Street in New Orleans; this is the same office used by Lee Harvey Oswald and Guy Banister for their anti-Castro operations. Hunt was also no friend of John Kennedy, who he felt betrayed the CIA by not supporting the Bay of Pigs invasion in Cuba (which now, in retrospect, we know was a false assumption). Many people remember E. Howard Hunt due to his involvement with the Watergate break-in, which was ordered by then President Richard Nixon. This burglary occurred at the Democratic Headquarters located in the Watergate Towers in Washington DC, just prior to the 1972 election (Maier 2012, Baltimore

Post Examiner).[205] The criminal team included another CIA superstar in the 1960s, Frank Sturgis. They were caught in the act by an alert security guard and subsequently arrested by the police at the scene of the crime. They were all charged and convicted, and some spent time in prison, such as G. Gordon Liddy and Chuck Colson, one of the planners of the event, whom Nixon hung out to dry.

Many researchers, including myself, believe that there was something more to the Watergate burglary. The story told by Nixon's men was that the burglars were after some democratic strategies for the upcoming election, but this makes no sense at all, because the 1972 election would have been a landslide for Nixon. So what was it they were really after? I feel that it had something to do with the murder of JFK or Robert Kennedy. Robert Kennedy had just won the California primary in 1968 when he was shot down in the kitchen of the Ambassador Hotel in Los Angeles; his win all but secured an upcoming presidential battle between himself and Richard Nixon. It would have been another Nixon/ Kennedy bloodbath at the polls.[206]

---

[205] Police arrested Hunt, a former White House aide, as one of the "plumbers" during the Watergate scandal. He was directly linked to Sturgis and the other four men who broke into the Watergate Hotel. He was charged with burglary, conspiracy, and wiretapping. He served thirty-three months. Hunt worked in the CIA from 1949 to 1970. On January 23, 2007, he died in Miami of pneumonia (Maier 2012).

[206] Now there is no evidence that President Nixon was involved in the murder of RFK (yet), but I can say that the RFK investigation was also poorly conducted. I have reviewed that assassination and the autopsy, as well as talked to officers who were there at the scene, and there is no evidence that Sirhan-Sirhan fired the fatal shot. He was there, of course, and he did fire his weapon, but he was never close enough to deliver a fatal contact wound to the back of Kennedy's head, which was clearly visible and verified in the autopsy by Medical Examiner Thomas Noguchi (Noguchi was actually fired for a period of time because he would not go along with the official LAPD version of the story). According to researcher Joseph Geringer (1999, *The Assassination of Robert Kennedy*), Noguchi released a sixty-two-page report stating the facts involving the fatal shot that killed RFK, which "entered through the mastoid bone an inch behind the right ear and traveled upward to sever the branches of the superior cerebral artery."

It is clear to me that Nixon could not have handled losing to yet another Kennedy and may have been involved to make sure that this battle did not take place.[207] Now this is all *speculation,* of course, but what isn't speculation is that Nixon knew a lot more about the JFK assassination, more than the American public ever knew. According to researcher Randolph Polasek, Nixon actually had a code he used when he referred to the JFK assassination. In his book *Powers behind JFK Assassination,* Polasek states, "So Nixon could deny any association with the assassination, or conversation pertaining to it, he used code words whenever he spoke about the JFK assassination; those code words were 'Bay of Pigs thing'" (Polasek 2010, 143). We have, thanks to Nixon himself, many taped conversations from the White House; it is almost like Nixon wanted us to know the truth, after he was gone. In a conversation with H. R. Halderman and another one with Nixon's White House boys, he stated the following regarding Hunt and his arrest for the Watergate job (please excuse the poor English, it's a direct quote): "Very bad

[207] Geringer goes on to explain one of the biggest stumbling blocks the LAPD could never overcome were the witness statements concerning the proximity of Sirhan, the supposed gunmen, to Robert Kennedy. He explains, "One more issue remained, one that neither Noguchi, the LAPD, nor the witnesses at the crime scene could explain—and one that continues to haunt theorists and historians of the assassination to this day. The shot that both Noguchi and the Los Angeles Police conclude killed Kennedy—the one that entered the back of his head, fragmented upon impact, and lodged in his brain stem—it was fired so close that it left thick powder burns on the skin. Coroner Noguchi estimates (and the LAPD concurs) that the shot was fired at a range no more of a distance than one-and-a-half inches. Yet, according to all the witnesses at the scene of the murder, Sirhan-Sirhan was shooting in front of Kennedy, and as far as anyone knew, the senator never had the chance to turn his back towards Sirhan."... Even though Noguchi remained tight-lipped and diplomatic at the time, in his biography that he penned a decade later—entitled *Coroner*—he wrote, "Until more is precisely known ... the existence of a second gunman remains a possibility. Thus, I have never said that Sirhan-Sirhan killed Robert Kennedy" (Geringer 1999). That was just a little taste of information on the RFK assassination to provoke your curiosity; more to come on that topic in another upcoming book.

to have this fellow Hunt, ah you know, ah, it's, he, he knows too damn much and he was involved, we happen to know that. And that is gets out that the whole, this is all involved in the Cuban thing, that it's a fiasco, and it's going to make the FBI, ah CIA look bad, and it's likely to blow the whole, uh—Bay of Pigs thing—which we think would be very unfortunate for the CIA and for the country at this time,[208] and for America foreign policy, and he just better tough it and lay in on them" (Polasek 2010, 143).[209]

There was also H. R. Haldeman himself, who was Nixon's chief of staff. He had some interesting things to say about Nixon's probable involvement in the JFK assassination as well in his own book, *The Ends of Power*. Referring to the Nixon White House tapes, Haldeman stated, "In all of these Nixon references to the Bay of Pigs, Nixon was actually referring to the Kennedy assassination.... After Kennedy was killed, the CIA launched a fantastic cover-up.... The CIA literally erased any connection between Kennedy's assassination and the CIA ... in fact, Counter Intelligence Chief James Angleton of the CIA called Bill Sullivan of the FBI and rehearsed the questions and answers they would give to the Warren Commission investigators" (Benson 1993, 166).

Okay, let's back up and digest this information. What is Nixon really talking about here? First, there are his coded words, "Bay of Pigs thing," which, according to Halderman, means the JFK assassination. Next, we have the line that the FBI and CIA are going to be embarrassed and made to look bad; what does that mean? It means that ugly secrets will come out about how the president was killed. That's what it means. It means their dirty laundry will be aired out for the entire world and, most of all, for the American people to see. Oh sure, there is no doubt at all he is also referring to many of the secrets regarding Cuba, the Mafia, and other connections

---

208 Can this be any clearer? Nixon was concerned that the whole story, which Hunt admitted to before his death, would come out to the whole world and destroy the reputation of US intelligence.

209 Polasek, R. J. (2010). *Powers behind the JFK Assassination.* (2nd ed.). Raleigh, NC: Lulu. www.powersbehindjfkassassination.com

that Nixon had as well. So we know that Hunt knew all about the assassination, because he was involved; Nixon himself confirms this in his tapes. We will further analyze Hunt's involvement when we discuss Sam Giancana, and we'll also see just how deep Nixon's involvement went in the murder of JFK.

So long before he was breaking into buildings for Richard Nixon and running his spy ring known as the "Plumbers," Hunt was very much involved in the JFK assassination. The strongest and most incriminating evidence for this was his own deathbed confession, which he recorded while he was hospitalized toward the end of his life. His testimony was extremely powerful indeed, for a man who really had nothing left to gain, no money, no fortunes, no more book or movie deals. He knew his life would be over very soon; because of this, I feel you can, and should, consider this pretty incriminating evidence of his involvement in the death of President Kennedy.[210] Here is some vital information from his testimony regarding the major players in the assassination:

1. **Lyndon B. Johnson** (1908–1973): LBJ directed the CIA-led hit team and helped guide the Warren Commission's lone gunman cover-up.
2. **Cord Meyer** (1920– 2001): He was a CIA agent and the architect of the disinformation apparatus known as Operation Mockingbird. He was married to Mary Meyer, who reportedly had a relationship with JFK and ended up murdered herself.[211]
3. **David Atlee Philips** (1922–1988): Bay of Pigs operative who recruited fellow CIA member William Harvey and Cuban exile militant Antonio Veciana.[212]

---

210 Hunt, http://www.youtube.com/watch?v=96FDflK_Iug

211 There is an excellent book out regarding the murder of Mary Pinchot: *Mary Mosaic: The CIA Conspiracy to Murder John F. Kennedy, Mary Pinchot Meyer, and Their Vision for World Peace.*

212 There is also solid evidence that Philips was the CIA contact for Lee Oswald in Mexico City. See the eighth episode of *The Men Who Killed Kennedy: The Love Affair.*

4. **William Harvey** (1915–1976): Another CIA and Bay of Pigs operative who was linked to Mafia figures Santos Trafficante and Sam Giancana.
5. **Antonio Veciana**: He was a Cuban exile and founder of CIA-backed Alpha 66. He told *Esquire* magazine that he had some "hot stuff" on the JFK case but was holding it for "life insurance."
6. **Frank Sturgis** (1924–1993): Sturgis was a CIA operative, a mercenary, a Bay of Pigs operative, and later a Watergate figure; he all but admitted his participation in the JFK assassination as well.
7. **David Morales** (1925–1978): CIA hit man and Bay of Pigs operative and was possibly involved in the RFK assassination (he was seen at the location of the murder). He also admitted to several friends and coworkers that he was in Dallas on November 22, 1963.
8. **Lucien Sarti** (1931–1972): Sarti was a Corsican assassin and drug trafficker who may have been the "French gunman" on the grassy knoll dressed in a Dallas police uniform (Maier 2012).[213]

The footnotes include a link to Timothy Maier's online article, which has a video portion that you should watch. Then, after you watch Hunt in the video, watch the last episode of *The Men Who Killed Kennedy,* called *The Guilty Men*; you won't be disappointed.[214] Hunt's information is very much in line with information in that DVD. Remember, we will never have *all* the truth regarding this murder, which happened fifty years ago. Some information was wiped clean by the CIA and the FBI, according to Victor Marchetti, a CIA officer and former assistant to Richard Helms. We can, however, look for confirmation in the statements and testimonies of the witnesses and the major players.

---

213 This excellent article by Maier covers many vital points. Although Maier feels Hunt may have been stretching the truth, you decide for yourself. Here is the link: http://baltimorepostexaminer.com/deathbed-confession-who-really-killed-jfk/2012/07/02

214 Take me seriously on these documentaries. Get them and watch them; they are powerful.

The preponderance of evidence does indicate that the Texas connection was involved, especially when you consider the deathbed confession of E. Howard Hunt. His statements of the CIA's involvement, along with the cover-up ordered by Lyndon Johnson, are confirmed by others as well, such as Madelyn Brown, who was LBJ's mistress for many years.[215] Brown stated many times that LBJ admitted to her he knew all about the assassination; although he never said that he ordered the murder, he said he knew who did. According to Brown, Johnson maintained his internal hatred for JFK and was overjoyed by his murder.[216]

Sam Giancana and the Mob

The story of the Mafia's involvement in the assassination of the president must start with this man. Sam Giancana was the most prominent Mafia godfather in the United States for several decades. Chuck Giancana, his younger brother, said that Sam confided in him many times over his lifetime about the Mafia's dealings with the CIA and certain American politicians. One day, Sam told Chuck this story (once again, this is a verbatim quote): "That's what we are, the Outfit and the CIA ... two sides of the same coin. Sometimes they need a little trouble somewhere or maybe they need some bastard taken care of ... Jesus, they can't get caught doin' shit like that. What if people found out? But we can provide guns, a hit, muscle ... whatever dirty work needs to be done. We're on the same side, we're workin' for the same things ... we just look different. So ... we're two sides of the same coin" (Giancana and Giancana 1992, 215).[217] He stated that

---

[215] Not to mention Hoover, who was in charge of the FBI, was one of his best friends and had firm control of the Dallas investigation as well as the Dallas Police Department. Both of these men went to their graves with many dark secrets.

[216] Well, one thing that is absolutely certain is, there was a conspiracy. The doctor's statements alone prove that there were shots coming from in front of the limo. This proves there were at least two shooters.

[217] Giancana, S., and C. Giancana (1992). *Double Cross: The Explosive, Inside Story of the Mobster Who Controlled America.* New York: Warner Books.

the CIA and the Mafia were two sides of the same coin; the government (the CIA) and the Mob were working together on the same team.

Let's finish this quote from Chuck's book (once again, excuse the grammar): "Right now we're workin' on Asia, Iran, and Latin America. Someday, Chuck, we'll be partners on everything. If you think we had Truman ... let me tell you ... we got this deal sewn up. Ike [President Eisenhower] all he does is play golf, so that's what you like about that guy. Shit, he's a pigeon...*it's Nixon that's got the power.* He's the one with the backing of the big money, like Hughes and the guys in California and the oilmen in Texas.... Hump says Nixon's gonna call us if he needs a little hardball behind the scenes" (my emphasis) (Giancana and Giancana 1993, 215).[218]

After reading the words of Sam Giancana, how can anyone not clearly see the relationship that had been going on between the American Mafia and the CIA? You must really be in a state of denial to not understand the implications here, but if you need more verification, read on. In his book *Double Cross*,[219] Chuck Giancana further lays out his brother's role in the murder of President Kennedy and the involvement of many political figures, such as Richard Nixon and LBJ. There is actually so much great information in this book, it is impossible to cover all of the items completely here, but know for sure that Giancana had all the connections and help he needed to get the job done. What job? It was the job that E. Howard Hunt referred to as "the big event."

Many people have always wondered what the connection was between Guy Banister, David Ferrie, and Lee Oswald. Ferrie knew Oswald in his younger days, when they both lived in New Orleans; they joined up later with Banister's operation. Where did Banister fit in? Well, he was a friend of Sam Giancana, who of course owned Chicago back in the 1950s and 1960s, when Guy was in charge of the FBI there. Banister and Sam

---

218 Do I have your attention now? Pretty impressive information.

219 This is an excellent book with great inside stories; it is one of the books I review later.

go way back, as pointed out by Chuck Giancana in describing Oswald's return from Russia: "Once back in New Orleans with his Russian wife, he was directed by the CIA to a man very well known to Mooney, [220]former Chicago FBI agent and Commie-buster Guy Banister" (Giancana and Giancana 1993, 332).

This next segment of Chuck Giancana's statements ties so many aspects of the JFK murder together that I had to include them. Those of us who have studied this case for decades have always tried to fill in the missing pieces the best we could, but in *Double Cross,* many of these pieces come together clearly. As I mentioned in past chapters, a good investigator will always try and tie things together while confirming the facts and testing the evidence against other aspects of the case.

As an example, the Warren Commission said they could not find any connection between Oswald and Ruby, which we know now to be ridiculous. Many people testified to seeing them together, but we know the Warren Commission was not interested in the truth; they were only interested in the story they were ordered to come up with, namely the lone gunman theory. Here is some hard evidence of this fact, provided in a statement by Chuck Giancana (it confirms once again that Oswald and Ruby knew each other): "When Oswald was sent to Dallas by his intelligence superiors, he met with Mooney's Dallas representative, Jack Ruby, at Ruby's Carousel Club and reestablished his relationship with David Ferrie. Oswald was also put in contact with another of Mooney's associates, a man Mooney dealt with through both his Haitian and Dallas dealings, the Russian exile and CIA operative George de Mohrenschildt."[221] Referring to de Mohrenschildt, Sam told Chuck Giancana, "That guy helped me make a lot of money in oil; man, oh man, did he have the contacts with Texas oilmen back then. He introduced me to a lot of 'em, too" (Giancana and Giancana 1993, 332).

---

220 This was Sam Giancana's family nickname; Chuck refers to him by this name many times in his book.

221 Remember that de Mohrenschildt had ties to Oswald and the first President Bush. He also died in Miami under suspicious circumstances; http://www.youtube.com/watch?v=lx8t-CJNsjQ

So now we see that Sam Giancana was also connected to de Mohrenschildt and other Texas oilmen. As you remember, de Mohrenschildt was a real player in all the action in Dallas; in 1977, he was apparently trying to set the record straight when he was found shot to death just before he was to testify before the Select Committee in Washington. In his book, Chuck Giancana continued to drop names and describe some of the other players in the president's murder. He said that Sam told him that each man involved received $50,000, which was a lot of money in 1963. He also said that all of the top men, Carlos Marcello, Santos Trafficante, and even Jimmy Hoffa, were all excited to get rid of Kennedy and get his little brother off their backs. Sam also implicated a CIA man named Frank Fiorini, who was none other than Frank Sturgis, E. Howard Hunt's partner on the Watergate burglary. Sturgis was a true CIA warrior and a trained killer. Many have thought he was involved in the shooting of the president.[222]

In another quote, Sam Giancana told his brother just where the top of the ladder was with regards to the JFK conspiracy. Chuck stated, "Mooney said the entire conspiracy went right up to the top of the CIA. He claimed that some of its former and present leaders were involved, as well as a half dozen fanatical right wing Texans, Vice President Lyndon Johnson, and the Bay of Pigs Action Officer under Eisenhower, Richard Nixon" (Giancana and Giancana 1993, 333). Well, there is Richard Nixon's name again; I think if America knew just how involved Richard Nixon was in domestic covert operations, they would be shocked. However, even after the Watergate scandal, we still buried him with honors, like some kind of hero; God help us all.

J. D. Tippit and Roscoe White

Another interesting tidbit of information: Chuck mentioned that Sam told him the Dallas police had supplied two shooters who were assigned to kill Oswald before he could

[222] According to Chuck, Frank Sturgis was working both sides for Giancana; he was one part CIA and one part mobster.

make his getaway. They were Roscoe White and J. D. Tippit. Tippit, we know, was gunned down in the street after the assassination. I have always felt there was more to that story, and indeed, there are entire books on just that aspect of the assassination. You should research the Tippit shooting; it was very much tied to the assassination. In his recent book, *Into the Nightmare*, author Joseph McBride points out many aspects and details of the bizarre events surrounding the Tippit shooting.[223] He has studied the shooting of Officer Tippit for over twenty years and believes that there is a possibility that Tippit was one of the shooters. Here is a quote from his book:

The location of the Tippit shooting in Oak Cliff. Photo Credit: Author.

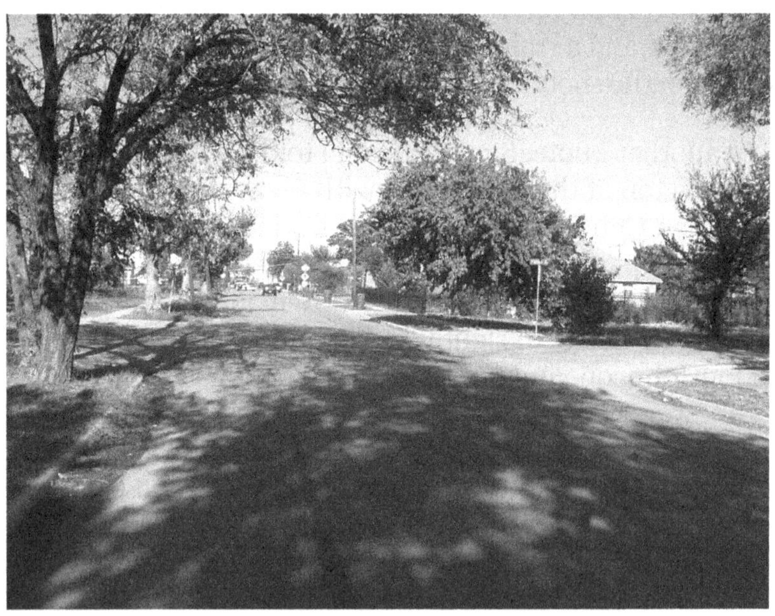

"We've already learned how Tippit, contrary to the story put out by the police and the Warren Commission, was busy chasing the elusive patsy in the assassination, Lee Harvey Oswald, around Oak Cliff in the twenty-plus minutes before

223 McBride, J. (2013). *Into the Nightmare: My Search for the Killers of President John F. Kennedy and Officer J. D. Tippit*. Berkeley, CA: Hightower Press.

the officer's death. But we also know now that Tippit was not entirely innocent. He was part of the conspiracy to frame, capture, and perhaps eliminate the patsy. Whether Tippet's involvement in the conspiracy went further than that is a matter we need to consider. Perhaps it would explain his execution" (McBride 2013, 500).

East 10th Street and North Patton Avenue. Photo Credit: Author.

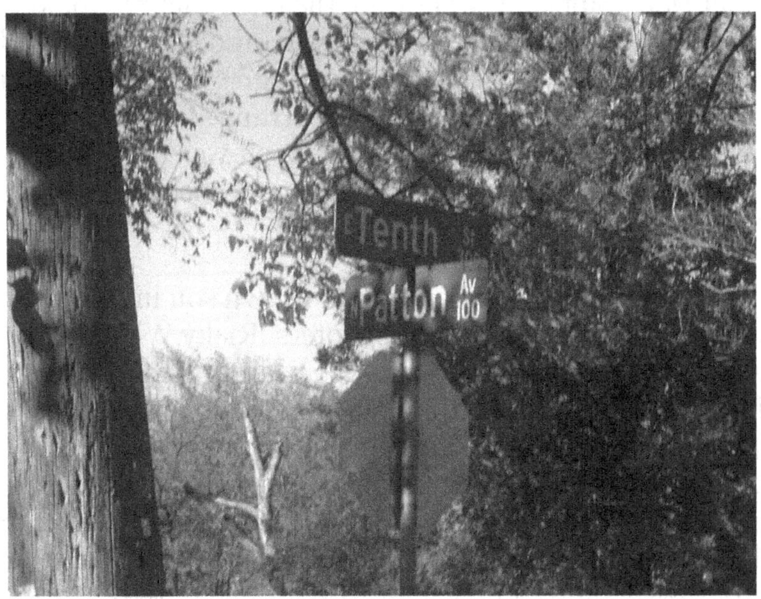

In another overview of the Tippit shooting, Jesse Ventura and his fellow authors point out these facts, which they claim makes it impossible for Oswald to have murdered Tippit: "Oswald's whereabouts at 1:04 p.m. were pinpointed by his landlady, who looked out of the window and saw Oswald standing at the bus stop at that time. At 1:06 p.m., only two minutes later, Officer Tippit, by some reports, had already been shot and lay dead on the ground. District Attorney Jim Garrison figured out that it wasn't logistically possible. He put the time of the shooting at 1:06 p.m. Garrison knew that there wasn't enough time for Oswald to have made it to that crime scene" (Ventura, Russell, and Wayne 2013, 131).

Of course, Oswald never stood trial for the Tippit murder, because he was killed by Ruby. But some witnesses to the Tippit shooting say the shooter looked nothing like Oswald, and some said there was a second man at the scene, a heavyset, shorter man who did the shooting and a bystander who looked more like Oswald. Well, however that went down, I always wondered what Tippit was doing in that area when all the other cars had been ordered to the Dealey Plaza area. As McBride points out, what were the odds that he would run into the so-called presidential assassin, and on a very small side street miles away from the shooting?[224] You think about those odds for a while; that is a very strange fact indeed. I have had suspicions all along that Tippit was involved somehow, and Chuck Giancana adds more than some intrigue to that theory.

With regards to Roscoe White, his own son implicated him as one of the grassy knoll shooters. Ricky White made the talk show circuit a few years ago, claiming that he found evidence in his father's old Dallas home that he was involved in the president's murder. This included some type of diary and notes on the assassination; another strange fact in this case? Maybe, maybe not. Oswald's longtime friend Ron Lewis did state that Oswald told him clearly that Roscoe White was one of the shooters, a very interesting detail indeed.[225]

Jack Ruby

We covered Jack Ruby fairly extensively earlier in the book, but he was truly one of the most colorful actors in the Kennedy assassination. You could write an entire book just on the life

---

[224] Another lost fact was that Earlene Roberts, Oswald's rooming house landlady, stated that she saw a police car pull up in front of the rooming house while Oswald was in his room; she said the police car sounded its horn twice, like it was some kind of signal to Oswald. Shortly after the Warren Report came out, Roberts simply disappeared and has never been found, dead or alive.

[225] It seems that Oswald was aware of some of the details of the assassination, which may indicate (as some have speculated, including Lewis) that he was trying to prevent the assassination.

and times of Jack Ruby. Really, what we need to focus on with regards to Jack at this point includes who was he working for when he killed Oswald and did he have a part in the murder of the president? So let's see what information is out there on the man who silenced Oswald.

According to John Canal, in his book, *Silencing the Lone Assassin*, Ruby was a mobster.[226] That's right, in a book written to show that Oswald acted alone and that there was no conspiracy, the author admits and provides solid evidence that Ruby had strong ties to organized crime. Canal points to the fact that Ruby's murder of Oswald was clearly a hit ordered to silence him for good. He states, "The Mob was especially fearful not only because Oswald was in a position to bargain with authorities or trade information for his life, but also because most of the world was waiting to hear what he had to say! ... Meanwhile in Dallas, within three hours after the assassination, Jack Ruby, an associate of Marcello's[227] underboss, Joe Civello, had gathered up seven thousand dollars in cash, making it legal for him to carry his pistol. By no later than 8:00 p.m., he had started to stalk Oswald" (Canal 2000, 112).

Let's turn back to Chuck Giancana's book while we are on the subject of Ruby. In *Double Cross,* Giancana states the following regarding Ruby's murder of Oswald: "Ruby's murder of Oswald, an act that placed Chicago's outfit and its leader squarely in the middle of the assassination cover-up for anyone who understood the Outfit hierarchy, was, as Chuck had already suspected, not inspired by a sudden outburst of patriotism on the part of a two-bit racketeer" (Giancana and Giancana 1993, 330). He further states that Ruby was not the bumbling idiot strip club owner that the Warren Commission made him out to be:

---

[226] Canal, J. (2000). *Silencing the Lone Assassin: The Murders of JFK and Lee Harvey Oswald.* St. Paul, MN: Paragon House.

[227] Remember, Carlos Marcello was the Louisiana Mafia boss who was also in control of Dallas. Jack Ruby was certainly under his control.

Mooney told Chuck that he'd kept Johnny Roselli [228]*as his liaison to Marcello, Trafficante, and the CIA, while concurrently directing his lieutenants to put Ruby in charge of overseeing the Outfit's role in the assassination, collaborating in Dallas with the government agents. So it came to be that another Jack Ruby—a smart, clever man, one very different from the person erroneously portrayed by the media as an overzealous yet bumbling nightclub owner—played a major role in the events surrounding the murder of the president. But there was another reason Mooney said he selected Jack Ruby for the job: His relationship with Dallas law enforcement officers were unusually good. Since first coming to Texas, true to his Chicago Outfit training, he'd massaged the local cops and politicians, gradually getting to know most on a first-name basis. As the person representing the Outfit in Dallas, the task had quite naturally fallen to Ruby to silence Oswald when he was unexpectedly captured alive.* (Giancana and Giancana 1993, 330)

So we can clearly see once again that Ruby was acting on orders. When you really think about it, everything fits into place. Oswald was completely set up and he knew it, which is why he led his pursuers to such a public place as a movie theater. He was smart enough to know he was about to be gunned down, especially after Tippit had possibly just encountered him. Even when he was about to be shot, you could see in Oswald's face that he recognized Ruby as he approached him in the Dallas police station basement.[229]

---

228 Johnny Roselli was the link between the CIA and the mob, he goes way back and also helped the CIA with their plots to kill Castro in Cuba.

229 If you really want some food for thought, who was the short stocky guy who shot Tippit? He was obviously with Oswald and somehow protected him from being killed or captured by Tippit. I have seen video testimony of some CIA members who were not happy with the plan to kill the president and actually tried to stop it. Was this one of them?

We then have information from Don Fulsom, which fills in even more blanks on Ruby's involvement;[230] Fulsom states, "Jack Ruby was a busy man in Dallas on November 22nd. Only hours before Kennedy's arrival, the debt-ridden striptease club operator met with Mafia paymaster Paul Jones. Shortly after Kennedy was shot, Ruby showed up at Parkland Hospital, where the president had been taken—though he later denied being there at that critical time. Minutes after Kennedy was pronounced dead, Ruby phoned Alex Gruber—an associate of one of Jimmy Hoffa's top officials, and a man with known connections to hoodlums who worked for racketeer Mickey Cohen. Ruby and Gruber had met 10 days earlier in Dallas.[231] When he was arrested for killing Oswald two days later, Ruby had $2,000 on his person and authorities found $10,000 in his apartment" (Fulsom, n.d.).[232] Fulsom goes on to explain on his website that Ruby and Oswald knew each other and that many people had seen them together prior to the assassination: "More than a dozen people claim to have seen Ruby and Oswald together during the four months prior to the Kennedy assassination. In 1994, Dallas reporters Ray and Mary La Fontaine claimed that, shortly after Oswald's arrest on November 22, he told a cell mate that he and Ruby attended a meeting in a local hotel just days earlier" (Fulsom, n.d.).

Fulsom also connects the dots between Johnny Roselli (the mob connection to the CIA) and Jack Ruby; Roselli and Jack Ruby are reported to have met in hotels in Miami during

---

230 Fulsom, D. (n.d.). *Richard Nixon's Greatest Cover-Up: His Ties to the Assassination of President Kennedy*. Retrieved from http://surftofind.com/mob

231 Also don't forget the small fact mentioned earlier that Ruby called the Dallas Police Headquarters the day before he murdered Oswald and warned them not to move Oswald, stating that "we are going to kill him." This was verified by Dallas Police Officer Billy Grammer, who took the call from Ruby.

232 In the two months before President Kennedy's assassination, Jack Ruby was in telephone contact with Murray Miller and Barney Baker. The latter was once described by Robert Kennedy as "Hoffa's ambassador of violence." Ruby was also in touch with key figures from the Marcello, Trafficante, and Giancana crime families.

the months before the JFK assassination. Years later, Roselli told columnist Jack Anderson, "When Oswald was picked up, the underworld conspirators feared he would crack and disclose information that might lead to them. This almost certainly would have brought a massive US crackdown on the Mafia. So Jack Ruby was ordered to eliminate Oswald" (Fulsom, n.d.).

There were also many witnesses who saw Oswald inside of Ruby's strip club in Dallas. Perhaps the most shocking of these accounts was that of Carroll Jernigan. Jernigan went so far as to write a letter to the FBI just after the assassination, in which he describes a conversation he overheard while in the club between Ruby and a man who called himself H. L. Lee. The following is the actual letter:

Dear Mr. Hoover

On Oct. 4, 1963 I was in the Carousel in Dallas, Texas, and while there I heard Jack Ruby talking to a man using the name H.L. Lee. These men were talking about plans to kill the Governor of Texas. This information was passed on to the Texas Department of Public Safety on Oct. 5, 1963 by telephone. On Sunday Nov. 24, 1963 I definitely realized that the picture in the Nov. 23, 1963 Dallas Times Herald of Lee Harvey Oswald was a picture of the man using the name of H.L. Lee, whose conversation with Jack Ruby I had overheard back on Oct. 4, 1963. (Benson 1993, 217)

The Warren Commission never called Carroll Jernigan as a witness; I know it is hard to believe, but they thought he was making up this story. Even District Attorney Henry Wade said he thought he was not telling the truth and therefore no action was ever taken on this information.[233] It should have

---

233 Of course, if you watch Mark Lane's movie *Rush to Judgment,* you will hear a witness, a former Ruby bartender, who clearly states that Henry Wade was a frequent visitor to Ruby's club as well. Maybe that is why he did not act on the information.

been questioned why anyone would make up such a story. First of all, he made this complaint prior to the assassination, when no one was considering Ruby a suspect in any crime.

I could go on for several more pages, but do we really need more to connect Ruby to the American Mafia (and to Oswald, for that matter)? As I mentioned, the Warren Commission could find no connection; amazing right? Ruby was a hit man on an assignment; to see anything less in his actions is to simply ignore basic intelligence (which many people have done over the years). Be the investigator; you don't even need a gut feeling on this one. As a final note on Ruby, after he was convicted of murdering Oswald, he gave a short but sweet confession to the media; you can find it in the footnote. I would watch that segment; in it, Jack Ruby explains that he was forced into the position of having to kill Oswald because of a much larger conspiracy. He says that these forces "will never let the true facts come above board to the public."[234] What more do we really need? It amazes me that people still believe that Ruby was just another lone assassin himself. If you're not convinced that Ruby was part of a conspiracy, what can I say? You may be a lost cause.

Trafficante

This was the Mafia chief over Florida and Cuba in the 1950s and the 1960s; he was heard by Jose Aleman threatening the life of President Kennedy. Aleman, a wealthy Cuban exile, was called before the House Select Committee on Assassinations. On May 12, 1977, he testified that Trafficante was upset about the treatment that Jimmy Hoffa had received from the Kennedys. He was quoted by Aleman as saying, "JFK doesn't know that this kind of encounter is very delicate. Mark my words, this man Kennedy is in trouble, and he will get what is coming to him. He's not going to be reelected; he's going to be hit" (Benson 1993, 6).

234 Ruby's confession, http://www.youtube.com/watch?v=we2eucWXqjg

Those who have been investigating the assassination for many years know of the hatred that Trafficante and his cronies, Hoffa and Marcello, had for the Kennedys. They simply despised them. There is no doubt that the Kennedys received help from organized crime; certainly in winning the election in 1960. Actually, the election was a battle over who had more connections, the Kennedys or Richard Nixon. Well, we see who won that fight. At least in 1960, Kennedy had more contacts, but in a matter of three years, JFK would lose most of those powerful connections. Many in the Mafia felt that Kennedy had bitten the hand that helped him win the election. This may be true, but it was actually Bobby Kennedy who went after organized crime with a passion. The president could have told him to back off, of course, but he never did. This might be the reason that Robert Kennedy refused to really search out the president's killers, because he thought his own efforts might have contributed to his death. Of course, this line of thinking is pure speculation. It did seem strange that RFK never did anything at all to investigate the conspiracy that killed his brother, which I hope now seems pretty obvious. RFK's own son, Robert Kennedy Jr., admitted in Dallas earlier this year that his father told him when he was a teenager that he never trusted the Warren Report; he considered it a poorly conducted investigation.

The Secret Team

Finally, I want to briefly cover a group that is really a compilation of groups who all seem to have the same interests. For the purpose of this book, I will touch very lightly on this subject, but you can get more information if you read *The Secret Team: The CIA and Its Allies in Control of the United States and the World*, by L. Fletcher Prouty. In the most recent edition, there is a great foreword by Jesse Ventura.[235]

---

235 Prouty, L. F. (2011). *The Secret Team: The CIA and Its Allies in Control of the United States and the World.* New York: Skyhorse Publishing.

Colonel Prouty was an expert on the Secret Team. He referred to them as a powerful cabal, the invisible government, or the Secret Elite. He says, "The Secret Team (ST) being described herein consists of security-cleared individuals in and out of government who receive secret intelligence data gathered by the CIA and the National Security Agency (NSA) and who react to this data, when it seems appropriate to them, with paramilitary plans and activities, e.g. training and advising" (Prouty 2011, 3). Prouty knew what he was talking about with regards to the Secret Team and black ops; he was, after all, in charge of black ops for years as part of his duties in the military. He saw the inner workings of the secret cabals. He states, "The Secret Team has very close affiliations with elements of power in more than three-score foreign countries and is able when it chooses to topple governments, to create governments, and to influence governments almost anywhere in the world" (Prouty 2011, 3). Prouty's first book on the JFK assassination, *JFK: The CIA, Vietnam, and the Plot to Assassinate John F. Kennedy,* is a powerful work with regards to the elements of the assassination and its connection to the Vietnam War. He is convinced that some form of this secret group may have assisted in the assassination of President Kennedy and in the cover-up as well.

Final Notes

In his book *Final Judgme*nt, Michael Collins Piper points out an additional group of players who many have simply overlooked.[236] Before explaining his logic behind this group, Collins points out this concise list of tantalizing facts:

- That there was a conspiracy to kill John F. Kennedy.
- That the conspiracy itself involved elements of the US intelligence community, the CIA in particular.
- That organized crime figures played a major part in the conspiracy.

---

236 *Piper, M. C. (1993). Final Judgment: The Missing Link in the JFK Assassination Conspiracy.* Washington DC: The Wolfe Press.

- That anti-Castro Cubans were actively participating in the conspiracy, at the urging of or manipulated by the CIA and elements of organized crime.
- That somehow Lee Harvey Oswald (wittingly or unwittingly) was brought into the conspiracy and that the conspirators planted false evidence to link Oswald with Fidel Castro and the Soviets.
- That Oswald was directly involved in some manner of US intelligence community activities and that he was a knowing participant in those activities.
- That Jack Ruby either was an active participant in the assassination conspiracy itself or was used in some fashion to manipulate Oswald prior to the assassination of JFK.
- That Ruby was actively involved in the organized crime activities and that he was, as a consequence of that involvement, also linked with organized crime activities that operated in conjunction to (or ran parallel with) US intelligence community activities.
- That the Central Intelligence Agency was cognizant of the activities of both Oswald and Ruby and certainly manipulated both.
- That Oswald was executed by Jack Ruby for the purpose of silencing Oswald forever.
- That a major cover-up of the JFK assassination conspiracy was undertaken following the events in Dallas.
- That the cover-up involved elements of the federal government (including the CIA).
- That the Warren Commission and the House Assassinations Committee were deliberate participants in the cover-up.
- That the cover-up conspiracy was conducted for a wide variety of motivations, both ostensibly "patriotic" and otherwise, including but not limited to the following:

    1) Burying intelligence community connections to the assassination conspiracy.
    2) Protecting organized crime elements involved.

3) Preventing hostilities between the United States and foreign nations (whether it be the Soviet Union or Castro's Cuba).
4) Resolving questions about the assassination in the public's mind, both here and abroad.
5) That the controlled media actively encouraged or participated in the cover-up due to its links to the CIA, the intelligence community in general, and organized crime. (Piper 1993, 6-7)

Chapter 13

Cast of Characters in the JFK Assassination

"The great enemy of the truth is very often not the lie—deliberate, contrived, and dishonest—but the myth, persistent, persuasive, and unrealistic. Belief in myths allows the comfort of opinion without the discomfort of thought."
—President John F. Kennedy

Abraham Bolden: This former Secret Service agent was the first African American agent to work on the White House detail. He authored the book *The Echo from Dealey Plaza*. Agent Bolden had firsthand knowledge regarding many aspects of the cover-up and certainly some solid information surrounding the mysterious Secret Service agents seen hanging around behind the grassy knoll area after the shooting of President Kennedy. He also had ideas on how those phony agents got their hands on real Secret Service agent badges, which they produced for the Dallas police officers behind the fence. His statements are a great example of how the pieces of information begin to fit together like a giant puzzle.

Abraham Zapruder: He took the most famous film of the assassination from a pedestal in Dealey Plaza. His film included the fatal head shot of the murder. According to sources, he sold this film only a few days later to Time-Life, but evidence has been shown that the film was copied and potentially altered prior to Time-Life taking possession of it. Very few people have ever seen the true original film, which is said to have many more details of the assassination; at this point, it may be lost to history.

Al Bogard: He was the car salesman who test-drove a car with Lee Oswald (at least he said he was Lee Oswald). This was in Dallas just prior to the assassination. The funny thing was Oswald did not drive and never had a license—ever. According to Bogard, the so-called Oswald drove like an expert racecar driver. So what happen to Bogard? Well, after the assassination, he was hounded by federal agents, who tried to get him to positively ID Oswald as the man he drove in the car with; he would not do so at first, and then he was threatened by local thugs in Dallas. He was pretty much harassed for some time over this. What the Warren Commission failed to bring up was the real Oswald had an alibi for November 9, the day he supposedly visited the car dealership; he was with family and friends all day. On February 15, 1966, Bogard was found dead from carbon monoxide poisoning, thereby eliminating him from the picture; they said it was a suicide. I guess we will never know the whole story there, will we?

Allan Dulles: The former head of the CIA, Dulles was another direct enemy of the president; he was fired as the director of the CIA shortly after the Bay of Pigs fiasco, when Kennedy cleaned out what he thought were rogue problems within the agency. Dulles had thousands of contacts throughout the spy world, and it is not surprising that Johnson put him on the Warren Commission. Even the HSCA said that it was clear that the CIA had covered up many facts that the Warren Commission never even knew about. Earlier in the book, Judge Burt Griffin, who was a Warren Commission member, verified this fact.

Allen D. Graf: Graf, an often overlooked figure, was Oswald's platoon sergeant in the Marine Corps. He stated that Oswald never appeared to be against capitalism, nor did he promote communism while under his command. He said Oswald was even tempered and smart, and he learned very quickly.

Alex Gruber: Gruber was a friend of Jack Ruby's from Chicago. He was one of the individuals Ruby called on the day of the assassination; this was even confirmed by the Warren Commission. When questioned by the Warren

Commission, Gruber had several memory lapses regarding his communications with Ruby prior to the assassination.

Arlen Specter: He was the inventor of the magic bullet theory and counsel for the Warren Commission; he interviewed many of the witnesses for the commission. Specter passed away during the editing of this book. Even he began to admit before his death that there were holes in the Warren Commission's findings, such as the fact that he regretted using artist drawings of the president's autopsy to form their conclusions, rather than the actual photos. Despite this, he clung to his ridiculous magic bullet theory until the very end.

Arnold Rowland: Rowland was the witness who was standing in front of the Texas School Book Depository, waiting for the president to drive through Dealey Plaza. According to Rowland, he saw a man with a rifle standing in one of the windows of the building, just before the arrival of the motorcade. The problem for the Warren Commission was that the man Rowland saw was standing in a window on the west side, not the southeast corner, which is where they said Oswald fired all three shots. In that window, Rowland reported to the commission that he saw a black male leaning out of the window, looking down in the plaza. After this testimony, the commission then began to refute his observations.

Aubrey Bell: Aubrey was a Parkland Hospital supervising nurse; she saw the wounds of the president and concurred with all of the doctors that the president's head wound was a large exit wound. She also worked on Governor Connally and was actually there when they removed the bullet fragments from his wrist. She maintained until her death that the fragments of the bullet taken from the governor's wrist clearly outweighed the lead that was missing from the so-called magic bullet. Also, there was the fact of a second bullet being found on the governor's gurney when he was wheeled into surgery; this bullet was given to a Texas Highway

Patrolman, who claims he gave it to the proper authorities, but it was never seen again.

Austin L. Miller: This witness to the assassination saw a shot hit the street and saw smoke coming out of the trees on the grassy knoll.

Bernard Barker: A former CIA agent who had dual citizenship in both Cuba and the United States. Barker was a colorful figure involved with the Bay of Pigs invasion and later went to prison as one of the Watergate burglars. He was also seen behind the famous grassy knoll on the day of the assassination by Dallas Deputy Constable Seymour Weitzman, who clearly pointed out Barker as the fake Secret Service agent who showed him a badge behind the fence. Two other Watergate spies later confessed to being involved in the assassination, including Barker's one-time boss, E. Howard Hunt. Barker was said to have lived in fear the rest of his life, most likely because his cover was blown in Dallas.

Barney Baker: Barney was an associate of Teamsters leader Jimmy Hoffa in the 1960s. Ruby called Baker two weeks before the assassination and once more when he contacted another Hoffa crony. There was no love lost between the Kennedys and Baker; Bobby Kennedy called Baker Hoffa's "ambassador of violence," and Baker hated both Kennedy brothers.

Betty McDonald: One of many dancers and strippers who worked for Jack Ruby and ended up dead or missing shortly after the assassination. What did they know? What did they hear? We will never know, but Betty was found hanging in her Dallas police cell after she was arrested for a very minor offense. They said she hung herself with her pants (yes, really, her pants). It turns out she was also the alibi for a man who tried to kill another assassination witness; coincidence?

Beverly Oliver: One of the key eyewitnesses to the assassination, she was one of the closest witnesses to the shooting. Beverly was also an acquaintance of Jack Ruby and had many friends who worked in his club. She worked at the club next to Ruby's, the Colony Club. She claims to have seen Lee Oswald in Ruby's club before the assassination and said she also saw David Ferrie there on several occasions. Oliver's Super 8 film she took of the assassination was confiscated by the FBI and never returned. This video would have been even more valuable than Abraham Zapruder's because of her location at the time of the shooting.

Billy Grammer: This former Dallas police officer knew Jack Ruby very well. Grammer has stated, without question, that when he was working the desk the day before Oswald was to be transferred, Jack Ruby called him and told him they needed to change the plans to transfer Oswald because, he said, "We are going to kill him," and then Ruby hung up. Grammer always maintained he is absolutely certain that it was Jack Ruby he talked to that night.

Bobby Hargis: He was a Dallas police motorcycle officer who was riding to the rear of the president's limo; he was splattered with brain and blood matter. Right after the limo took off, Hargis dismounted his unit and ran up the grassy knoll to look for suspects, because that was where he thought the shots originated from.

Bonnie Ray Williams: He had lunch on the sixth floor of the Texas School Book Depository right next to the so-called sniper's nest. His empty lunch bag can be seen in photos that were taken right after the shooting. He said he left at 12:20, only ten minutes before the assassination, and never saw Oswald up there when he left. Maybe because Oswald was in the lunchroom, where he said he was at that time, witnessed there by several others, including a Dallas police officer.

Buddy (Eddy) Walthers: Buddy Walthers was a deputy sheriff who was on duty in Dealey Plaza; he was very much involved in two incidents. He was the first officer who reported that James Tague had been struck in the face by a ricochet right after the rifle fire in the plaza; both Tague and Walthers located the section of the curb where the bullet struck. Walthers also observed two federal agents at the scene who located a spent projectile in the grass over by the curb and walked away with it. In a famous picture, Buddy Walthers is seen with these agents when they were picking up the spent round in the grass.

What happened to that bullet? Why wasn't it ever processed as evidence? Could it be that it would have revealed another shooter in the plaza?

Buell Wesley Frazier: Coworker and friend of Lee Oswald; Frazier would frequently give Oswald a ride to work, and November 22nd was one of those days. Frazier picked up Oswald before work; he said he noticed nothing unusual about Oswald that morning. This is strange, considering the fact that the Warren Commission claims Oswald was about to murder the president of the United States. Frazier said that Oswald was carrying a small package with him, which he explained were some curtain rods he needed for his apartment. Frazier was certain that there was no way that the package he saw could have contained a dismantled rifle, because it was far too short and thin. He claims to have seen Oswald holding the package up under his armpit, with the bottom of the package cupped in his hand. If this is true, there is no way that was the rifle, considering that even broken down; the rifle was nearly three feet long.

Carolyn Arnold: The vice president of the Texas School Book Depository, who stated that she saw Lee Harvey Oswald in the lunchroom at approximately 12:15 p.m., just moments before the shooting. Her observations were confirmed by other witnesses, including Officer Baker of the Dallas Police Department, who found Oswald right in that same location just seconds after the shooting.

Carolyn Walther: Walther worked at the Del Tex Building, which was directly behind the School Book Depository building. Just prior to the president's turn onto Elm, she saw two men in one of the windows of the Depository. One man had a rifle, which he was pointing down onto the street, and she said that she assumed this was a security person who was protecting the motorcade. The other man she said had a much smaller rifle, and he was in the same window. Neither of her descriptions fit Oswald, not to mention she claims to have seen these men in a fourth or fifth floor window.

Carlos Marcello: The Mafia boss of New Orleans as well as the Dallas area, he had a working relationship with Jack Ruby and other Oswald associates, such as David Ferrie. He hated the Kennedys because Bobby Kennedy had him deported to the jungles of Guatemala. Marcello made several statements with regards to having the Kennedys murdered; he once stated, "If you want to kill a dog, you don't chop off his tail, you chop off his head." This meant that by killing the president, he would get rid of his brother Bobby as well.

Carroll Jernigan: Carroll was a Dallas attorney who saw Lee Oswald with Jack Ruby on October 4, 1963, at Ruby's strip club. He said he overheard them discussing a plot to murder Governor John Connally. He further claims Ruby was upset because Connally was being too aggressive with organized crime members in Dallas.

Carver Gaten: He was a former FBI agent who knew James Hosty. Hosty was the FBI agent Oswald was bringing the note to when he went to the Dallas FBI office just two weeks prior to the assassination. According to Gaten, Oswald was a paid informant for the FBI, even though he gave them very little hard information. We will never know what was truly in that note, which Hosty admitted destroying after Oswald was murdered. Many believed that FBI Director Hoover had ordered Hosty and his supervisors to keep their mouths shut about Oswald, which they certainly did for several years.

Charles Brehm: Brehm was standing on the street with his little boy when the shots rang out and told news reporters and Mark Lane that he felt the shots came from behind him. He also stated that he saw a piece of President Kennedy's head come flying off and land well behind the limo onto the curb. Researchers have concluded from his statements that the fatal shot could not have come from behind because of the direction Brehm saw the skull particle fly, which was clearly to the rear of the limo. If the shot had come from behind, how could this have happened?

Charles Cabell: He was a former deputy director of the CIA and brother of Mayor Earl Cabell of Dallas. Kennedy fired him over the Bay of Pigs disaster. He was also involved in plots to assassinate Fidel Castro in Cuba. Cabell hated Kennedy and his brother Robert, a feeling shared by Cabell's own brother, Earl.

Charles Killion: Charles Killion was an FBI firearms examiner who worked on the Tippit shooting case by trying to identify the bullets used to kill the officer. He could never conclusively determine if the shells found at the Tippit murder scene came from Oswald's revolver.

Christopher Dodd: Dodd was a House Select Committee on Assassinations member during the late 1970s. Dodd was a real thinker and did not agree with many of the other members; he pointed out the acoustic evidence indicated that two of the shots came within only 1.66 seconds of each other. So Oswald could not have been the only shooter. This information is right in line with dozens of witnesses listed in this book (including many police officers and Secret Service agents), who clearly heard shots coming right on top of each other.

Clint Hill: Mrs. Kennedy's personal Secret Service agent, who is seen in the Zapruder film running and catching up to the presidential limo right after the fatal head shot. He is the only agent to respond in any way to the shooting of the president. All of the other agents were frozen in time during the seven and a half seconds of the shooting. Agents are even seen on video clips being ordered off the president's car. This was a clear indication of a massive plot to leave JFK unprotected during his drive through downtown Dallas.

Clint Murchison: Oil baron from the Dallas area, he was said to have held a party the night before the assassination that was attended by Richard Nixon, FBI Director Hoover, LBJ, and other prominent people; there is solid evidence that the party actually did take place.

Courtland Cunningham: Courtland was also a ballistics expert for the FBI Crime Lab; he tried to identify the slugs from the Tippit shooting to see if they could link them to Oswald's 38 revolver. He was unable to do so and stated as much to the Warren Commission, but he claimed he was able to match one of the shell casings found at the scene to that weapon with some reasonable certainty.

Chuck Colson: While working in the Nixon White House, he helped plan the Watergate break-in and went to prison for it. He was also E. Howard Hunt's boss and was known to have planned several other crimes during the Nixon administration.

Chuck Giancana: Chuck was Sam Giancana's own brother; he and Sam's godson stated many interesting facts in their book, *Double Cross,* which is an excellent read. The book describes the direct involvement of Giancana in the assassination, his relationship to the other conspirators, and the Jack Ruby connection.

Chuck Nicolette: Famous Mafia hit man who was part of the Chicago syndicate under Sam Giancana. Nicolette has been suspected of being involved in the president's murder by several researchers and probable players over the years. It is reported that he was one of the actual shooters and fired from behind the motorcade. James Files, who has admitted to being involved in the assassination (although the jury is still out on that), told researchers that he was certain Nicolette was a shooter and fired from the Dal Tex Building.

Cyril H. Wecht: Dr. Wecht a world renowned pathologist and forensic expert, has always been a sharp critic of the WC conclusion of a lone gunmen in the murder of President

Kennedy. He is the author of *Cause of Death*, and many other books on the subject of forensic investigations and medical legal autopsies. His final conclusion regarding the JFK assassination speaks for itself, "But from all the physical evidence I have reviewed, using all the forensic knowledge and experience I have, there is no doubt in my mind that Lee Harvey Oswald was not the lone gunman. Indeed, the hard evidence strongly indicates that he did not shoot at either Kennedy or Connally".

David Lifton: He wrote the best-selling book, *Best Evidence*, which promoted the body alteration theory. He was able to bring together several witnesses who saw the president's body arrive in a cheap shipping casket, zipped up in a body bag. He also found witnesses who were at Bethesda Naval Hospital and saw the two separate caskets arriving at the hospital. He was a key figure in helping us all understand just what occurred after the president's body left Dallas.

Dave Powers: Dave was a personal aide of President Kennedy and his most trusted advisor (other than Bobby). He was riding in the follow-up car, filming the event, but ran out of film just as the motorcade turned onto Elm Street. This was seconds before the first shot. When the shooting started, Powers was heard to say, "We have driven into an ambush." He fully believed that they were being fired on from in front of the motorcade and stated as much numerous times, including in his statement to the Warren Commission.

David Ferrie: Ferrie was a friend and acquaintance of Lee Harvey Oswald in New Orleans. Ferrie was a soldier of fortune, so to speak. He was also friends with Carlos Marcello, the Mafia crime boss of New Orleans. He was a main character in the Jim Garrison investigation. Ferrie was heavily involved with Clay Shaw and Guy Banister, also from New Orleans, and was one of Oswald's controllers. When Oswald was arrested, Ferrie's library card was said to be found among his possessions.

Dennis David: David was a Navy Petty Officer First Class who was chief of the day at Bethesda on November 22, 1963. David was one of the best witnesses to the extreme depth of the conspiracy and confirms that the president's body arrived much sooner than the motorcade containing the official party. He said that he and his men had already unloaded the body almost forty-five minutes before Jackie Kennedy arrived; it seems clear she was in that ambulance with an empty casket. David Lifton was the first researcher to get Dennis David on record as to what really went on that day in Maryland.

Diana Hamilton Bowron: She was a nurse at Parkland Hospital who was there when the Kennedy limo arrived. She stated that she observed a very large hole in the back of the president's head. She was also one of the nurses who prepared him prior to being placed in the bronze casket.

Don Adams: As a retired FBI agent who worked on the assassination, following up on leads, he has a great story to tell about a man named Joseph Milteer, who was a right wing radical who predicted the murder of President Kennedy with incredible accuracy. Milteer's statements were captured in an undercover audio by the Miami police. The audio was then given to the FBI and the Secret Service a week prior to the Dallas trip, but they did nothing to alter the president's plans.

Donald Rebentisch: One of the sailors who helped unload President Kennedy's body from the back of the black ambulance which arrived way before the official motorcade containing Jackie Kennedy and Bobby Kennedy and the bronze Dallas casket. Rebentisch was working with Dennis David that night and confirms his story about the cheap gray casket he and his other men unloaded that night into the back of the hospital. This casket really did contain the body of JFK, which we learned was inside the cheap casket, zipped in a body bag.

Dorothy Kilgallen: She was a very colorful figure, a news reporter and columnist by trade; she even appeared on popular game shows in the 1950s and 1960s. She reportedly told friends that she was going to break the JFK case wide open, that she had solved the case. Was it true? Well, it is very possible, because she landed an interview with Jack Ruby shortly after the events in Dallas; she was one of many reporters who were trying to get the story from Ruby, but he chose her—maybe because of her hard-nosed reputation. On November, 8, 1965, Dorothy was found dead in her bed; the police said it was a suicide or an overdose, another victim of the mysterious death syndrome. There is a large amount of information on her death and her life; she clearly felt she had information on the president's murder.

Dr. Charles J. Carrico: The first doctor to attend to the wounded president, he actually wrote in his report at the hospital that the president's head wound was a frontal entrance wound that exited the back of his head.

Dr. Charles A. Crenshaw: Crenshaw was the Parkland doctor who worked on President Kennedy and may have had the longest and closest observation of the president's head wound. He coauthored a book, *JFK: A Conspiracy of Silence,* in which he clearly describes the fact that the bullet that killed the president entered the right temple area and went through his head and blew a large portion of his brains out of the back of his head. He further pointed out that the fatal shot had to have come from the front, based on his observations of the president's wounds. He has always assumed it was a shot from the grassy knoll area that caused the damage to President Kennedy's head. He also confirmed what all the Parkland doctors stated: that the throat wound was an entrance wound, not an exit wound.

Dr. Evalea Glanges: Dr. Glanges was one of those wonderful witnesses who just happened to see something she should not have. She was standing outside Parkland Hospital while the president was being treated inside; she was standing very close to the presidential limo when she observed a through-and-through bullet hole in the front windshield of the limo. She said firmly that it was clearly a round bullet hole that appeared to have entered from the front of the vehicle. Glanges, who was an avid hunter and firearms hobbyist, claims that one of the agents saw her looking closely at the hole and drove the vehicle away to a better protected area.

Dr. Gene Coleman Akin: Dr. Akin, another Parkland doctor, stated publicly that the president was shot from the front, that the right occipital-parietal portion of the president's head was shattered, and that he saw brain matter seeping out through it. He maintained that the rear wound was an exit wound.

Dr. J. Thornton Boswell: Autopsy doctor at Bethesda Hospital, who assisted in the autopsy. He stated that the president's back wound was only two to four inches deep, but the track was never totally explored.

Dr. Robert McClelland: A true warrior and one of the best Parkland witnesses, who always maintained that the president's wounds came from a frontal assault: one to his right temple and one to his midline throat area. Very outspoken, Dr. McClelland always believed that both wounds were entrance wounds, based on the vast number of gunshot victims he treated over the years.

Dr. Victor Weiss: He was the psychiatrist who treated Rose Cherame after she was pushed out of a car near New Orleans. Cherame was a prostitute with ties to Jack Ruby who told local authorities that someone was going to kill President Kennedy. Weiss, a well-trained psychiatrist, said that he felt Cherame was telling the truth about having foreknowledge of the assassination.

Dr. William Kemp Clark: The chief of neurosurgery at Parkland Hospital who signed the president's death certificate; he clearly stated that the shot to the president's throat was an entrance wound. He said that shot entered near the necktie but never did exit his body, according to his examination of the president's body.

Dr. Earl Rose: The Dallas Medical Examiner at Parkland Hospital, who tried to follow Texas law and have the president's autopsy done in his office. According to Rose and several witnesses at the hospital, the Secret Service pulled out pistols and automatic weapons and forced their way out of the hospital with the president's body and then drove it to the airport in clear violation of the law. Jim Garrison said that the departure from Love Field was more like a getaway than anything else.

Dr. Pierre Finck: An Army lieutenant colonel who was a gunshot expert and was at the autopsy of the president. He made several statements over the years that the autopsy was controlled by nonmedical staff such as Army generals and Navy admirals. He also stated that he was ordered not to examine the throat wound or to trace its path, nor were they allowed to examine the president's clothing, which he considered a dereliction of a proper investigation.

Earl Warren: Warren was chief justice of the United States during the Kennedy and Johnson administrations; he was later put in charge of Johnson's investigation into the assassination of JFK. This committee would later be called the Warren Commission; they also produced the official Warren Report.

Earlene Roberts: She was the landlady at Oswald's rooming house in Dallas and told an interesting story to the Warren Commission. Roberts told the commission that about thirty minutes after the assassination, Oswald returned home and went into his room. While he was in his room, Roberts claims that a Dallas police car pulled up right in front of the rooming house and honked its horn twice. She said she saw two uniformed police officers in the car and the vehicle number: 207. (This car 207, just prior to the Tippit shooting, was being operated by officers Jim Valentine and Gerald Lynn of the Dallas police.) Right after the police car departed, she said Oswald came out of his room wearing a jacket and left the house. The last time she saw Oswald, he was standing across the street, waiting for the bus. All this information is very important, because if Oswald was the person who shot Officer Tippit eight to ten minutes later, then he must have received a ride to Tippet's location, or it was clearly not Oswald. This is because the shooting location was at least one mile away from Oswald's rooming house. Also, who was in the police car that pulled up in front of his rooming house? How in the world did anyone know where Oswald lived when he wasn't even a suspect yet?

Ed Hoffman: One of the most forgotten witnesses to the murder of JFK is Ed Hoffman; not only did Hoffman see the shooters behind the fence, he also saw their accomplices, who helped remove one of the rifles from the scene. From his view high up on the freeway overpass, Hoffman also got an excellent view of the inside of the presidential limo as it passed under the triple overpass. He said he could clearly see the back of the president's head was missing. He was featured in the documentary, *The Men Who Killed Kennedy*.

Eladio del Valle: He was a friend and fellow CIA operative of David Ferrie's; they were both killed at the same time and on the same day. Ferrie claimed there was a death warrant out for him because Jim Garrison had named him in his 1967 investigation into the assassination of President Kennedy. Both del Valle and Ferrie were involved in anti-Castro CIA operations.

Esther Ann Mash: Esther worked for Jack Ruby in his Dallas nightclub and said she saw Lee Oswald in Ruby's club with six other men one night; they stayed there until one o'clock.

Floyd Riebe: Riebe was the official medical examiner autopsy photographer, who backed up the observations of the Parkland medical personnel regarding the wounds he saw during the autopsy.

Forest Sorrels: As the lead Secret Service agent in Dallas on the day of the assassination, he rode in the lead car of the motorcade. He later told Orville Nix, his friend who had filmed the murder, that he felt the rifle fire came from behind the fence in front of the motorcade and not the Book Depository. He was also the only Secret Service agent to ever go back to Dealey Plaza after the shooting; no other agents ever went back to investigate what really happened there and determine how they lost the president. The entire investigation was left up to the FBI and the Dallas Police Department. In Mark Lane's documentary *Rush to Judgment*, you can hear Orville Nix state clearly that both he and Agent Sorrels were clear about the location of the gunfire; it was in front of the motorcade and behind the wooden fence.

Fletcher Prouty: Prouty was a former colonel in charge of black operations during the 1950s and 1960s; he was the coordinator between the military and the CIA. He claims that the president was killed by a black operation in much the same fashion that was used around the world to eliminate other world leaders. He wrote two very powerful books, *The Secret Team and JFK, The CIA, Vietnam, and The Plot to Assassinate John F. Kennedy.*

Fidel Castro: Due to his role as president of Cuba for several decades, he was the target of many assassination attempts himself during the 1960s by the Mafia and the CIA.

Frank Sturgis: Sturgis, also known as Frank Fiorini, was a very colorful soldier of fortune; he worked for the CIA for decades. He was heavily involved in the attempts to overthrow Castro in Cuba. He was also a Watergate burglar, partnering with E. Howard Hunt and G. Gordon Liddy. Toward the end of his life, he hinted to being involved in the murder of the president in Dallas. He spoke to reporter Jack Anderson on several occasions about what his partner Hunt called "the big event."

Gary Underhill: Former CIA agent during the 1960s, who claimed he knew too much about the JFK assassination and feared for his life. He became one of those witnesses who "shot themselves" in the back of their head; in his case, the bullet wound was behind his left ear, even though he was right handed.

G. Gordon Liddy: Liddy was another CIA man who was involved with Frank Sturgis and E. Howard Hunt in the Watergate burglary, which he also served time for. He was known to have been a bag man for the Nixon White House; in later years, he became a conservative talk radio host.

George de Mohrenschildt: Count de Mohrenschildt was a complicated character who had several connections, including Lee Oswald, George W. Bush, and several oilmen in Texas. He died under very suspicious circumstances just before he was to testify to the Select Committee in the late 1970s; his death was ruled a suicide by shotgun (very suspicious indeed). Just before his death, he had begun to work on a book about Lee Harvey Oswald entitled *I'm Just a Patsy, I'm Just a Patsy*. He had also reached out to then CIA director George H. W. Bush, telling him that someone was stalking him and he feared for his life. Researchers believe that he had begun to have loose lips about the assassination and the role that Oswald played in Dallas, which may have contributed to his early demise. He was, in fact, responsible for getting Oswald the job at the Book Depository weeks before the assassination.

George Hickey: Hickey was the Secret Service agent riding in the follow-up car and the one seen standing up in the back of the car with the AR-15 rifle as the limo sped away. His observations and witness statements clearly state that two shots were fired right on top of each other, with one of these being the fatal head shot. There was also wild speculation that he had accidently shot the president with his semiautomatic weapon; this, of course, is complete nonsense.

Glenn Bennett: Bennett was a Secret Service agent in the follow-up car that made direct statements as to the location of the shot that hit JFK in the back. He said clearly that the shot entered way too low in the back to be the magic bullet later postulated by Specter, which then became the official story of the Warren Commission.

Gordon Arnold: One of the grassy knoll witnesses who reported that shots were fired over his head while he fell to the ground in front of the picket fence. His story of seeing a policeman with dirty hands who confiscated his camera that day has been confirmed by the discovery of "Badge Man," firing from behind the fence in the Mary Moorman photo. He was also seen by Senator Yarbrough, who claims he saw Arnold hit the deck during the shooting. Gordon Arnold gives a gripping testimony on an episode of *The Men Who Killed Kennedy* by Nigel Turner.

Governor John Connally: The second victim in the car that day in Dallas, Governor Connally was riding in the jump seat with his wife, directly in front of the president and Mrs. Kennedy. He suffered several wounds that nearly killed him, including a punctured lung and bullet wounds to his chest, wrist, and his leg. Connally insisted until his death that the Warren Commission got it wrong and that he could not have been hit by the same bullet that hit the president in the back; he felt he was clearly hit by a separate bullet, because the president was struck first. This is confirmed by his wife, who was sitting right next to him, but once again the Warren Commission decided not to believe the victims or the eyewitnesses in this case. As we know, much of the evidence that could have determined the direction of the gunfire was distorted or destroyed. As an example, the governor's suit with the bullet holes was sent from the hospital directly to the cleaners, where it was cleaned and pressed. Have you ever heard of anything more ridiculous? What was the governor going to do, wear that suit again, which of course was now riddled with bullet holes? Someone was destroying evidence here; you decide who to blame, but it was someone who had the power and the control to do so.

Guy Banister: Banister was the former special agent in charge of the Chicago FBI office who moved to New Orleans and created a front business for his anticommunist activities.

Out of his private investigating office, he managed a private war funded by the CIA and Clay Shaw, who would later be prosecuted for conspiracy by Jim Garrison. He also sheep dipped Oswald, who was working out of Banister's office on Camp Street in downtown New Orleans, as a procommunist sympathizer. Numerous witnesses who worked with Banister and were in and out of that office saw Oswald with him over a period of several months. As a sidebar, E. Howard Hunt also had an office there, for one of his spook agencies he was running for the CIA. Hunt's printing company actually billed the CIA for all the printed material used at this location, including Oswald's Fair Play for Cuba pamphlets.

Hale Boggs: A Warren Commission member who always seemed to have reservations about the commission's findings and was perhaps the most outspoken against the lone-gunman theory; in 1972, he disappeared on a plane trip to Alaska and was never heard from again; his body was never recovered, and the plane's wreckage was never found.

Hawk Daniels: A former agent involved in the FBI's 1960s wiretapping project conducted on members of organized crime. According to Daniels, Jimmy Hoffa personally ordered plastic explosives for the purpose of killing Robert and possibly John Kennedy. Daniels said he was absolutely certain that Hoffa and the Mob planned on killing the Kennedys after hearing all the phone conversations during his wiretapping assignment.

Henry Wade: The Dallas district attorney who seemed to think the case was closed the afternoon of the assassination. He went on TV several times that day, stating they had the right man and there was no conspiracy. Wade, who apparently had more skills than any investigator in history, came to this conclusion before even 10 percent of the evidence had been collected. It is very clear to most researchers that Wade, who was also a friend of Jack Ruby's and was seen in Ruby's club numerous times, was clearly trying to cover up the facts of the case right from the start. His goal seemed certain from his first public statement that there was one lone gunman and his name was Lee Harvey Oswald.

Howard Brennan: Brennan was a key Warren Commission witness whose story was full of more holes than a punch board. It has been picked apart over the years by many researchers and investigators. Brennan saw a man in one of the sixth floor windows, but he said the man was standing up and was able to provide a height description of the suspect. Well, how could this be when pictures of the so-called sniper's window show it was closed at least halfway down? How could he see anyone standing there? Also, the Warren Commission said that he could positively identify Oswald as the man in the window, but Brennan was unable to pick Oswald out of a police lineup later that day. Brennan's description was even used to advise all police units to be on the lookout for this suspect; the Dallas police later gave this as the reason Officer Tippit stopped Oswald on the street thirty minutes after the shooting in Dealey Plaza.

S. M. Holland: Perhaps the best grassy knoll witness of all time, Holland was a railroad supervisor who was standing on the triple overpass with several of his men that day. He was the most outspoken critic of the Warren Commission's lone gunman theory, claiming he was certain that someone was firing from behind the fence line. He told Mark Lane in an interview that he was absolutely positive that at least one shot came from behind the picket fence; he saw the smoke and heard the report of the rifle fire. He also stood his ground with regards to the so-called magic bullet, claiming that the president and Governor Connally were not hit with the same bullet; he saw with his own eyes that they were hit by separate bullets. What a great witness. See and hear his testimony in Lane's *Rush to Judgment*.

J. D. Tippit: Tippit was the officer killed approximately thirty minutes after the shooting in Dealey Plaza. His murder remains a huge mystery and is a subject unto itself. Who killed him? Why was he killed? What was he doing near Oswald's rooming house? These questions have never been answered. Some witnesses said there were two suspects at the scene of Tippit's murder. Some researchers go as far as to say that Tippit was somehow involved in the conspiracy himself. These questions may never be answered.

Jack Martin: He was a private investigator who worked for Guy Banister, the former FBI chief of Chicago. Banister was the CIA contact who was controlling Oswald in New Orleans; they both shared the same office on Camp Street. Jack Martin was a witness to the goings-on in that office and claims to have seen Oswald, David Ferrie, and Clay Shaw all together at that location on many occasions.

Jack Ruby: The now-famous nightclub owner and murderer of Lee Harvey Oswald. It has been confirmed by hundreds of sources that Ruby was connected to the Mafia in many ways and that the murder of Oswald was clearly a hit. It has also been established that Ruby knew Oswald very well; they were often seen together before the assassination in Ruby's Carousel Club. In the two weeks prior to the assassination in Dallas, Ruby made several phone calls to Mafia members all over the country, including Chicago, Miami, and Los Angeles. The Warren Commission could not deny these calls existed, so they said that Ruby was merely carrying on friendly relations with old friends, talking about business deals and the weather. I kid you not; they really said that. Ruby also knew hundreds of members of the Dallas Police Department and was very good friends with Henry Wade, the district attorney who would later be forced to prosecute his old buddy in court for the murder of Oswald.

Jack Van Laningham: FBI informant who was locked up with Carlos Marcello in the same state prison during the late 1980s and early 1990s. Van Laningham was able to record hundreds of hours of conversations with Marcello in which the Mob kingpin admitted to being involved in the assassination of President Kennedy. Marcello said he was one of the organizers of the assassination and provided some of the resources in Dallas, such as Jack Ruby. Van Laningham was also able to get other valuable details regarding organized crime activities in the United States.

James Hosty: Hosty was a former FBI agent working out of the Dallas office in the 1960s who was assigned to watch the movements of Lee Oswald and his wife Marina. Hosty clearly did not watch Oswald close enough, because Oswald, if he truly was considered a threat, was everywhere he shouldn't have been with the president coming to town. Hosty never told the Warren Commission that Oswald dropped off a note to him just two weeks before the assassination. We may never know what the note said. This information did not come out until the 1970s. Hosty told the HSCA that it was a message to leave his wife alone, but the clerk at the FBI office who gave the note to Hosty said Oswald had threatened to blow up the Dallas FBI office and the Dallas police station. I think the most important point about this note is, why in the world would a rabid, bloodthirsty communist who was planning to kill the president of the United States go anywhere near the FBI building in the city where he was preparing to carry out this crime? That should be your question. More than likely, the note was a warning about the assassination, because it has been proven that Oswald was an FBI informant; just put the pieces together. It should be noted that around the time of Oswald's visit to the FBI office, the agency issued a warning that stated a right wing militant group would attempt to assassinate President Kennedy on his trip to Dallas. This message went out to all the FBI offices across the country. Hosty later testified that on orders from Agent in Charge Gordon Shanklin, he ripped the note up and flushed it down the toilet at the FBI office in Dallas on November 24.

James Jarman: Jarman worked with Lee Oswald in the Book Depository. He is an important witness because he told the Warren Commission that he saw Oswald in the lunchroom at 12:20. If that is correct, he not only confirms the statement of Carolyn Arnold, who also saw him around the same time in the same location, but clearly establishes the location of Oswald in the building minutes before the shooting.

Additionally, Jarman had gone to a fifth floor window to watch the motorcade go by and claims he heard shots coming from below him, not above him. This observation then confirms the claims made by Carolyn Walther; she was down on Elm Street and said that the shooters were possibly in the fourth or fifth floor windows and not the sixth floor window, as maintained by the Warren Commission.

James Jenkins: He was a technician at the autopsy who along with Paul O'Connor removed the president's body from the cheap metal casket and the gray body bag. He confirmed O'Connor's recollections that the president's head wound had a frontal entry point. He also said that the president's head was wrapped in towels, which did not come from Parkland Hospital, according to all the witnesses there.

James Simmons: Simmons was a railroad worker and key grassy knoll witness who saw the shot from the fence line; he said he saw the smoke come out from behind the fence, just like S. M. Holland. He later ran over with the rest of the employees and found several muddy footprints in the exact spot where the smoke came out.

James Tague: Tague was the third victim of the shooting in Dealey Plaza; he was hit in the face by a ricochet off the curb. Tague was standing under the railroad underpass across from Elm Street and the grassy knoll; he was told by a police officer that he had blood on his face right after the shooting; he had been hit by gunfire. He told Mark Lane in the film *Rush to Judgment* that he felt that the shots came from the fence behind the grassy knoll as well. His injury forced the Warren Commission to come up with the ridiculous magic bullet theory in order to still have a single shooter in the plaza.

James Wilcott: An often-overlooked witness who claims that Oswald was recruited by the CIA out of the Marine Corps. He further testified that Oswald was a double agent and that he was responsible for handling the financial aspect of his recruitment.

Jean Hill: Jean was another grassy knoll witness who was very close to the shooting and claimed that the shots came from behind the grassy knoll, having seen the muzzle flash and the smoke from the shot that killed President Kennedy. She was accosted by federal agents and had her film taken from her; she describes these events in her book, *The Last Dissenting Witness.*

Jerrol F. Custer: Jerrol was a Bethesda Hospital technician who took the x-rays of the dead president. Custer would later be shown the x-rays that were used by the Warren Commission in David Lifton's film, *Best Evidence.* Custer told Lifton that there was no way those were the x-rays he took. He said over and over, "No way, these are not the ones I took." When Lifton asked him where they came from, Custer said, "I have no idea, but those were not the ones I took that day." Custer also stated that he had already taken all of the x-rays of the president when the official ambulance with Jackie Kennedy and Robert Kennedy arrived in the main entrance. He said he was shocked because he was standing with the x-rays in hand and wearing a blood-stained gown. He said he had no clue what was in that ambulance, because the president's body had already arrived much earlier in another black ambulance.

Jesse Curry: The Dallas police chief during the 1960s; Curry rode in the lead car of the motorcade and was there when LBJ was sworn in on *Air Force One.* In 1969, he wrote a book called *JFK Assassination File.* He had a lot of reservations about the claims that Lee Oswald was the lone gunman; he had access to a lot of firsthand information, much of which was in his book. He was also a highly intelligent and educated police officer; his book has some solid information in it. It is clear he knew there was another shooter firing from the grassy knoll.

Jim Garrison: The New Orleans district attorney who made the only attempt to prosecute any of the conspirators. He charged Clay Shaw with conspiracy to murder the president of the United States; the trial took place in New

Orleans and captured a worldwide audience. Shaw was found not guilty, but Garrison really turned up the heat on the government as well as others who were involved in the murder. The trial was the first public viewing of the Zapruder film, clearly showing that the president was killed from a shot fired from in front of the limo and proving that JFK and Governor Connally were hit by different bullets. This information confirmed the statements of the governor as well as his wife, who both insisted that the president and the governor were shot with different projectiles.

Jimmy Hoffa: The infamous Jimmy Hoffa was the Teamsters Union president during the time of the assassination; Hoffa was involved in organized crime and helped to finance loans for the Mafia through the millions of dollars that were brought in through Teamster Union dues. He hated the Kennedys perhaps more than anyone else, having gone to war with them on many occasions. He also made death threats against them on a regular basis, and if he had had the resources, I am certain he would have tried to kill them both. Hoffa disappeared in the 1970s; he had served time in prison and then was pardoned by Nixon. He made the mistake of trying to regain control of the union; he was never seen again.

Joe Civello: Civello was the Mafia lieutenant reportedly in charge of the Dallas underworld; he was close friends with Jack Ruby and Carlos Marcello. He was also very close, as was Ruby, with most of the Dallas police officers in the 1960s.

Joe Smith: Joe Smith was the *Fort Worth Star News* reporter who took the famous pictures of the three tramps in Dealey Plaza; some people claim that one of the tramps was E. Howard Hunt, and another tramp was accused assassin Charles Harrelson, who had killed a federal judge and others as well. He died in prison in 2007. Chauncey Holt claimed to be one of the tramps as well; he said he unwittingly became part of the conspiracy to kill JFK. Holt said himself many times that the tall tramp was in fact Harrelson.

Johnny Roselli: He was good friends with Jack Ruby; their friendship went way back. Roselli supposedly made statements to journalist Jack Anderson that the Mafia used Ruby to silence Oswald. Roselli was about to testify to the Select Committee on Assassinations in the 1970s when he was murdered. His chopped-up body was found floating in a drum off the coast of south Florida. After his body turned up, Florida Mafia boss Santos Trafficante began to refer to him as "Johnny in a Drum."

Joseph Dulce: He was a wound ballistics expert who made a report in April 1964 that Governor John Connally could not have been struck with the magic bullet, because it was impossible for Connally's wrist bone to be shattered in such a way and for the bullet to remain in pristine condition.

Julia Ann Mercer: On the morning of the assassination, around eleven o'clock, Mercer observed a truck parked up on the curb in front of the grassy knoll on Elm Street. As she passed by, she got a really good look at the driver, who she later positively identified as Jack Ruby through a series of mug shots at the sheriff's office. Ruby was letting out a passenger, who according to Mercer was carrying a gun case and headed straight for the wooden picket fence, where she lost sight of him. She reported this to the authorities, but of course nothing was ever done with this information. The Warren Commission even twisted her words in their final report, stating that she could not identify the driver of the truck. Had Ruby been picked up by law enforcement that day, he would not have killed Oswald the next day at police headquarters.

Lawrence Angel: Angel was a forensic expert who was asked by the HSCA in the 1970s to explain how the piece of the president's skull, which was found on the curb well behind the limo, had come from the rear of his head and not the front. The official autopsy photos and x-rays indicated this fact. Angel, a well-known forensic expert, told the HSCA that he could not explain this anomaly.

Lee Bowers: From his perch high up in the railroad tower behind the picket fence, Lee Bowers was in a perfect position to observe all that was going on in Dealey Plaza the morning of the assassination. Although he was one of the few witnesses called by the Warren Commission, they failed to ask him any pertinent questions, thereby wasting a chance to find out the truth of what went on behind the grassy knoll. Bowers said that he saw at least two men right at the spot where all the other witnesses saw the same shooters; two of these men, he said, were wearing police uniforms. This is also the same location where there was a flash of light and smoke that came out from under the trees and also where Gordon Arnold said he was standing as a bullet whizzed past his ear. Bowers saw the spotters driving around right before the assassination and said they were speaking into what appeared to be microphones. He also heard the shots going off and swore that two of the shots he heard came right on top of each other, which is also what so many other witnesses heard that day, including law enforcement officials.

Lee Harvey Oswald: The accused assassin of the president, according to the FBI, the Dallas police, and District Attorney Henry Wade. He was never put on trial, having been executed by Jack Ruby. It is clear that had Oswald gone to trial, he would have not been convicted, due to the lack of almost any real physical evidence, including the fact that nitrate tests conducted on Oswald were found to be negative, despite the statements of the district attorney. There were also no true fingerprints on the weapon, according to the FBI. There were also no witnesses who could put him in the window with the rifle, and most of all, he had absolutely no motive whatsoever to kill the president. In fact, according to the FBI, he was at their Dallas office two weeks before the assassination. What likely assassin would do such a thing? No eyewitnesses, no direct evidence, and no motive almost always ends in a not-guilty verdict.

Lee Rankin: Chief Counsel for the Warren Commission. During the commission's investigation, it is known that Rankin received vital information (such as proof that Lee

Oswald had worked for the FBI) that was never used in the investigation.

Lewis McWillie: McWillie was a Mafia member who was friends with Jack Ruby and other mobsters like Carlos Marcello and Santos Trafficante. He worked out of Cuba; Ruby would go down and meet up with him there, and there are facts to back this up. He was also good friends with a Mafia associate named Pat Kirkwood, who owned the Cellar, the bar where some of the president's Secret Service detail partied the night before the assassination.

Madeline Brown: Brown stated many times over the years that she had seen Lee Oswald in Jack Ruby's club in the fall of 1963. She was also a longtime mistress of Lyndon B. Johnson, with whom she had a child; prior to her death, she told many stories that incriminated Johnson and his cronies in the murder of President Kennedy and the cover-up.

Malcolm Summers: Summers was a grassy knoll witness who ran up the slope with many others in an attempt to locate the shooter they had seen on the knoll. Summers said when he reached the top of the knoll; he was confronted by a man in a suit with a coat over his arm, holding a weapon. According to Summers, this individual told him, "You better get out of here or you're going to get hurt." Summers was frightened when he saw the weapon and decided to back off. Other witnesses claimed to have seen this same person as well; some said he told them he was a CIA agent.

Malcolm Wallace: Wallace was a close friend of LBJ's and also a convicted murderer. He was used by LBJ to get rid of people, including, some think, the president. It is a clear and solid fact that Malcolm Wallace's fingerprint was found in the so-called sniper's nest on the sixth floor of the School Book Depository the day of the president's murder. How did it get there?

Margaret M. Henchliffe: Margaret was a nurse at Parkland Hospital who attended to the wounded president.

She was well experienced with gunshot wounds and told the Warren Commission flatly that the wound to the president's throat was unequivocally an entrance wound.

Marin Baker: He was the police officer who rushed into the Texas School Book Depository within seconds of the shooting. Accompanied by the building manager, Baker encountered Lee Harvey Oswald in the lunchroom on the lower floor. He was drinking a Coke at the time; Baker pulled his pistol on him and asked the building manager, "Does this man work here? Is he an employee?" Once he was told that Oswald worked there, Officer Baker resumed his search of the building.

Mary La Fontaine: She was the author of *Oswald Talked* and a Dallas researcher who managed to locate John Elrod, who claims to have been locked up in the Dallas police station with Lee Oswald the day after the assassination. He said Oswald revealed to him an aspect of the conspiracy involving Jack Ruby: that Jack Ruby and Oswald knew each other and that Ruby was part of the conspiracy.

Maryanne Mooreman: Mooreman was another roadside witness who was taking pictures at the time of the assassination. She captured one of the most infamous pictures, which was actually returned to her by the FBI because they said it had no real evidentiary value. Many years later, this same picture, with the help of new technology, revealed many new clues, such as the figure firing a rifle from behind the wall on the grassy knoll.

Mary Pinchot Meyer: She was the wife of a very high CIA official and also a mistress to JFK; on October 12, 1964, she was found shot to death, execution style. What she knew she took to the grave, but many believe she was the victim of a hit surrounding the murder of President Kennedy. For more information, see the new book by Peter Janney, *Mary's Mosaic: The CIA Conspiracy to Murder John F. Kennedy, Mary Pinchot Meyer, and Their Vision of World Peace.*

Mary Woodward: Mary worked as a reporter for the *Dallas Morning News*. She was on Elm Street the afternoon of the shooting; throughout the years, she maintained that the head shot that hit President Kennedy came from the front and behind the grassy knoll or close to the underpass area. She said she was forced to change her story because it did not fit with the official version. She said the *Dallas Morning News* did not want to make waves, but what she observed and heard that day was the truth. She gave her story to Nigel Turner in episode 3 (*The Cover-Up*) of his documentary, *The Men Who Killed Kennedy*.

Mark Lane: One of the most famous authors involved in the search for the truth of the JFK assassination; he has written several books, including *Rush to Judgment* and *Plausible Denial*; his most recent book is *Last Word*. Lane is a true hero, in my opinion; he was a research pioneer who laid the groundwork for all of us. He was also able to get many of the important assassination witnesses on video, many of whom were murdered or died shortly after *Rush to Judgment* came out. I have dedicated this book to him.

Marina Oswald: The Russian wife of Lee Harvey Oswald. She came back with Oswald when he returned from the Soviet Union. They had two children, who are now very active in proving that their father was an innocent victim.

Nellie Connally: The First Lady of Texas was sitting right next to her husband, Governor John Connally, when he was nearly killed that day in Dallas. She was a key witness because she was so close to the gunfire and claimed until her death that her husband and the president were hit by separate bullets. She said over and over that the so-called magic bullet theory was simply rubbish. She made several appearances over the years, once going on *Oprah* and explaining that she saw the president clearly hit first before her husband was even shot. She said her husband was turning around when the president was struck and did not get hit until he had turned back toward the front of the car.

Orville Nix: Nix was a solid witness to the assassination and took both moving film and still pictures of the murder. He was asked to turn in his film to the FBI, which he did, and was later told it had been lost. When it was returned, it was missing several frames, including critical moments during the head shot; it does not take very much imagination to figure out why. Nix said he was certain that the shots came from in front of the motorcade, and his friend Forrest Sorrels, the Secret Service agent in charge of Dallas (who was also in the motorcade), confirmed this. Of course, their story changed after the Warren Report came out.

Orlando Martin: Martin is a ballistics expert and author of the book, *JFK: Analysis of a Shooting: The Ultimate Ballistics Truth Revealed,* a very solid book and worth reading. I have cited some of his information in this book.

Oliver Stone: Movie producer and writer who created the film *JFK* in 1992. This film was so powerful that it began a new outcry by the public over the discrepancies in this case, so much so that President Bill Clinton created the JFK Assassinations Records Review Board, which released thousands of pages of information on the assassination. Much of this information had been kept hidden from the public, such as Lee Harvey Oswald's CIA personnel file.

Paul Chambers: Chambers is author of the book *Head Shot,* which offers even more perspective on the shots that were fired at the president. The book is a great read indeed.

Paul O'Connor: He was an excellent Bethesda Hospital witness who actually handled the president's body during the autopsy. He gave several statements to David Lifton regarding his eyewitness accounts of the autopsy and what he observed regarding the president's wounds. This included the massive rear exit wound that blew out the back of his head, and the fact that the president's brain had been removed from his skull and was no longer with the body. He also gave his account of how the president's body arrived in a cheap metal casket and was zipped in a gray body bag. His eyewitness accounts make it clear that the president's body was removed from the original casket seen leaving Parkland Hospital, altered, his brain removed, and then put back in a body bag, the way O'Connor found him when the body arrived at the autopsy.

Pat Kirkwood: Kirkwood was a personal friend of Jack Ruby's; he owned the Cellar, the nightclub where many of the president's Secret Service agents partied long into the morning hours the night before the assassination. Many of these agents were drunk, which is why some of their credentials were lost that night and then used by the assassins the next day.

R. B. Denson: Ruby's defense investigator during his trial; he investigated Ruby's contacts prior to the assassination. According to Denson, Ruby had contact with some very undesirable underworld characters prior to the assassination; he passed this information on to Ruby's defense attorney Melvin Belli.

Richard Dodd: Dodd was another railroad employee who was standing on the triple overpass and observed what all of them saw that morning: a shooter firing from behind the picket fence.

Richard Case Nagell: A noteworthy CIA operative who died in 1995, just after the Assassination Records Review Board requested records he still possessed regarding the assassination. Nagell was also the subject of Richard Russell's book, *The Man Who Knew Too Much*, published in 1992.

Robert Groden: He is a researcher and author who has truly carried the torch for many years in an effort to get the truth out about the murder of JFK. His books, *The Killing of a President* and *The Search for Lee Harvey Oswald*, have become classics and are still very popular research tools to this day.

Roger Boyajian: On November 22, 1963, Marine Corps Sergeant Roger Boyajian was in command of the security detachment at Bethesda Hospital. He is an important witness, because he confirms that the real casket containing President Kennedy's body came into the back of the hospital forty-five minutes before the official motorcade arrived. This information totally confirms the testimony of Dennis David, chief of the day, who helped to unload the cheap gray casket.

Roger Craig: One of the most important and overlooked witnesses of the whole event was Roger Craig; he was a deputy sheriff in Dallas and was on duty the day of the assassination. Craig paid a high price years later, because he knew too much. He saw that the rifle found was a Mauser and not the Oswald rifle and also claims to have seen Lee Oswald leave the Book Depository with a dark-skinned man driving a green station wagon (this dark-skinned man was also seen by many people that day in and around the depository). Craig died in 1975, almost certainly murdered, but of course authorities said it was a suicide. Mark Lane did a wonderful documentary on Craig's life, which includes an interview with the deputy; it is called *Two Men in Dallas*.

Roscoe White: White was a former deputy sheriff from the Chicago area; prior to that, he was in special operations in the military. At the time of the president's murder, White was a patrol officer for the Dallas Police Department. He was good friends with Officer Tippit and was suspected by his own family as having been involved in the shooting of the president. Some claim he is the Badge Man from the Mary Mormon photo, seen shooting a rifle from over the wall. He might have been the police officer encountered by Gordon Arnold on the grassy knoll just after the shooting. Remember, Arnold stated that a man in a police uniform pointed a pistol at him and took the film out of his camera. White was also good friends with Jack Ruby. Actually, his wife Geneva was a dancer at Ruby's Carousel Club, and it is said that Jack Ruby and Geneva White were also good friends. Geneva made many claims after the death of Roscoe White. She said she heard her husband discussing plans to murder the president with Jack Ruby. After his father died, Ricky White, Roscoe's son, was said to have found incriminating evidence that his father was involved in the murder, such as a diary describing the plans of the assassination and an original copy of the Oswald backyard photo.

Also, it should be mentioned that Oswald himself told his friend Ron Lewis that Roscoe White was in fact supposed to be one of the trigger men in the assassination of President Kennedy.

Robert Frazier: FBI firearms expert who tested the rifle the Warren Commission claimed was used by Oswald. Frazier concluded that it took at least 2.3 seconds to cycle the rifle; this was without adding time to aim at a moving target. His results contributed to the necessity for Specter to create the ridiculous story of the magic bullet, because a single shooter could not have pulled off the assassination.

Robert F. Kennedy: Robert was the brother of President John Kennedy and the United States attorney general at the time of the president's murder. He was also the president's number one advisor, and they shared the disdain of many organized crime members in the United States. After the murder of his brother, RFK gave up his pursuit of Mafia members in the United States.

Ron Lewis: Ron Lewis worked with Lee Oswald in New Orleans; they both worked for Guy Banister and Clay Shaw. He has stated this fact many times and even wrote his own book, called *Flashback: The Untold Story of Lee Harvey Oswald.* He claimed that Oswald knew Ruby very well and that they had worked together on certain projects for Banister and Shaw.

Rose Cherame: Rose was a prostitute who claims to have overheard several men on their way to Dallas planning the murder of the president. She said the group had left New Orleans on a road trip to Dallas, and they subsequently threw her out on the road with her belongings after they were done with her. She was found by authorities, who tried to piece her story together, but it was too late when she was finally believed by her psychiatrist.

Ruth Paine: Former friend and housemate of Marina Oswald, Ruth Paine is a rather mysterious individual. Her husband worked for Bell Helicopter at the time they met the Oswalds at a get-together, but then they later separated. She allowed Marina and the children to move into her home; Lee would come to visit at times. The Dallas police said they found incriminating evidence in her garage linking Oswald to the assassination.

Sam Giancana: At one time, the most powerful Mafia boss in the United States; he worked out of the Chicago office and was also in charge of the Dallas area through another Mafia boss, Carlos Marcello. Sam's own brother and godson stated many interesting facts in their book, *Double Cross,* which is an excellent book. In the book, they describe the direct involvement of Giancana in the assassination, his relationship to the other conspirators, and the Jack Ruby connection.

Sam Kinney: He was the Secret Service agent who drove the follow-up car in the presidential motorcade in Dallas.

Sandra Styles: A friend of Vicki Adams; both women were coming down the rear staircase of the Texas School Book Depository just after the shooting; they never saw Lee Oswald coming down, as the commission stated. The reason: because Oswald was in the lunchroom, where he said he was, having been seen there by several witnesses.

Santos Trafficante: Santos was the Mafia chief for the state of Florida (and also Cuba) in the 1950s and 1960s; he was one of the Mafia leaders many researchers feel could have been involved in the assassination. He hated the Kennedys in more ways than one; he also had close relations with Carlos Marcello and Jimmy Hoffa. Both of these men were Kennedy haters themselves. Trafficante was actually jailed in Cuba shortly after Castro shut down the

Mafia-controlled casinos there. While in jail, he had a very interesting visitor: Jack Ruby, and the Warren Commission admitted this information through their own investigation, but they ultimately concluded Ruby had no Mafia ties. I can't make this up.

Seth Kantor: Kantor was a local Dallas newsman who was an acquaintance of Jack Ruby; he remained solid in his statement that he talked with Jack Ruby at Parkland Hospital after the shooting. He said he saw Ruby in the hallway with the empty stretchers used to take the wounded president and Governor Connally from their vehicle. This is also where the so-called magic bullet was found.

Seymour Weitzman: Deputy Seymour Weitzman was a key witness on the day of the assassination; he was outside during the shooting, recovered some evidence, and interviewed witnesses in Dealey Plaza. Weitzman was also inside the Book Depository when the rifle was found. Weitzman originally identified this rifle as a German Mauser; he even signed an affidavit to that effect. Later, the Mauser somehow turned into an Italian rifle that matched the one Oswald apparently owned.

Silvia Odio: What a great witness Odio turned out to be: she was not in Dealey Plaza that day, but she was visited shortly before the assassination by two Cubans and a man she described as Lee Harvey Oswald. Of course, the Warren Commission denied this, saying that Odio was mistaken because Oswald was in Mexico at this time, but she has always maintained that it was Oswald she saw that day.

Thomas Dowling: He was the first chairman of the House Select Committee on Assassinations; he told the other committee members that he was convinced there was more than one gunman.

Thomas Kimmel: FBI special agent in charge of the investigation involving Carlos Marcello, when he was incarcerated at the Texarkana Federal Prison in the 1980s.

Using an informant, Kimmel was able to get hundreds of hours of covert recordings in which Marcello openly admitted to being involved in the assassination of President Kennedy, as well as his personal relationship with Jack Ruby, whom he ordered to kill Lee Oswald.

Vicki Adams: A very critical witness at the Texas School Book Depository, who was in the rear staircase right after the shooting, which was the time the Warren Commission said Lee Oswald was running down those same stairs to the second floor lunchroom after shooting the president. Adams emphatically stated that she and her friend Sandra never saw Oswald. Adams was harassed by the Warren Commission and the Dallas police to the point that she disappeared for many years, staying out of the limelight. Vicki's statements and her observations are backed not only by her friend Sandra Styles, who was there, but also her supervisor, a Mrs. Garner, who confirmed Vicki's story to Assistant US Attorney Martha Joe Stroud. This information was later passed on to Warren Commission General Counsel Lee Rankin.

Victor Marchetti: A former high-ranking CIA member who was an assistant to Richard Helms, the CIA director. Victor was the highest ranking official to spill the beans on the JFK assassination, implicating the agency and E. Howard Hunt in the assassination. He also verified the fact that the agency went after Jim Garrison during his prosecution of Clay Shaw in order to protect Shaw, who was an agency facilitator.

Warren Reynolds: Reynolds was one of the witnesses to the murder of Officer J. D. Tippit. He did not see the actual shooting, but he got a clear and up close look at the shooter who ran from the scene, whom he said was not Lee Oswald. He gave a very different description of the man running that day, that is, until someone tried to blow his head off one night when he was leaving work. He was shot in the head, and the bullet caused serious and permanent damage; not long after that, he identified Oswald as the assailant of Officer Tippit. Surprised?

Will Hayden Griffin: Griffin was another FBI agent who said that Oswald was an FBI informant. He interviewed Oswald's landlady, who said that a Dallas police car pulled up to her house and honked its horn twice while Oswald was in his room. She said she saw two police officers in the vehicle; they left seconds before Oswald came out of his room and left the house.

William Matson Law: Law conducted an incredible and detailed interview with Perry Raymond Russo, who was a Jim Garrison witness. Perry had a lot of first-hand knowledge regarding the CIA activities in New Orleans during the 1960s.

William Bruce Pitzer: Pitzer was a Navy lieutenant commander who filmed the autopsy of JFK. He was found dead in his office at Bethesda Hospital just months before he was to retire from the Navy. The official story was suicide, but little evidence supports this claim. For one, he was said to have shot himself with his off hand; also, his family says he was looking forward to retirement. There is evidence that Pitzer was planning to continue working in the media after retirement, which may have led to his murder. He made the mistake of showing some of the film of the autopsy to friends. The film, according to Dennis Davis, a coworker and one of those friends, clearly showed that the president had been shot in the head from the front and not from the rear, as the official story states. What other evidence this film might have shown may never be known, because there were no films found in his possession at the time of his death.

William Goday: This was a journalist in the New Orleans area around the time of the assassination. He knew Guy Banister pretty well and spent time around Banister's office. He stated for the record that he saw Lee Harvey Oswald with Banister in the summer of 1963 but never knew Banister's involvement in the assassination; he was sure he had something to do with it, based on the fact that Banister had a relationship with Oswald, and they knew each other well.

William Greer: Greer was the Secret Service agent who was driving JFK's limo in Dallas; he has been criticized, and rightly so, for bringing the presidential limo to a near stop during the gunfire. Greer actually put his foot on the brake and looked back at the president just before the fatal head shot, giving the sniper a perfect view of the president. His security tactics that day were simply deplorable. It is amazing they let him drive the Navy ambulance to Bethesda Hospital (of course, we now know it did not contain the body of the president). It should be noted that Kennedy's normal driver had died of a heart attack prior to the Dallas trip; Greer was the replacement.

William Westbrook: A Dallas police captain during the time of the Kennedy assassination, he was involved in the arrest of Lee Oswald but is most notably known for finding a wallet near J.D. Tippit, who was killed within an hour of the president's murder. The strange thing to note is that when Oswald was arrested, he already had a wallet in his possession, which was booked into evidence and contained all of his personal information and ID cards. So what about this other wallet? If Lee Oswald was the killer of Officer J. D. Tippit, then who owned the wallet found at the murder scene by Captain Westbrook?

Winston G. Lawson: Lawson was a Secret Service agent who rode in the lead car of the motorcade with Secret Service Agent Forrest Sorrells. Strangely, Agent Lawson was responsible for lowering the protection details that surrounded the president's motorcade, such as cutting down on the motorcycle outriders. But he has always claimed that he heard the final shots in rapid succession, which of course could not have been made by the Oswald bolt-action rifle.

Chapter 14

The Real Spin on Killing Kennedy: The End of Camelot: Fair, Balanced, and Simply Ridiculous

"The Truth will ultimately prevail where there is pains to bring it to light".
—George Washington

Around the time I was concluding my book, Bill O'Reilly and Martin Dugard released *Killing Kennedy: The End of Camelot.* [237] After reading this book, I felt it was important to comment on it in my final chapter. Although the first part of the book covered a fairly good historical overview of the Kennedy presidency, as I read on, it became apparent to me that this book falls into what G. Paul Chambers, the author of *Head Shot,* classifies as "irresponsible." Chambers points out the following: "Almost a thousand books have been published on the Kennedy assassination; most have uncovered serious flaws in the official version of events, but some are, in my view, irresponsible and play into improbable and impossible themes. Among these are certain critical and influential books such as Gerald Posener's *Case Closed* and Vincent Bugliosi's *Reclaiming History*, which, I would argue, paint a distorted picture of the truth" (Chambers 2012, 8). Well, Mr. Chambers, *Killing Kennedy* will most certainly be included in your next list of irresponsible books. It turns out that O'Reilly's book is another regurgitation of the old bullet-ridden official version put forth by the Warren Commission in 1964, including the ridiculous tale of the magic bullet. Interestingly, Mark Fuhrman, another Fox News personality,

---

237 O'Reilly, B., and Dugard, M. (2012). *Killing Kennedy: The End of Camelot.* New York: Henry Holt and Company.

published his own book in 2006, *A Simple Act of Murder.*[238] This book does a great job of discrediting the magic bullet theory, so why would O'Reilly continue to side with that old official story after it has been completely discredited over the years? It escapes common-sense reasoning.

All you need to do is to read the Warren Report, and with a little speculation, and some true bloviating, you have pretty much the same conclusions you find in O'Reilly's new book. Also, I must mention the total and complete lack of any true references in the entire book (aside from a few endnotes); sadly, this book is a big disappointment, in my opinion of course, and maybe yours as well, once you have read this chapter.[239] Although I will point out that O'Reilly's *Killing Lincoln* was very well done. Bravo for that one!

So let's take it from the top. First, O'Reilly went on *Fox & Friends* to talk about his book and stated that it was based on the facts. It reminded me of Sergeant Friday of *Dragnet*, who used to say, "Just the facts, please." Well, they sure are the facts: the facts based on the discredited, moth-eaten, and simply embarrassing official version of the assassination.[240] As a matter of "fact," over the last several years, just about the only people who still believed the official story were Gerald Ford, George H. W. Bush, Gerald Posener, and Vincent Bugliosi, who have always supported the fictionalized story of

---

[238] Mark and I actually worked together on the LAPD in the early 1980s at West L.A. Station. He is a great guy, and I have fond memories of working with him. I was a rookie officer back then, and he was always fun to work with. I remember he always had thoughts of conspiracy in this case and discussed it openly with me and other officers. He says as much in his introduction, although he has changed his views over the years.

[239] When books do not contain references in the text or have a reference page or footnotes, then the authors are free to add whatever they want and call it the truth. This is the case with *Killing Kennedy,* which only provides a very short list of sources toward the rear of the book.

[240] Just as recently as the second week of January 2013, Robert F. Kennedy Jr. stated during an interview that his father knew that the Warren Report was poorly constructed and apparently did not develop all the facts.

the lone gunman.[241] But now there seems to be a resurgence of sorts supporting the official lone nut story, thanks to books like *Killing Kennedy*.

Perhaps the biggest downfall of the Warren Commission was that they were being fed their facts through only one agency: the FBI. They relied solely on this investigative agency to provide them with what they thought were the total and complete facts of this case.[242] We have also seen that the Warren Commission only interviewed around 10 percent of the witnesses in Dealey Plaza. This alone tells you that their investigation was flawed from the start, but this is the same information O'Reilly relied upon in his new book.

If you rely on flawed and false information, you force yourself to come to the same incorrect conclusions over and over again, and *Killing Kennedy* is a perfect example of this, because there was clearly more than one shooter in Dealey Plaza; even the last official version established this fact in 1979. They also came to the conclusion that there was a conspiracy to kill the president; maybe the authors failed to read that version.[243]

Another point to keep in mind was the so-called magic bullet, supposedly found on a stretcher in Parkland Hospital,

---

241 Also, how could I have forgotten Arlen Specter (who actually passed away while I was completing this book)? I always wanted to confront him on his single bullet theory nonsense.

242 Although we have seen that James Sibert's report of the autopsy was a God-send; through his report, we can conclude that there was more than one gunman in the plaza, that the president was shot from the front as well, and that the magic bullet was a piece of fiction made up by Specter.

243 Of course, the magic bullet theory was not believed by several members of the Warren Commission. Allan Dulles and Senator Long, to name two, refused to believe that Kennedy and Connally were hit by one bullet. They just went along for the ride on that one, never being fully convinced, based on the film of the assassination, which showed that Kennedy reacted much sooner to being hit than Connally. Connally himself told the Warren Commission that he and the president could not have been hit by the same bullet; he stated over and over again, "That the first shot did not hit me, I am certain of that."

was the only direct piece of evidence linking the Oswald weapon to the shooting. Of course, there was no chain of evidence regarding the stretcher bullet, known to some as the pristine bullet, and this bullet was the cornerstone of the Warren Commission's lone gunman theory. However, we learned in previous chapters that this bullet may not have even come from Governor Connally's stretcher but was more than likely found on the president's stretcher at Parkland Hospital, according to the Secret Service. We also learned that this bullet fell out of Kennedy's back wound, according to the FBI agents present at the autopsy and the FBI ballistic laboratory information provided by Agent Killion, their ballistics expert.

So let's move on to other evidence. In any real murder investigation, there must be proof beyond a reasonable doubt that someone committed the murder. Keep in mind that no one could even identify Lee Harvey Oswald as being the shooter in the window on the sixth floor of the Book Depository.[244] As a matter of fact, the best that anyone could do was to conclude that someone with a weapon was in one of those windows and provide a very sketchy statement regarding their clothing. We must remember that there were several boxes stacked up around the window; O'Reilly himself states that the shooter was in a kneeling position; if that was the case, how in the world could anyone but Superman see someone in enough detail to describe them to a point beyond a reasonable doubt? It would be impossible to accurately see anyone at a distance of about a hundred yards if that person was kneeling down.[245]

---

244 Even the Warren Commission's star witness, Howard Brennan, stated that he could not with any certainty identify Oswald as the man he saw in the window before the shooting, and he could not pick Oswald out of a lineup at police headquarters later that day.

245 Actually, I am not sure how O'Reilly knows what truly happened up there. Was he a fly on the wall? Oswald never admitted to being up there, therefore, if it was Oswald, he died before he could give an account of his actions (or anyone else's, for that matter).

How about the other evidence that was originally touted as solid proof of Oswald's guilt, like the infamous paraffin tests? District Attorney Henry Wade and the Dallas police were all quick to tell the media that Oswald had tested positive on the test conducted on him, but this was simply not the truth; the test was actually negative. In fact, the commission had to deal with this big problem of the negative paraffin results, so they simply decided to shoot down the reliability of the paraffin test itself by stating that it was very poor evidence in any shooting incident. Here is a quote from the Warren Commission regarding the use of the paraffin test: "The unreliability of the paraffin test has been demonstrated by experiments run by the FBI. In one experiment, conducted prior to the assassination, paraffin tests were performed on seventeen men who had just fired five shots with a .38-caliber revolver. Eight men tested negative in both hands, three men tested positive on the idle hand and negative on the firing hand, two men tested positive on the firing hand and negative on the idle hand, and four men tested positive on both their firing and idle hands" (Lane 1964, 151).

Mark Lane also points out, "Furthermore, nitrates which ordinarily might be present after firing an old and cheaply constructed rifle were not found on Oswald's face" (Lane 1964, 150). So if Oswald's case had gone to court, the paraffin tests conducted on him would have, at the minimum, been found to be unreliable and inadmissible, but the real facts appeared to prove that there were no nitrates found on Oswald's face.

There is so much I could discuss about O'Reilly and Dugard's book, but I am trying to get my book closed out and put into production, so I will leave it to another researcher to totally dismantle this mostly fictionalized book; I am very sure someone else will, and soon. Let me continue to hit the high points for you now. O'Reilly is advertising his book as a piece of academic literature, a work of true history, which should be used in our public schools; really, Mr. O'Reilly?

On p. 139, the authors discuss the Secret Service detail that was guarding the president. They state, "The Secret Service motto is 'Worthy of Trust and Confidence,' and the agents reinforce that message through their poise and professionalism. They are athletic men, many of them possessing college degrees and military backgrounds. Drinking beer on duty is out of the question"[246] (O'Reilly and Dugard 2012, 139). Well, what do you do with all the negative information out there that many of these same agents were drunk the night before the assassination? Let's look back a little at some of the information that was uncovered: "In Fort Worth the night before the visit to Dallas, the majority of the president's Secret Service agents had a boisterous party that lasted into the early hours of November 22. The party was held at a local nightclub, the Cellar, that was owned by Pat Kirkwood, a friend of another Dallas nightclub owner, Jack Ruby. Back at his hotel, the president's protection was provided by only two unarmed Fort Worth fireman" (Groden 1993, 9). This behavior if true was simply disgusting and disgraceful.

Furthermore, let's not forget Secret Service Agent Bolden's comments involving the previously mentioned party and its ramifications. Bolden said what he saw was a lack of concern for the president, which he felt was widespread within the agency. He said, "The women and booze mentality of the presidential detail was putting the president at risk" (Bolden 2008, 73). He felt that suspects could have exploited these weaknesses in the president's protection, which of course makes complete sense. You have just read that the presidential detail was seen at an all-night party the night before in Fort Worth, and Agent Bolden confirms this many times over in his book. He also gives a solid explanation as to how the conspirators managed to get their hands on official

---

[246] Well, as we have seen over the last year, this is not always the case with regards to the Secret Service scandals, like the ones recently uncovered in South America involving hookers and booze. The same was true in 1963. Of course, not all the agents act in such an unprofessional manner, and I am sure the recent scandal was just a small group of losers whose behavior discredited the entire Secret Service.

Secret Service badges and credentials. He states, "I firmly believed that the officer who confronted the unknown suspect behind the picket fence immediately after the assassination was indeed shown an authentic Secret Service commission book, the book that had been lost by, or taken from, an alcohol-impaired agent the night before. Further, I was convinced that the Secret Service leadership acted to conceal or at least obstruct this fact by providing new commission books for all the agents in the Service. The Service has, of course, publicly denied this" (Bolden 2008, 73).

I guess the authors of *Killing Kennedy* must have overlooked all these facts; there is much more if you dig into it. Many others have verified the above information, but for the sake of time, I have just included a few of the facts and details here.

So how effective was the Secret Service protection that day? Well, I think you have the answer to that question with the end result: one very dead president and one nearly dead governor. But according to the authors, "Once the president leaves the White House, eight agents form a human shield around him as he moves" (O'Reilly and Dugard 2012, 140).[247] Gentlemen, you are kidding, right? If that is how they form a human shield, they need to revamp their training, which of course I know they have. Today's protection of the president provided by the agency is nothing less than stellar.

Also, there is this statement: "Any crazed lunatic with a gun and an agenda can easily take a shot during moments like those. Should that happen, each agent is prepared to place his body between the bullet and the president, sacrificing his own life for the good of the country" (O'Reilly and Dugard 2012, 140). But I seem to remember the frozen squad of agents that day as the shots rang out for several seconds; with the agent in charge of the follow-up car telling all his agents to stay put. In addition, there was a lack of outriders on the president's limo, and no agents were posted

247 Now that is a proper reference on my part. Their book has almost no references within its pages. Why is that?

on the rear of the car, which should have been standard for that time, especially given the very slow speed of the motorcade and the multiple threats against the president in Dallas. Let's face the facts: the president's protection was extremely weak in Dallas, and if you can't see that, then it is obvious that you are protecting some reputations here.

As you read earlier, Special Agent Clint Hill was the only agent to respond at all. All the other agents were like statues, frozen in time. Then we have William Greer, the driver, who after hearing several gunshots hitting the vehicle, decides to bring the limo to a near stop, giving the assassins a sitting target. Just where did Agent Greer get his training from? This is a good question, although I did find out that the president's regular driver had a heart attack and died just prior to the Dallas trip.

I will always give credit where it is due, and on page 143 the author's state, "Right here in Washington, the CIA is none too happy about the rumors that JFK would like to place the agency under closer presidential supervision by putting Bobby Kennedy in charge" (O'Reilly and Dugard 2012, 143). This is exactly true and therefore provides the CIA with a perfect motive_to eliminate Kennedy, a strong motive, which the authors later admit was completely absent in the case of Lee Oswald, who had no reason to kill President Kennedy. Also, the authors note that the president was going to pull out of Vietnam. This is a point that many historians refuse to believe, despite a large amount of evidence supporting this conclusion. On p. 156, the authors state, "John Kennedy believes that America needs to end the Vietnam conflict, though he is not quite ready to go public with this. 'We don't have a prayer of staying in Vietnam' he will tell Pulitzer Prize-winning journalist Charles Bartlet off the record" (O'Reilly and Dugard 2012, 156). This is also very true and an excellent point; this is further evidence of a motive for the Central Intelligence Agency and the Pentagon to relieve the president of his life. However, there is still no motive for Oswald, who according to the authors was a rabid procommunist. If true, why would he be upset with the president for pulling our troops out of Vietnam, a communist country?[248] It would seem to me that a procommunist person would have wanted President Kennedy right where he was, rather than remove him from power and then put Johnson in charge. Johnson, we know, was much less liberal regarding American foreign policy than President Kennedy.

I would now like to make a quick comment regarding the author's version of the General Walker shooting. First off, this is still an unsolved crime. No suspects were ever questioned, and no one was ever charged in that crime. Despite this, the authors seem certain that Oswald did the shooting. Maybe if we try hard enough, we can get Oswald posthumously charged with the Black Dahlia murder in Los Angeles and the sinking of the USS *Maine*. O'Reilly says that Oswald was only forty yards away, shooting at a sitting target, and he missed? Despite this lack of accuracy, he still claims that Oswald, "the expert shot" and highly trained former marine, was able, under extreme pressure, to hit the president with two out of three shots while firing at a moving target that was over five times the distance of the Walker shooting. He was firing through foliage, as well.

On a final note, General Walker hated John Kennedy; as a matter of fact, he had planned a huge demonstration against JFK in Dallas. So really, Oswald and the general would have been on the same team, they both hated Kennedy correct? So why would Oswald want the general dead if they both did not like JFK? Oh wait, I forgot: according to O'Reilly and Dugard, Oswald liked and admired JFK; well, maybe a lot of people go out and murder people they like and admire. Okay, I'm being sarcastic, sorry, but does this truly make any sense to anyone? If it does, please tweet me and fill me in so I'm not left in the dark any longer.

---

248 Look, my dear readers, there is nothing about Oswald killing Kennedy that really makes any sense. Even Bill O'Reilly admits that he had no motive and did not want to see the president killed. So because he has marital problems or can't find a good job, he one day decides to kill the president, ridiculous really, isn't it?

Okay, where were we? So did Oswald shoot at the general or not? It's doubtful, and even Chief Jesse Curry had his own doubts. According to the chief (as well as the FBI), Oswald's rifle could not be linked to the Walker shooting. He states, "The FBI report was inconclusive but indicated some unique similarities" (Curry 1969, 1). Of course it was possible. No one knows, but no one saw him do it. It's just like the Kennedy murder. It is all speculation, and both authors seem very good at speculating.

So now we turn to page 233, where there is an interesting statement made by Special Agent James Hosty of the FBI. Hosty was assigned to keep an eye on Oswald, who was supposedly a crazy and bloodthirsty killer who was psychologically depressed because he did not have a decent job and could not have sex with his wife.[249] Because of these problems, he was now on the prowl to kill the president of the United States, all without a motive. So what does Hosty, a well-trained, intelligent, and very experienced FBI agent, say about the threat that Oswald posed to the public? Here is their quote: "Special Agent Hosty now mentally assigns a low priority to the Oswald investigation. He's concluded that Lee Harvey Oswald is just a young guy with marital problems, a fondness for communism, and a habit of drifting from job to job" (O'Reilly and Dugard 2012, 233). So much for the rabid mad-dog killer who was an expert marksman with murder on his mind. Are you getting the picture here? The whole thesis of this book is simply mad; they want you to believe something they themselves disprove throughout their entire book, which is that Oswald had a motive to commit this crime; he didn't, and they prove this very clearly in their own words.

Next is a section on Secret Service Agent Winston G. Lawson, who was the lead planner for the president's trips. My point here is not to beat up on Agent Lawson, but to point out two main issues. First, let's start with a quote from the book: "Lawson, a Korean War veteran [why that matters, you

249 These are all points brought out in the book.

tell me], in his early thirties [another strange point but okay], specializes in planning Kennedy's official travels. As with all such visits, his primary responsibilities are to identify individuals who might be a threat to President Kennedy, then to take action against anyone considered to be such a threat, and plan security for the president's speeches and motorcade route" (O'Reilly and Dugard 2012, 233). Okay, so we have the Secret Service agent in charge of looking for potential threats. Well, I guess this means that Oswald was not a threat, because he did not shake him loose from the depository that day or any of the days prior to the presidential visit. Then we have Hosty stating that Oswald was not a threat at all, and that's one *huge* mistake if you think Oswald did kill the president. They further state in their book that Hosty only provided the Secret Service with the name of one person he considered a troublemaker in the area, and it wasn't Lee Oswald. Why? Because once again, Hosty had determined that Oswald was *not a threat to anyone*, including the president. They further state that this unknown person Hosty pointed out had no plans to kill the president. So then there were two people in Dallas with no plans to kill the president. Can you see how ridiculous this sounds?

Now those of you who did not skip ahead read about a man named Jack Ruby. Remember good old Jack the gangster? He was the guy who blasted a hole right through the middle of Oswald's torso, hitting all his major organs with a .38 caliber round.[250] Well, we have seen the background of good old Jack; he was a gunrunner, mobster, bookie, pimp, strip club owner, and friends with at least two enemies of John and Robert Kennedy: Santos Traficante and Carlos Marcello (not to mention Sam Giancana, who was the head of the Chicago Mafia). So why wasn't Ruby on Lawson's

---

250 Jack Ruby's brother told the press that Jack only intended to hurt Oswald. His brother said he never meant to kill him. You know, like a mobster would do if you owed him money. He might break a leg, shoot off a testicle or a toe, a little maiming but nothing like murder, right? But Ruby shot Oswald in a perfect location to cause the most damage possible, right through all those major organs. The doctors never really had a chance to save Oswald once Ruby did his dirty work.

or Hosty's list? Good question, right? Conveniently, Ruby ends up shooting Oswald. So Oswald, the wanna-be killer with blood on his mind, and Jack Ruby, the biggest mobster within two hundred miles of Dallas, are both overlooked by these professionals who are so keenly set on protecting the president.

Well, what about the parade route? Was that protected? Here is another quote regarding Lawson's pretrip protection plans: "There is still discussion over whether there is to be a motorcade through downtown Dallas, which will be a security nightmare, thanks to the more than twenty thousand windows lining the city's major thoroughfares. The more windows, the more places for any gunmen to aim at the president's limousine. But Lawson temporarily sets that question aside.[251] He begins his investigation of potential threats by combing through the Secret Service's Protective Research Section (PRS). These files list all individuals who have threatened the president or may be potentially dangerous to him; Lawson's review of the PRS on November 8 shows that "*no such person exists in the Dallas area*" (O'Reilly and Dugard 2012, 233). Hmm, well, those of us researchers who have spent decades looking into this investigation know that they missed several people. Ruby was one; what about the grassy knoll shooters seen by dozens of people, including many police officers, and the fake Secret Service agents behind the picket fence; how about the Latinos seen on both ends of the sixth floor of the Book Depository and some of the lower floors; and the list goes on. But who's counting? That might only be a dozen or so suspects. I mean, you can't catch everyone in that steel net that was thrown around the city of Dallas, but one might have been good enough to save the president's life, right? Or certainly Oswald's life, because he was also killed by someone who

[251] Of course, why not set that question aside? We are only talking about the life of the president, right? I mean, they did such a great job protecting him during his death ride through Dallas. All you could see were open windows everywhere and people hanging out of most of them, not to mention that Lawson removed several Dallas police outriders who would have been riding on the side of the limo, protecting the president from gunfire.

should have been on that list, a person who was picked out of a mug shot book the day before he killed Oswald.

Okay, I have to mention this section on p. 241 of the book, which involves a young man named Sterling Wood, who was around twelve in 1963. This young man claims to have seen someone who looked like Oswald at a shooting range before the assassination.[252] Well, to set the record straight, there are so many different stories about this so-called rifle range appearance. I frankly cannot tell truth from fiction. For the sake of time, I will let you research that incident on your own. It's long and rather boring, but I will conclude that there is no way, and I mean no way, any one of these people, including the twelve-year-old, would have stood up under cross-examination in a court of law. No way! They changed their stories several times; two of the other people who claimed Oswald was there never had the correct date for this occurrence. They would have been an absolute nightmare for the prosecution in a case against Oswald; most likely, they would never be called as witnesses because of this. These same witnesses saw this man, who might have been Oswald, hanging out with other men that day, and two of the witnesses said one man they saw with this Oswald character was an employee of Jack Ruby's nightclub. That's right, he was not alone. He was, according to the witnesses, at the range with at least one other person, firing rifles together that day, and they were also seen loading a car with several weapons. So if you believe that was Oswald at the range, then *you must believe in a conspiracy,* because he clearly had company that day at the range. Okay then, you have three choices: take my word that this story is full of holes, believe the authors of *Killing Kennedy* that this twelve-year-old boy absolutely recounts this incident correctly, or research it

[252] Actually, much research has been done on this subject, and most people come away feeling that, at best, the person at the range was an Oswald look-alike; at worst, these three or four witnesses (who, as I said, could not get their stories straight) did not see Oswald there.

yourself. It is very, very weak and flimsy evidence at best and not the slam dunk that the authors make it out to be.[253]

Also, on p. 241, O'Reilly and Dugard make some very speculative statements about Lee Oswald. What they are doing is helping you form an opinion of Oswald as you are reading the book; clearly they have done very little research on the real Oswald. They state, "Oswald turned twenty-four just one month ago. He has little to show for his time on earth. He is losing his wife and children. He works a menial job. And despite his keen intellect, he has no advanced education.[254] He doesn't know whether he wants to be an American, a Cuban, or a Russian. Still he longs to be a great man. A significant man. A man whose name will never be forgotten" (O'Reilly and Dugard 2012, 241–242). This is *all* speculation. Oswald knew who he was, and all this psychobabble by the authors is what O'Reilly would call "bloviating" on his show. There is no evidence here, of course, just speculation. They then go on to compare Oswald to John Wilkes Booth. What? Where is the reasoning here? They just wrote a book on the killing of Lincoln, and they want to compare Booth to Oswald. That is simply preposterous. I could talk about those differences for several pages, but let us not forget that O'Reilly and Dugard have already reasoned, as we will soon see, that Oswald *had no motive here*. They also admit that he fostered no ill will toward JFK and did not

---

253 On a further note, many anti-conspiracy authors have tried over the years to use this information to prove that Oswald was out there at the range training with his weapon before the murder, but did you know that this evidence is so weak they would not even use it in their books? Wood, along with the other range witnesses, will not even confirm their stories. For decades, they have been hounded and chased by writers and researchers, who all come away truly believing that these witnesses, including Wood, did not see Oswald that day. Also, as I have pointed out, if Oswald was with confederates that day, especially the Jack Ruby employee, then this puts this shooting into a whole new perspective for sure.

254 He was a sergeant in the Marine Corps; he worked at a top secret base and had a high security clearance. He also spoke at least two languages, one being Russian. Have you ever tried to master that extremely complex language?

want to see him hurt. Well, that is a far cry from Booth, who hated Lincoln with all his heart and considered him a traitor of the highest order. Now, I have studied a lot of history and have even taught history in high school, but I am no expert on the murder of President Lincoln. Despite this, even I am able to see a huge difference between Oswald and Booth; keep in mind, O'Reilly has been all over the air waves the last several weeks, selling this book as a piece of history. I would say the opposite: this book is a distortion of history.

Okay, first off, Oswald was not a loser. Do some research! He was a sergeant in the US Marine Corps. Are there any marine sergeants reading this right now? How many of you former sergeants out there consider yourselves losers? Not many, I'm sure. Was it easy to make sergeant? Of course it wasn't. Did you know that Oswald actually had a higher security clearance at his base in Japan than his commanding officer? Well, I guess the authors left that point out of their book. Consider the fact that Oswald was an expert at reading, writing, and speaking Russian; when he went to Russia, everyone there thought he was Russian, because he had nearly perfected their language. Have you studied Russian, Mr. O'Reilly? I know I haven't and would not want to try. Trust me; it takes more than a loser to learn Russian as a second language. Then we have Judith Baker. Now I am sure most of you have never heard of Judith Baker, but she was a biologist who worked with Oswald in New Orleans (it has also been reported by many sources, and Baker herself admitted, that she had an ongoing affair with Oswald).[255] In *The Love Affair,* one of the final episodes of *The Men Who Killed Kennedy,* she recounts all of the information regarding her time with Lee Oswald. You need to get that episode and watch it. It will amaze you; she discusses Oswald's role in a much larger and deeper scenario than these authors admit in their book. Oswald was no loser; he was a smart man working for an intelligence agency. He may have had some

---

[255] This could explain Oswald's lack of sexual performance with his wife, but of course, this is speculation (see, I tell you when I'm speculating, unlike some people).

issues in his marriage, as FBI Agent Hosty pointed out, but a loser, far from it.

Let's get back to that point of Oswald having no motive. Here is a quote from the authors: "Oswald does not hate the president. He has no reason to want JFK dead. He is, however, bitter that a man such as John Kennedy has so many advantages in life. Oswald well understands that it's easier for men born of privilege to distinguish themselves. But other than that small amount of envy, he does not speak unfavorably about the president. In fact, Oswald would very much like to emulate JFK" (O'Reilly and Dugard 2012, 248). That is about the weakest motive I have ever heard for a murder, especially a murder of this magnitude; really, you have to do better than that. I saw hundreds of murders on the streets of Los Angeles over the years. I did not investigate every one of them, but I have studied many crimes and heard many motives for murder; most of them fall into an array of categories, but the above statement only solidifies my view that *Oswald had no motive to kill the president.* Another thing I have learned over the years is that people do not go to the extent of planning and carrying out a murder without a solid motive (unless, of course, they are mentally deranged, which we know was not the case with Oswald).

Now I am only assuming this, but I don't think the authors went through any formal police training, have gone to any investigative schools, or have ever worked on the streets as an officer or investigator. That being said, I think they were pretty honest here in admitting that Oswald had no motive. I have said in this book as well, if Oswald were a true socialist (and I am not convinced of that fact by any means), he would have liked President Kennedy, because Kennedy was trying to make peace in the world. By the way, no one knew at this time that the president had been trying to knock off Castro through a plan called Operation Mongoose.[256] This

---

256 Operation Mongoose was the code name for the CIA operation against Castro and his regime in Cuba, with the ultimate objective being his demise; of course, this never happened.

did not come out until many years later. So even if Kennedy was not a Castro fan, and there is evidence to support this fact, only people in his inner circle, like his brother Bobby, would have known this fact in 1963, and Oswald most certainly would not have been in that group.

At the end of chapter 22, the book once again speculates on what Lee Oswald's activities were on the day before the assassination. The Warren Commission, being fed false information from the FBI, said the infamous brown paper bag Oswald took to work on November 22nd contained the rifle they found upstairs after the shooting.[257]

There are problems with this story. One such problem is that the bag was way too small. That bag was too small to hold the rifle, period; even if it was broken down, it was several inches longer than the bag, which according to the best eyewitness was only two feet long. The rifle, disassembled, was around three feet long, so the bag was much shorter than that. Then there was that cheap scope as well; not to mention the rifle had a shoulder strap, making it even thicker. The authors also mentioned Wesley Frazier, who was a friend of Oswald's at the time. Frazier gave Oswald a ride to work on some days, and if you watch episode 3 of *The Men Who Killed Kennedy*, you will hear him state on camera that he felt that the package was way too small to contain the rifle.[258] He said that when Lee walked away from his car on the morning of the assassination, he was holding the package underneath his armpit and had it cupped with

---

257 The authors make the statement that Oswald spent the whole day at work creating this perfect bag that was to be used to carry the rifle into work. Well, first of all, who in the world can testify to that? Also, what do you think Oswald's boss would have said to him if he found him working on this paper bag in the shipping department instead of completing his own duties? This was 1963, after all; people showed more integrity in their work back then. You were expected to pull your weight, not spend a good part of your day on the Internet. This makes no sense at all, and again, it is simple speculation (with no witnesses and no common sense added in).

258 Wesley Frazier, http://www.youtube.com/watch?v=iDWaOjFqgHk

his hand at the bottom.[259] There is simply no way he could have held a rifle this way; it would have been physically impossible. As I said, the bag was several inches too short to have contained the rifle, even if it was dismantled and broken down. They are grasping at straws here. You need to get the documentary *The Men Who Killed Kennedy*; after watching all nine episodes, you will never look at this murder the same way again. The funny thing is, for several years, they played these episodes over and over again on the History Channel and A&E, but now those channels only run shows about ridiculous computer animations. Over a fifteen-year period, I watched more than forty documentaries that contain solid and relevant research on the assassination. What happened to the History Channel over the years? Someone tell me, if you know.

On p. 252, the authors once again engage in mere speculation regarding Oswald's movements and actions the morning of November 22nd. How in the world do they know what he had for breakfast and what he was thinking that morning? They state, "Oswald's trip home was primarily to get his rifle. But he is willing to set aside his dark plan if Marina agreed to live with him" (O'Reilly and Dugard 2012, 252). What? This is more of a book of fiction, supposition, and speculation. Really, how in the world would they know these things, even if they were true? After all, Oswald was murdered; he never even admitted to the crime as I have pointed out throughout this book. So how could they know what he was thinking and feeling? Really, if Marina said she would take him back, then he wouldn't shoot JFK? Does that ring true to any of you, even those who do not believe in a conspiracy? This so-called Marxist and trained assassin who, according to District Attorney Henry Wade, had planned this murder for weeks or months in advance, and then his wife

---

[259] Jesse Ventura in his new book points out that he is six foot four, and he tried to carry the Mannlicher broken down under his arm but was never able to "cup it in my hand and get it under my armpit" (Ventura, Russell, and Wayne 2013, 51).

says one day, "Okay honey, you can stay," and he calls off the murder? Their theory is simply preposterous.

The authors' whole breakdown of Oswald's movements and actions the day of the murder are completely without merit and, once again, just plain speculation; they act like someone was following Oswald around with a movie camera. It is simply impossible for them to know such things as what Oswald's movements were within that building that day. As an example, they state, "Lee Harvey Oswald peers out the first-floor window of the Depository Building, assessing the president's route by where the crowds stand" (O'Reilly and Dugard 2012, 256).[260] We do know Oswald was seen less than twenty minutes before the shooting, eating in the lunchroom; he was seen in that same lunchroom in the exact same spot approximately ninety seconds after the shooting. He was confronted there by Officer Baker and the building manager, who were searching the building. These movements and locations of Oswald we are certain of. Why? Because we have hard evidence—eyewitness statements—to prove his location in the depository just before the shooting and within ninety seconds after the shooting. This is the type of evidence that these authors seem to be lacking. Simply put, all other movements of Oswald that morning, other than those seen by witnesses, are speculative and not history; Remember now it is O'Reilly who has been stating on Fox News that his book is historically accurate.

On p. 259, the authors mention Chief Jesse Curry and his planning of the parade route and the president's trip. What they leave out is the chief's description of the sequence of

---

260 It seems that the authors are also indicating that Oswald was unaware of the actual parade route taken by the president. If they believe this, how in the world could Oswald have planned this whole event then? What if they took another route to the Trade Mart? Also, how in the world could he then have been in the lunchroom just before the shooting if he was still planning out the shooting? It is simple. Oswald was not up in that window; he was in the lunchroom, right where he was seen by three independent witnesses, one of them being a police officer, and another his boss, the building manager.

events during the shooting; it is clear from their statements about the chief that they feel his qualifications were impeccable. They state he is a lifelong law enforcement man who is greatly educated in the art of police work and police science. Okay, so let me reiterate the chief's observation that day while he was riding in the motorcade. Also, once again consider what I said earlier in this book: it took 2.5 seconds just to cycle the Oswald bolt-action rifle. Chief Curry states, "For a brief moment I almost started to relax. I made the left turn west and proceeded at a speed of approximately eight to ten mph toward the triple underpass. I did see a few unauthorized people on the overpass and wondered how they had gotten up there. About halfway between Houston and the triple underpass I heard a sharp crack. Someone in the car said, is that a firecracker. Two other sharp reports came almost directly after the first. All of the reports were fired fairly close together, but perhaps there was a longer pause between the first and second reports than between the second and the third" (Curry 1969, 30).[261] Once again, over and over, witnesses stated that two shots came too close together to have been fired from the same weapon. Here, the chief also confirms this fact; how many witnesses do we need to completely confirm this fact? There were two shooters ... at least, period.

Chief Curry also had other things to say about the real evidence that his department was digging into with respect to Oswald's guilt or innocence. When the chief was interviewed after Oswald's arrest, he was asked, "Do you have an eyewitness who saw someone shoot the president?"

---

261 When the Warren Commission was questioning Lee Bowers about his observations, he told them that he felt that two of the shots came too close together to have come from one rifle. The commission's counsel then reminded Bowers that he was not a trained expert and that he should leave that to the experts. Okay, what about Chief Curry? Was the chief not a well-qualified police officer? Was he not an expert? Of course he was, he was once in charge of the entire investigative section within the department, and he heard the exact same thing as Lee Bowers (so then maybe Lee Bowers was an expert; he was definitely a great witness who was also ignored).

His answer was, "No sir, we do not" (Smith 2008, 40).[262] He was, as they confirm, an honorable man. Indeed, you should read his book. Take some time and go back through my book, comparing my information, which is properly referenced, to the new O'Reilly book, which is nearly unreferenced. It is clear that there were multiple shooters that day; to deny this is to ignore simple logic and any form of reasoning. I truly doubt that these authors would have qualified as police investigators, but they seem to be doing a great job of mixing history with speculation.

It should be noted that the authors left out a large amount of information that was also provided by the Warren Commission and the FBI. Some of this information included statements and paperwork submitted to their superiors by special agents of the FBI. This included information provided by Special Agents Sibert and O'Neil, who were both present at the president's autopsy. In an official report, both of these agents reported that the doctors at the autopsy said they saw signs of surgery on the president's head. That's correct, surgery on the president's head: surgery that did not occur at Parkland Hospital. They stated in their official report, "Following the removal of the wrapping, it was ascertained that the president's clothing had been removed and it was apparent that a tracheotomy had been performed, *as well as surgery to the head area*, namely, in the top of the skull" (Smith 2008, 53).[263] It seems they left out this information as well; I wonder why?

Also, we have information once again from Agents Sibert and O'Neil regarding a bullet or missile that was found in the president's body; of course, this projectile disappeared, but it was booked as evidence by the agents after the autopsy. This was most likely because it came from a different rifle, not the so-called Oswald rifle. The receipt for this missile (bullet) booked by the agents has been around for years

262 Smith, M. (2008). *JFK: The Second Plot* (2nd ed.). London: Mainstream Publishing Co.

263 You need to read *Best Evidence*; put it in your library. It's well worth it; it covers this subject in detail.

(Smith 2008, 57). This missile could have come from the back wound or from the president's throat wound, neither of which had an exit point. The receipt for this missile was placed in the official file of the autopsy after the agents booked it as evidence; the missile was never seen again. Neither the Warren Commission, nor the FBI, nor any of the nonconspiracy writers have ever explained what happened to that projectile. See for yourself; it is all in the record.

If this book was not touted as being real history, I would not have as big of a problem with it. Some books are a little fiction mixed with some facts, but exploiting this as accurate and documented history is clearly a massive stretch of the imagination. It is, in fact, a strange mix of some facts and a lot of speculation and, of course, some undocumented theories as well. It is a confusing overview, with almost no referencing at all. Where did they get this information? If one of my students turned in an assignment with no in-text citations, no footnotes, and no reference page, they would receive a failing grade on that assignment. Without references, authors can pretty much say whatever they want; this is poor academics at best and certainly not college- or university-level research writing. I would have expected more from a former teacher. Do your homework on this murder. Don't fall for the spin from the no-spin man, listen to the real experts on this subject, look at the real evidence, read the agent's report of Kennedy's wounds, and get the real facts. This was, after all, the murder of a United States president.

Conclusion

"Men occasionally stumble over the truth, but most of them pick themselves up and hurry off as if nothing ever happened."
—Winston Churchill

As I have mentioned before, the main question asked by most people with regards to the JFK assassination is, who was responsible? Who murdered our president in the streets of Dallas right in front of the whole world? To answer that question, you must read hundreds, perhaps thousands of pages of information. I have studied this subject for over thirty-five years now, and there continues to be more and more information coming out all the time. It is like a never-ending soap opera in which the characters remain the same, only the scenes change, but you can be sure more information is still out there and will continue to be uncovered piece by piece. It has been my goal in this book to introduce you to this in-depth, provocative subject by providing a solid overview of the assassination and the aftermath in a uniformed order. It is up to you to follow up and obtain as much information as you personally desire. I have planted the seeds; you must make them grow, if you wish.

In conclusion, the evidence provided in this book makes it clear that there was more than one shooter firing at President Kennedy in Dallas on November 22, 1963. We begin our overview with a look back at the president's wounds and what the Parkland Hospital doctors saw that afternoon. When the Warren Commission interviewed the Parkland medical staff, they spoon-fed them their version of the lone gunman story, which involved one shooter firing from behind the president. If you remember, their plan failed, and it failed badly, because these were professional medical doctors and nurses who saw the president's wounds that day. Much to the surprise of Arlen Specter, they were all experienced with treating gunshot wounds.[264] If you remember, they all stated that the president was shot from the front and that both the throat wound and the head wound were frontal entrance wounds. The throat wound did not have an exit wound from the body, but the head wound had a large gaping hole in the right rear of the president's head. You can see this in a few of the autopsy pictures that managed to get into the official record; a large portion of the right rear of the president's head is completely missing. You can also note that the front of his head and face is still fully intact. Now you probably never investigated a homicide before, but just based on these photos, if the Warren Commission's conclusions were correct (that the lone gunman fired from behind, hitting the president in the back of the head), then how is it that his face, forehead, and eye sockets are still clearly intact in the autopsy photos?[265]

It seems crazy to believe that a shot from a high-powered rifle traveling at 2,500 feet per second hitting the back of the head would not blow out a giant portion of the face or forehead. I have seen many homicide scenes where such injuries have occurred. But not one member of the medical staff at Parkland or the autopsy staff at Bethesda said there were any other wounds to the president's head except the massive rear exit wound, and a smaller wound in the temple area (most likely the entrance wound). Consequently, when asked, none of the medical personnel described any wounds to his face, only to the back of his head. Even the autopsy report did not show damage to the president's face. There

---

264 Parkland Hospital was the largest trauma center in the city.

265 Also, to reiterate, the official x-rays showed the right front of the president's head and eye socket was cracked and blown apart; so how can they have it both ways? Was his face intact, as seen in the autopsy photos? Or was it blown out, as evidenced by the x-rays? I would conclude that there were multiple conspirators and several collaborators at work in this case, which is why some of the fraudulent evidence was contradictory, because you had several people at work altering and eliminating evidence.

was damage to the temple reported, what appeared to be an entrance wound, but not the face.[266]

Here is a list of some of the medical personnel at Parkland Hospital who worked on the president and stated they observed his head wound to be located in the right rear of his head, in the occipital area; they all believed this wound was an exit wound. Also, they stated that his throat wound was clearly an entrance wound.

- Dr. Paul Peters
- Dr. Robert McClelland
- Dr. Charles Crenshaw
- Dr. Jones
- Dr. Gene Colman Akin
- Dr. Malcolm Perry
- Dr. Charles J. Carrico
- Dr. William Kemp Clark
- Dr. Ronald Coy Jones, chief resident of surgery

Here, once again, are some of the Parkland medical personnel statements to the Warren Commission regarding the president's wounds.

Dr. Akin

Dr. AKIN: The back of the right occipital parietal portion of his head was shattered, with brain substance extruding.

Mr. SPECTER: Did you have any opinion as to the direction that the bullet hit his head?

Dr. AKIN: I assume that the right occipital parietal region was the exit.[267]

[266] As a matter of fact, some medical personnel noted that the president's hair was still combed in the front of his head, as if he had just fixed it.

[267] Warren Commission, Testimony of Dr. Gene Akin, 1964.

Dr. Carrico

Mr. SPECTER: Approximately how many missile wounds, bullet wounds, have you had an opportunity to observe in your practice, Doctor?

Dr. CARRICO: I would guess 150 or 200.

Mr. SPECTER: Would you describe as precisely for me as possible the nature of the head wound which you observed on the president?

Dr. CARRICO: The wound that I saw was a large gaping wound, located in the right occipitoparietal area. I would estimate to be about 5 to 7 cm. in size, more or less circular, with avulsions of the calvarium and scalp tissue. As I stated before, I believe there was shredded macerated cerebral and cerebellar tissues both in the wounds and on the fragments of the skull attached to the dura.[268]

Dr. Clark

Mr. SPECTER: What, if anything, did you say then in the course of that press conference?

Dr. CLARK: I described the president's wound in his head in very much the same way as I have described it here. I was asked if this wound was an entrance wound, an exit wound, or what, and I said it could be an exit wound, but I felt it was a tangential wound.

Mr. SPECTER: Which wound did you refer to at this time?

Dr. CLARK: The wound in the head. [269]

---

268 Warren Commission, Testimony of Dr. Charles Carrico, 1964.

269 Warren Commission, Testimony of Dr. William Clark, 1964.

Dr. Ronald Jones, Chief Resident of Surgery

The hole was very small and relatively clean cut, as you would see in a bullet that is entering rather than exiting a patient. If this were an exit wound, you would think that it exited at a very low velocity to produce no more damage than this had done, and if this were a missile of high velocity, you would expect more of an explosive type of exit wound, with more tissue destruction than this appeared to have on superficial examination.... [There] appeared to be an exit wound in the posterior portion of the skull.[270]

The main point to take away from the Parkland Hospital witnesses is that they all saw a small entrance wound in the president's throat and a massive exit wound to the back of his head, (See Figure-1 page 34). This point is without question, and anyone who states or writes to the contrary of this fact is misleading people or, as in politics, simply covering up the facts.[271] Medical doctors throughout the country are considered expert witnesses in most court systems. After all, these were trained emergency room personal who had years of experience with gunshot wounds, and they knew what they were looking at that day in Dallas. Who are you willing to believe, the expert eyewitnesses who saw and handled the president's body, or the Warren Commission investigators who were not even there that day?

These are the medical personnel at Bethesda Hospital who observed the exact same wounds prior to the autopsy cover-up:

- Floyd Riebe
- Jerrol Custer
- Paul O'Connor

270 Warren Commission, Testimony of Dr. Ronald Jones, 1964.

271 Once again, the news media was told on the day of the assassination that the only two wounds mentioned by the Parkland doctors were entrance wounds.

- James Jenkins

The Grassy Knoll Shooter

Next, let's remember all of those civilian witness who saw the shooter, or shooters, behind the fence line; we have multiple witnesses who stated over and over that they saw rifle fire coming from the grassy knoll behind the picket fence. You could write a whole set of books just on the witnesses to JFK's assassination. I have mentioned many of them in this book, but there were many more. These witnesses became part of history by being at the right place at the wrong time. They witnessed an event that they never could forget. Many were persecuted, some were murdered, and there are still others out there who never came forward. I often wonder how much evidence we missed out on, or how many statements were never given because these witnesses never came forward because of fear of persecution by their own government.

Let's take the railroad men, S. M. Holland, Richard Dodd, and James Simmons, who clearly and unequivocally saw the shooter firing from behind the fence. How in the world could these witnesses be ignored? As a former police officer, I can tell you these witnesses would have been at the top of my list during my initial investigation. When you listen to their testimony given to Mark Lane in his documentary, *Rush to Judgment*, you can just hear the honesty and certainty in their voices. Their testimonies were ignored, altered, or simply left out of the official investigation. Remember, these railroad workers were only a small fraction of the grassy knoll witnesses, but they were solid on what they observed that day in Dallas.

What about Lee Bowers, whose life was cut short only three years after the assassination? He was actually one of my favorite witnesses. He was a no-nonsense type of guy who was simply telling the truth about what he had seen that day. If you remember correctly, he witnessed a lot. He saw the spotters driving around, watching the area; he saw the men in police uniforms behind the fence, one of which was possibly a shooter, while the other suspect warned people off from behind the fence. He also saw two other suspects: one dressed in a railroad outfit and one in civilian clothing. Bowers stated that he saw a flash of light behind the grassy knoll, which was of course the rifle fire. Very recently, a test was done by Mike Baker, the host of the Travel Channel's *America Declassified,* which proved conclusively that Lee Bowers would have had a perfect view of the grassy knoll from his location on the railroad tower. Baker was allowed into the railroad tower and stood in the exact spot where Lee Bowers was standing when he spotted the shooters behind the fence. Further, Baker conducted a test by having a shooter fire shots in the same location as witnessed by Bowers, and clearly the muzzle flash and the smoke expelled from the rifle were visible and lined up perfectly with the observations made by Bowers and other witnesses that day. Also, the smoke coming out from under the trees during this test was exactly what the other railroad men saw that day; this all fits together like a perfect puzzle. There was a shooter there; the nonbelievers need to face the facts.[272]

All in all, Bowers was an excellent witness, even pointing out that two of the shots he heard came right on top of each other; he told the Warren Commission that there must have been another shooter because of how close those shots were to each other. Sitting high up in the railroad tower, he had a fantastic vantage point of the whole event. It saddens me that he died so young, and his death was never fully explained. His car went off the road one night, and he was killed in the crash. The medical examiner said he was in a strange state of shock when he died, but he was unable to determine the exact cause of death.

Then we have Dave Powers, the president's best friend and political aide, who was riding with the Secret Service in

---

[272] Baker, M. (Performer) (2013). *Travel Channel's America Declassified: JFK Assassination* [Web]. Retrieved from http://www.youtube.com/watch?v=Atq7yfaHKXE

the follow-up car. Here, once again, is his powerful witness statement: “The total time between the first and third shots was about five or six seconds. My first impression was that the shots came from the right and overhead, but I also had a fleeting impression that the noise appeared to come from the front in the area of the triple overpass. This may have resulted from my feeling, when I looked forward toward the overpass, that we might have ridden into an ambush” (Warren Commission 1964).

Next, we think back on Gordon Arnold, who was almost shot himself, as a bullet was fired right past his head and went on to hit the president in his right temple. Arnold was in a state of shock when his film was confiscated by a man pointing a handgun in his face; the man was wearing a Dallas police uniform. Was this man Roscoe White or J. D. Tippit? Or was this an imposter officer?

One of the best civilian witnesses was Ed Hoffman, who was a deaf mute; Hoffman was standing on the freeway overpass and had a perfect view of what was happening behind the picket fence on the grassy knoll. He stated that he saw the shooters just after the shots were fired; he observed them dismantling their weapons and fleeing the scene. His testimony never made it into the Warren Report (big surprise, right?); he was totally and completely ignored by local and federal law enforcement authorities that day. They pretty much told him to hit the road and get lost.

We have just covered a handful of the non-law-enforcement witnesses. Earlier, we discussed dozens of police witnesses who were there and observed the shots coming from the grassy knoll. This included Dallas Police Chief Jesse Curry, who admitted in his own book that he heard shots coming from the right side of the triple underpass; he stated that two of the shots came right on top of each other. He surmised that there were at least two gunmen that day. He also based this on Dr. Perry’s statements regarding the president’s wounds that he observed that day.

Chief Curry put a lot of weight in Dr. Perry's observation, because he was considered a local expert on gunshot wounds at Parkland Hospital. Here are the chief's comments: "Dr. Perry examined the throat wound and assessed it as the entrance wound. He was no amateur at assessing wounds. By his later testimony he stated he had previously treated from 150 to 200 gunshot wounds.... Dr. Perry insisted that the president was shot from the front, entering at the throat and exiting out of the back of the head. Immediate speculation began about shots coming from in front of the motorcade from the grassy knoll or the triple underpass" (Curry 1969, 34). I feel that the chief knew all along that something funny was going on; he certainly did after the FBI took over all of the evidence from the Dallas Police Department, thereby ending their probe into the assassination.

There were many other law enforcement officers who clearly believed that the shots fired at the president came from in front of the motorcade. Here is a quick overview: Officer Joe M. Smith encountered a man in a suit behind the fence on the grassy knoll who identified himself as a Secret Service agent (but there were no Secret Service agents on the ground in Dealey Plaza). Police Officer Bobby Hargis, who was riding to the left rear of the president's limo, gave short but very powerful statements, once again clearly supporting the evidence of another shooter from the right side of the limo. Deputy Seymour Weitzman, like so many witnesses, said that two shots came close together, one on top of each other, almost to the second. He told the Warren Commission:

Mr. BALL: How many shots did you hear?

Mr. WEITZMAN: Three distinct shots.

Mr. BALL: How were they spaced?

Mr. WEITZMAN: First one, then the second two seemed to be simultaneously.

Weitzman was also the officer who found the German Mauser on the sixth floor rather than the Oswald rifle; he later changed his story, but this was long after he swore in an affidavit that the weapon he found, along with fellow officers Boone and Craig, was a German Mauser.

Secret Service Agent George Hickey stated the second and third shots were too close together to have come from the same weapon. Here is a segment of his testimony: "[When Kennedy] was almost sitting erect I heard two more reports which I thought were shots and appeared to me completely different in sound[273] than the first report and were in rapid succession;[274] there seemed to be practically no time element between them" (Benson 1993, 183).

Another Secret Service agent, Glenn Bennett, gave testimony that the shot he saw hit the president in the back was clearly well below the neck line, exactly where we see the hole in the president's shirt and suit coat (Fiester 2012, 275). This could not have been the so-called magic bullet. He states, "I looked at the back of the president. I heard another firecracker noise and saw the shot hit the president about four inches down from the right shoulder" (Benson 1993, 37).

We also heard from officials, including FBI agents, that there was a bullet taken from the president's body during the autopsy; this bullet later disappeared (along with the president's brain and, with them, any sense of justice in this case). The conspirators were clearly able to destroy much of the direct evidence in this case (Smith 2008, 57).[275] But

---

273 This was because these shots came from in front of the vehicle and from a different location than the first shot he heard. This is the same distinction heard by Holland, the railroad supervisor, who clearly noted the difference between the sounds of the shots he said came from behind, and the shot he heard from the grassy knoll.

274 Once again, we have another witness who heard two shots right on top of each other. This witness was a law enforcement officer who was at ground level, right behind the limo. Clearly, this is another solid witness.

275 Smith, M. (2008). *JFK: The Second Plot* (2nd ed.). London: Mainstream Publishing Co.

thanks to some excellent work by FBI Agent James Sibert, who was at the autopsy, we have the plain truth regarding the ridiculous magic bullet; simply stated, there was no magic bullet. Sibert confirms this in his notes: the doctors performing the autopsy said clearly that the back wound Specter and Ford said went through Kennedy did not go through the president's body; it never existed. And there was no other entry point found in the rear of his neck, either; nothing, no other hole, which tells us what, that the bullet which entered the president's throat came from the front, period. There simply were no other entrance wounds to the rear of his body, other than the back wound, which never exited; this was confirmed by the FBI and the Bethesda doctors. Now with this information, you not only lose the magic bullet, you prove that the president was shot from the front, so then you prove there was more than one shooter!

Then we have the Zapruder film, which was a lucky break in this case. The conspirators did all they could to eliminate all the movies and stills of the assassination. There is evidence, however, that the Zapruder film was altered to some extent; we do not have a complete recording of the original film.[276] Given the massive cover-up in this case and the destruction of many facts, we must consider what we have of the Zapruder film a blessing. If we just follow the film in slow motion, we can clearly see the effects of the rifle fire in the limo. It is also clear that there had to be a shooter in front of the vehicle, because the first indication that President Kennedy was hit was when he reached up and grabbed his throat, which can be seen in the film; at this point, you can see Governor Connally has not yet been shot.[277] So point number one is that they were

---

276 Also like Orville Nix's film, which was given to the FBI, lost, and then distorted by the agency. Nix had filmed the entire assassination, and there is no doubt in my mind this film would have proven very valuable.

277 Remember the statements by the witnesses on the railroad overpass, who saw the entire shooting; they clearly saw the shots coming from the grassy knoll, as well as the movements of the occupants in the limo, and stated that the president and the governor were hit by separate bullets. It is also clear in the film that the governor does jump up in his seat when a bullet flies by his head.

hit by separate bullets. That means there were at least two shooters, at the minimum. When we go to our best witnesses, the Parkland doctors, they tell us that the throat wound was a wound of entrance, without question; this is another indicator of multiple shooters.[278] The next thing we see in the film is that the president was hit from behind, pushing him forward in his seat. Remarkably, the original autopsy photos confirm this shot, and this was established by the pathologists themselves; this fact is clearly described in their notes indicating the bullet hole was in the middle part of the president's back. This wound was then probed by the pathologists, and their own notes verify that they could not find an exit point for this wound. This is another indication that the magic bullet theory was a complete farce; for one, this wound was much too low and was not anywhere near the president's throat, and two, it had no point of exit, which means the bullet never came out.

Moving on to the next volley of shots, we have James Tague, who was struck in the face by a bullet that made its way across the intersection and ricocheted off the curb. That is another shot; are you keeping score? How many shots is that? Then we have another shot, which hit Governor Connally's wrist; this was not the magic bullet, but another bullet fired from another rifle. It is clear once again in the Zapruder film that the governor was still holding his hat after he was shot the first time; the ridiculous magic bullet was proven bogus, once again. Then we have the final shot, which took off the back of the president's head; this shot unequivocally came from the right side, as visible in the film. It originated in front of the vehicle, evidenced once again by the Parkland doctors, who indicated over and over that the head shot came from the front, based on their observations of the president's head wound. Keep in mind that there may have

[278] Keep in mind that there were witnesses who reported seeing a hole in the windshield of the presidential limo. There were actually a few witnesses, including Dr. Evalea Glanges, a Parkland Hospital doctor, who saw the limo parked outside the emergency room. Also, there was the Ford executive who observed the employees at his Ford glass factory replacing the windshield and clearly noted the bullet hole in the windshield. He stated it was from a shot that originated from the outside of the vehicle.

been even more shots as well; we will never know, because the FBI and the Warren Commission would officially only admit to three shots, even though the FBI, at first, thought that the magic bullet was not a viable theory. There is also a picture in circulation of the rearview mirror of the limo, which has a distinct dent from an obvious bullet that went astray.

This shooting was obviously a well-thought-out operation; the crossfire brought to bear on the motorcade that day was a professional, military-style ambush, and the thought that people still want to blame this all on one man is simply illogical. Oswald was nothing more than a patsy in my opinion, just like he stated to the press after he was taken into custody. When the shots rang out in the plaza, he was downstairs in the lunchroom, just like he stated. Even the police admitted as much to the Warren Commission. They said around sixty to ninety seconds after the shooting, Dallas Police Officer Baker ran into Oswald in the lunchroom. How could it have been possible for Oswald to have run all the way across the sixth floor, stash the rifle under several boxes, run down five flights of stairs after zig-zagging through the boxes across each floor, run into the lunchroom, buy a Coke, open his lunch bag, and begin to eat his lunch and appear so calm and steady when Officer Baker confronts him, and all in around ninety seconds? I doubt all of that would have been possible in five minutes, never mind in a matter of seconds; I was getting tired just describing it.

In 1993, I made my first visit to Dealey Plaza as part of a college research project, and I spent a lot of time in the depository. Back then, you could get closer to the so-called sniper's nest than you can today. One thing I noted was how large the building was and how deep the floors were, and this is without thousands of boxes filling the aisles. The rifle was found about fifty yards away from the sixth floor window, and it was another fifty-yard run to the staircase. Look, Oswald could never have pulled this off, not even if he were an Olympic athlete. Don't be fooled, check it out yourself. Just running across the floor, burying the rifle in a row of boxes, and then running to the stairwell would have taken him at least one minute, never mind running down all those flights of stairs, and then there were dozens and dozens of workers in the building, none of whom said they ever saw Oswald running through the building or down the stairs. It was just physically impossible for anyone to do this and not be seen, and let's not forget, we received another gift that day: Officer Baker was in that building within seconds of the shooting, and he encountered Oswald almost immediately. This then set the time clock for everything that happened after the shooting.

During one of my visits to the Dallas, I spent many hours on the sixth floor of the Book Depository, trying to get a true feeling for what actually occurred there. I too was trained in the marines, as was Oswald, having gone through the same rifle training at Parris Island in the Marine Corps Reserves and later the Infantry Training School (ITS) in California. I was also a police officer for several years and investigated hundreds of shootings (which were all too common in Los Angeles). After spending all those hours at the scene of the assassination, I can say with a clear conscience that it would have been simply impossible for Oswald, or anyone else for that matter, to have done the entire shooting from the sixth floor window, simply and utterly impossible.[279] There may have been shots fired from that window, but not the earlier shots, because the occupants of the vehicle were not even visible to a shooter from that location, and the first shot that hit JFK in the throat came from the front, indicated by *all* the medical personnel at Parkland; really, could all of them have been wrong? Think about the odds of that happening. Time and space prevent me from exploring all the possible details in this investigation, but I hope I have succeeded in at least convincing you of the points I brought out here. There is so much more you can investigate; I have tried to provide you with as many references and resources as possible. This is a

---

[279] This is despite attempts by the FBI, the Warren Commission, the US Army, and hundreds of private investigations to repeat this impossible scenario. In fact, no one has ever been able to duplicate this feat, and it will never be done, because it is impossible, especially with an average shot like Oswald using an antique rifle.

case involving facts, evidence, and witness statements; it is not rocket science. After what you just read, I hope your minds have been profoundly affected. That was one of my goals.

My father, Bill Souza, used to tell me that one fact will always be certain: President Kennedy died that day in Dallas, along with the heart of our nation and its ability to fully trust its own government. Since that day, many scandals have rocked our nation, including the murders of Robert Kennedy and Dr. Martin Luther King Jr., the Gulf of Tonkin incident (which never happened), the war in Vietnam, Watergate and the fall of Richard Nixon, Iran Contra, and the list continues today with the events of 911 and the wars in the Middle East. The point is made perfectly clear: America has not been the same since November 1963.

I wish you all the very best in life. I leave you now with one of my favorite quotes from history:

"We are apt to shut our eyes against a painful truth.... For my part, I am willing to know the whole truth; to know the worst; and to provide for it."

—Patrick Henry

Ed Souza with Arnold Palmer.

Photo Index

All photos provided by author.

The criminal courts building; many people say there was a shooter located on the roof.

The grassy knoll with the Texas School Book Depository in the background.

Another view from the railroad overpass.

The Texas Theater, where Oswald was captured, had fallen into ill repair over the years but was recently refurbished to its grand old luster.

The entrance to the Texas Theater; that is my childhood friend Duane Cochrane in front.

The author on the railroad overpass.

View of the Texas School Book Depository in the background.

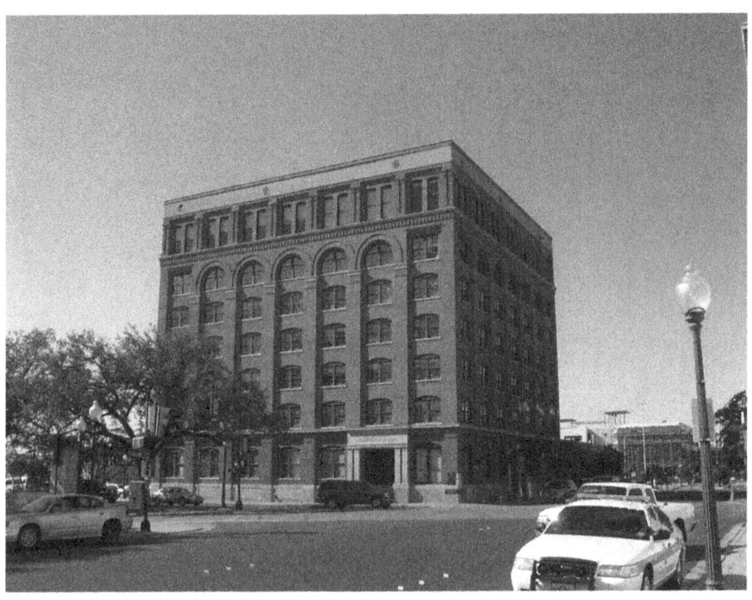

Memorial in Dealey Plaza.

Plaque of the memorial to JFK Dealey Plaza.

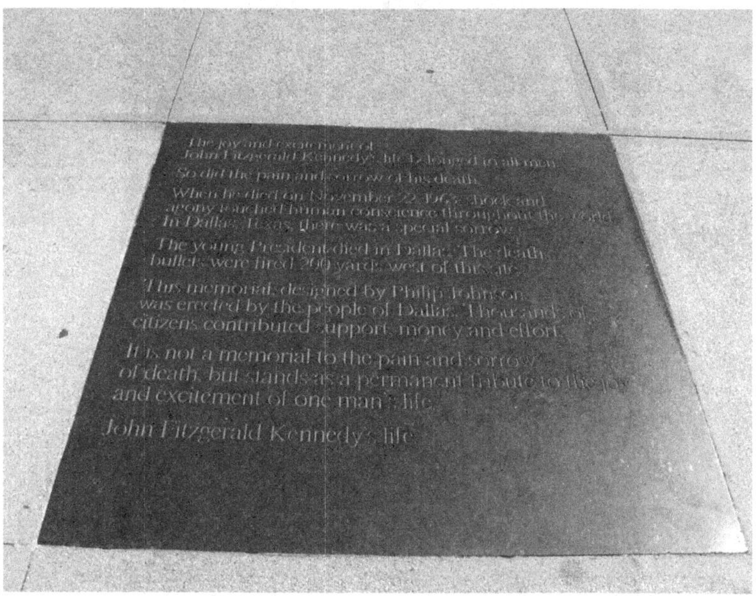

View from behind the picket fence

This is a very unique view through the trees from behind the fence

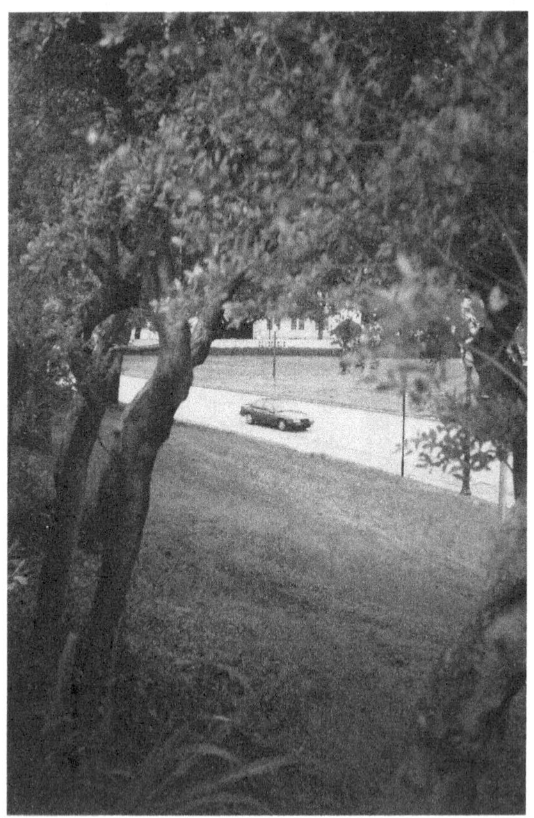

Here I am in the early 1990s behind the infamous grassy knoll picket fence

View looking up at the Book Depository

View from the center of Dealey Plaza

View from the railroad bridge overpass toward the School Book Depository

The view of the grassy knoll from Elm Street

View of the School Book Depository from Houston Street

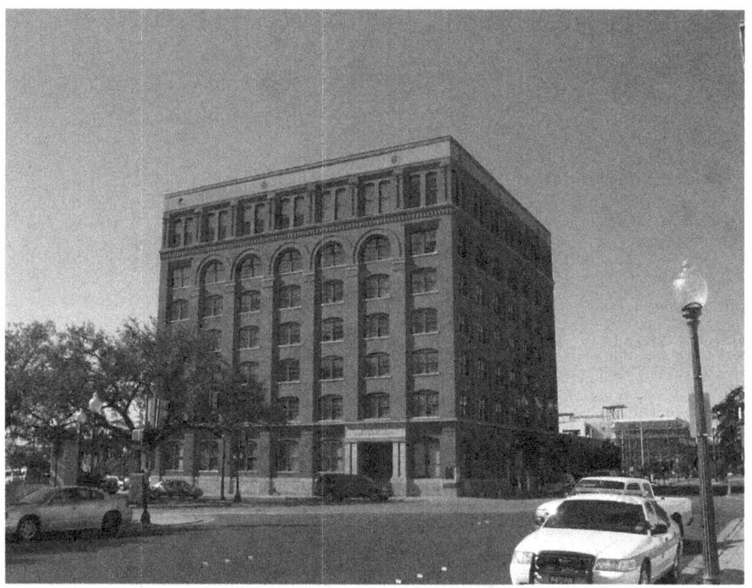

The Dal Tex Building

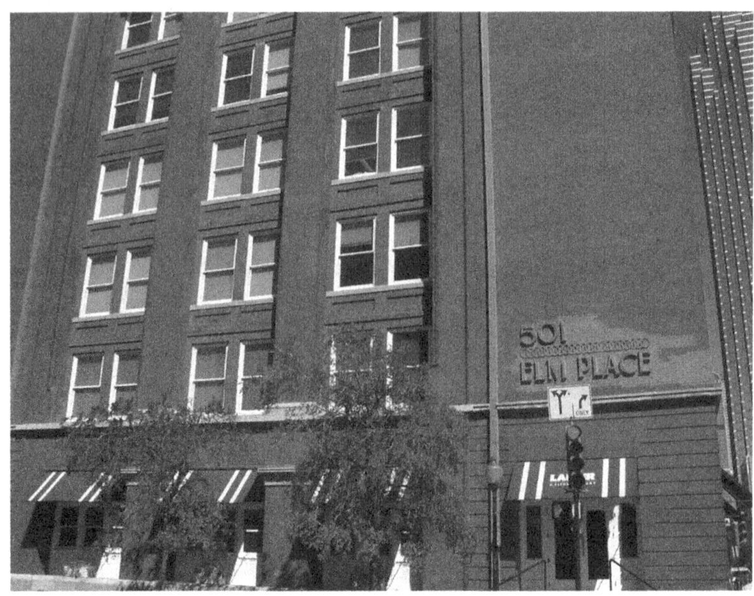

View facing the grassy knoll

View driving down Elm Street

Looking down from the railroad bridge overpass

A look behind the grassy knoll

The parking lot behind the grassy knoll

The grassy knoll, seen from across Elm Street

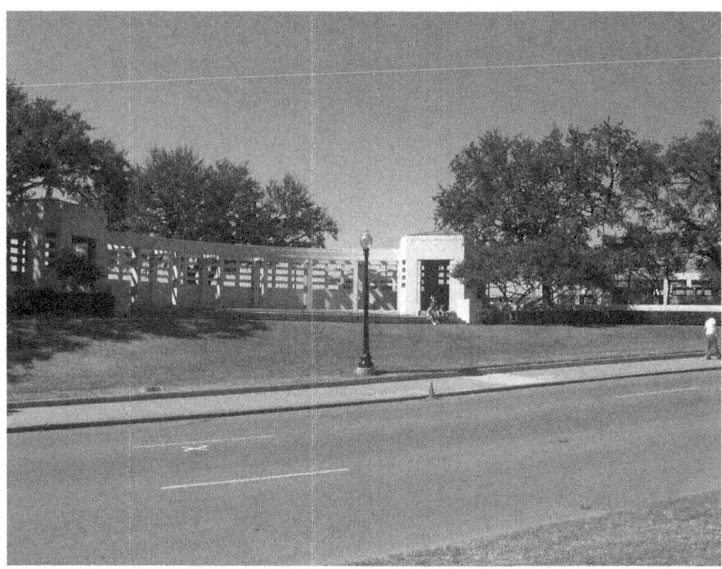

Looking down from the triple overpass

View of Dealey Park from Elm Street

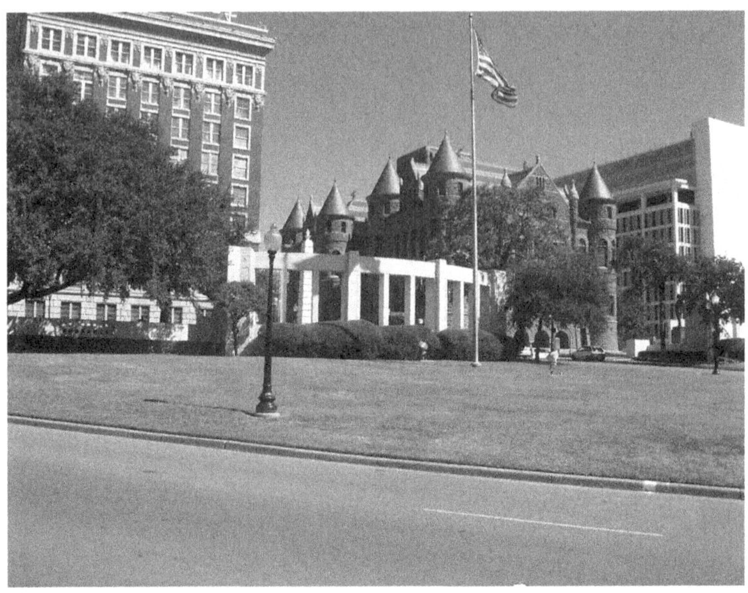

Full shot of Dealey Plaza

The location of the Tippit shooting

East 10th Street and North Patton Avenue

Selected Book Reviews

"The voyage of discovery is not in seeking new landscapes but in having new eyes."
—Marcel Proust

Belzer, R., and Wayne, D. (2013). *Hit List: An In-Depth Investigation into the Mysterious Deaths of Witnesses to the JFK Assassination*

Amazon book review: Richard Belzer and David Wayne are back to set the record straight after *Dead Wrong*; this time they're going to uncover the truth about the many witness deaths tied to the JFK assassination. For decades, government pundits have dismissed these "coincidental" deaths, even regarding them as "myths," as "urban legends." Like most people, Richard and David were initially unsure about what to make of these "coincidences." After all, events don't "consult the odds" prior to happening; they simply *happen*. Then someone comes along later and figures out what the odds of it happening were. Some of the deaths seemed purely coincidental; heart attacks, hunting accidents. Others clearly seemed noteworthy; witnesses who *did* seem to know something and *did* seem to die mysteriously. *Hit List* is a fair examination of the evidence of each case, leading to (necessarily) different conclusions. The findings were absolutely staggering; as some cases were clearly linked to a "clean-up operation" after the murder of President Kennedy, while others were the result of "other forces." The impeccable research and writing of Richard Belzer and David Wayne show that if the government is trying to hide anything, they're the duo who will uncover it.

Benson, M. (1993). *Who's Who in the JFK Assassination: An A–Z Encyclopedia*

This one book is an incredible resource and includes over 1,400 entries and explores many cracks and crevices surrounding the many witnesses and players involved in the assassination. This is a great book to have in your library and is a must-have for the serious researcher.

Blakey, R. G., and Billings, R. N. (1981). *The Plot to Kill the President: Organized Crime Assassinated JFK*

Robert Blakey was chief counsel and staff director of the House Select Committee on Assassinations. He's also an expert on organized crime in the United States and had worked for JFK's Justice Department under Robert Kennedy. He certainly knew his way around the circles of organized crime, and this book is very well written. As I have mentioned, there is no doubt that organized crime (the Mafia) was involved in some way with the murder of the president, but there is no way they could have organized, planned, and covered up this crime alone. They needed a lot of help. The book gives the Mafia a lot more credit for these actions than may be logically ascertained. Blakey, though, deserves a lot of credit for his research, although I do disagree with some of his committee's conclusions, such as their claim that the shot from the right front missed its target and that the autopsy photos were authentic, even though many showed no damage to the president's head in the occipital region, a total impossibility in my belief. I think the Dallas doctors and the Bethesda staff put that to bed very clearly. They also claim that Oswald was the shooter and fired the fatal shot from behind; based on the evidence in this book, it could not have happened the way he describes it in his conclusion. Finally, he does not in any way seem to suspect the CIA as a player in the assassination, and if you have read this far in my book, I hope you disagree with that conclusion.

Bolden, A. (2008). *The Echo from Dealey Plaza*

Former Secret Service Agent Bolden drops several bombshells in this book, describing just how relaxed the presidential protection was during 1963 and why he feels he was set up in order to remove his voice of dissent. He covers the party atmosphere that consumed the presidential detail and how some agents partied into the early morning hours the night before the assassination. He also covers, in detail, the loss of some Secret Service agent credentials, which may have been used by the suspects the next day in Dallas.

Brown, W. (1995). *Treachery in Dallas*

Walt Brown is a legend in his own right; he has focused his work over the years on the Texas connection and LBJ's involvement in the murder of JFK. This book is a classic in that subject area, delving into the oilmen who may have had a role in the assassination. His book is solid work, concise and compelling all the way.

Bugliosi, V. (2007). *Reclaiming History*

This book is simply a rehashing of the Warren Report. The author, much like the Warren investigators, ignores witness testimonies and other obvious evidence in this case. Paul Chambers, in his excellent book *Head Shot*, completely covers this text and is a very solid critic of the theories presented in Bugliosi's book. Here is just a very small quote from Chambers: "Bugliosi labors under the misguided belief that lawyerly tricks and the ability to steer a witness to a desired statement under cross-examination is a substitute for truth.... Though a brilliant prosecutor and author of many outstanding nonfiction books, Vincent Bugliosi advances and relies on arguments in *Reclaiming History* that sadly suffer from serious logical inconsistencies. This is the heartbreaking circumstance that has led Mr. Bugliosi to devote twenty years of his life to a flawed and hopeless cause, the rehabilitation of the Warren Commission findings and the establishment of Oswald as the lone assassin of John F. Kennedy" (Chambers 2012, 176, 177). I rest my case!

Chambers, G. P. (2012). *Head Shot: The Science behind the JFK Assassination*

This is a well-written book that looks at many ballistic aspects of the case; the author is an expert on ballistics and firearms and gives you a real-world perspective on this subject. He covers what was believable and what could have never happened, based on forensic science and ballistics.

Craig, R. (1971). *When They Kill a President* (self-published manuscript)

The story of Roger Craig is a sad one indeed; he started this book and never finished it. I have it listed here because it was interesting to read how his life transpired, in his own words. As I stated in my narrative, Roger talked a lot about what he saw that day in Dallas, and he also helped many of the early researchers; he then became a target himself. Many believe this cost him his life in the end. He was found shot to death; they ruled it a suicide, even though the weapon used was a rifle.

Curry, J. (1969). *JFK Assassination File*

This is one of the best books of its time, written by the chief of the Dallas Police Department, who was on the job and on the spot during the assassination. Curry, over the years, stated that he was very sure that the fatal shot came from the front. He was also a highly intelligent man, well trained and educated; this book is an excellent source of information.

Duffy, J. P., and Ricci, V. L. (1992). *A Complete Book of Facts: The Assassination of John F. Kennedy*

This is an excellent reference book for doing research; it includes important facts, short definitions, and biographies on many of the witnesses.

Fetzer, J. (2000). *Murder in Dealey Plaza: What we Know Now That We Didn't Know Then about the Death of JFK*

This is a fantastic book; when I read it, I had trouble putting it down. It has a chronological history that brings the reader through all the details surrounding the murder in Dealey Plaza. It then thoroughly covers many interesting aspects of the assassination, including the medical evidence, witness statements, and many important facts. You won't be disappointed with this book.

Furiati, C. (1994). *ZR Rifle: The Plot to Kill Kennedy and Castro*

Excellent overview of the plot to kill Castro and JFK as well; this classic book on the assassination covers many details not available in the 1970s; these facts are provided through many declassified Cuban files. Brazilian journalist and filmmaker Claudia Furiati does a fine job of bringing together many solid facts that point to the CIA's involvement in the murder of the president.

Giancana, S., and Giancana, C. (1992). *Double Cross: The Explosive, Inside Story of the Mobster Who Controlled America*

This is a powerful and very easy to read book. It is loaded with great historical information, and as I covered in this book, direct information implicating Sam "Mooney" Giancana and the CIA in the murder of President Kennedy. It also does a great job of covering the connection between the CIA and the American Mafia; it delves into the Texas connection, naming several members of the CIA and other sacred cows in American history who were part of the conspiracy.

Groden, R. J. (1995). *The Search for Lee Harvey Oswald*

This is one of the best and most comprehensive books written about Oswald, including perhaps the best pictorial record of the so-called lone assassin. Groden is an expert on this subject and provides a lot of related material throughout the book, along with some outstanding photographs. He makes the reader wonder just how many Oswalds there were by providing such a powerful visual history of Oswald, showing how his facial features were completely different from picture to picture; if there wasn't more than one Oswald, you explain how that could have happened and let me know.

Horne, D. (2009). *Inside the Assassination Records Review Board: The U.S. Government's Final Attempt to Reconcile the Conflicting Medical Evidence in the Assassination of JFK*

Amazon book review: Douglas Horne served on the staff of the President John F. Kennedy Assassination Records Review Board (ARRB) during the final three years of its four-year lifespan, from 1995 to 1998, and is the first US government official involved with the medical evidence to allege a cover-up in President Kennedy's autopsy, including the falsification of the autopsy photographs and x-rays. This book, the product of over thirteen years of writing and research, provides the best explanation yet offered of the true nature of the medical cover-up in the assassination of John F. Kennedy, and does so in meticulous detail, with scrupulous use of primary source material. It incorporates the latest information—much of it [sic] new evidence not revealed elsewhere—gleaned from the ARRB's depositions and interviews of medical witnesses, conducted from 1996 to 1998. With precise accuracy, and with a relentless focus on the massive fraud uncovered in the official records of the thirty-fifth president's assassination, Horne presents a persuasive case that the assassination of JFK was an "inside job," a true coup d'état in America, that was ruthlessly and brazenly covered up by those who "broke the back of the American century" in Dallas on November 22, 1963.

Kaiser, D. (2008). *The Road to Dallas: The Assassination of John F. Kennedy*

Kaiser's book does an excellent job of connecting the dots with regards to organized crime's involvement in the assassination. He also does the best job I have seen covering what he called "the Odio Incident." Silvia Odio was visited three months before the assassination by two Cuban exiles and, supposedly, Lee Harvey Oswald. The Warren Commission refused to believe her story, but it has been confirmed many times over, and Kaiser does a wonderful job of covering this fact. The only point I disagree with is that he still believes Oswald killed the president, which we have seen through numerous eyewitness statements and other reliable evidence simply cannot be the case. He does say there was another shooter on the grassy knoll, but that the shooter missed, which we also know could not have been the case. Here is another well-researched book by a great author with what I consider a flawed outcome, but worth reading for sure.

Krusch, B. (2012). *The Case against Lee Harvey Oswald (three-volume set)*

What an excellent set of books: very solid research on the real case against Oswald. This book is not only well written, it brings up many important points regarding the assassination of President Kennedy that are seldom mentioned. It provides some great reading on the subject and is entertaining as well.

Lane, M. (1966). *Rush to Judgment: A Critique of the Warren Commission's Inquiry into the Murders of President John F. Kennedy, Officer J.D. Tippit, and Lee Harvey Oswald*

There is so much to say about this groundbreaking book that never seems to grow old. I have watched the companion video by the same name over a hundred times. Lane's book came out in 1966, when the country was still under the influence of the Warren Commission. It took a lot of gumption for him to stand his ground and blast holes in the Warren Report. Lane was a true hero who was able to interview witnesses shortly after the murder while their memories were still fresh; many of these witnesses were killed off or died shortly after this work was published, Lee Bowers being one of them. This is a must read! When you read it and watch his video, you will know why I dedicated this book to him. You're the best, Mr. Lane!

Livingstone, H. E. (1993). *Killing the Truth*

This is a solid overview of the assassination, which includes a summary of the evidence and a look at the medical evidence comparing Dallas and Bethesda. This is a truly well-written book all the way around. Although it is over 700 pages, it is one of those books that will keep your interest; I have read it many times.

Prouty, L. F. (1992). *JFK, the CIA, Vietnam, and the Plot to Assassinate John F. Kennedy*

Amazon book review: Colonel L. Fletcher Prouty, the former CIA operative known as "X," offers a history-shaking perspective on the assassination of President John F. Kennedy. His theories were the basis for Oliver Stone's controversial movie *JFK*. Prouty believed that Kennedy's death was a coup d'état, and he backs this belief up with his knowledge of the security arrangements at Dallas and other tidbits that only a CIA insider would know (for example, that every member of Kennedy's cabinet was abroad at the time of Kennedy's assassination). His discussion of the elite power base he believes controlled the US government will scare and enlighten anyone who wants to know who was really behind the assassination of John F. Kennedy.

Sale, K. (1975). *Power Shift: The Rise of the Southern Rim and Its Challenge to the Eastern Establishment*

This is a well-rounded book that my very first political science professor asked me to read many years ago, and I have reread it many times since. It is not just about the JFK murder; it also contains some great historical information as well. Here is an excerpt relating to the assassination: "Even today the full story of that day is unknown, but enough has been uncovered by a small band of amateur sleuths and researchers to prove at the very minimum that the Warren Report was not justified in its bland conclusion that Lee Harvey Oswald was the sole assassin of President Kennedy. Serious questions still remain about the central details—the direction and number of the gunshots, the nature and location of the wounds, the background and politics of both Oswald and his assassin, Jack Ruby, the procedures of the Warren Commission in gathering and presenting evidence; even larger questions remain about the nature of the conspiracy behind it."

Smith, M. (2008). *JFK: The Second Plot*

Matthew Smith, who originally wrote this book in 1992, completed this new edition in 2008. It is an excellent read with a large amount of information. Smith provides many of the reference materials such as the autopsy chart, the receipt of the bullet taken from JFK's body, and even the statements from the FBI agents on duty at the autopsy. This book should be on your shelf.

Stone, O. (Producer) (1991). *JFK*

What a fantastic movie, and yes, of course there is some speculation in it, but the Warren Report wasn't speculation? Please. People who objected to this movie said it was not history; they are also members of the Church of the Lone Assassin and believers in the falsified evidence put out by the Warren Commission.

The movie fills in many of the blanks in the Warren Report and really tees off on the New Orleans connection. You have to love Oliver Stone; he speaks his mind. See the bonus disk for some great information on the true facts. In the words of Jack Lemmon, as Jack Martin (an associate of Guy Banister), "So what was history then, that fictional story by the Warren Commission, that pathetic piece of work by such a great man" (paraphrased). Get it and watch it.

Turner, N. (Producer) (1988). *The Men Who Killed Kennedy: The Coup D'État*

The first of nine episodes produced by Nigel Turner from 1988 to 2003 on the conspiracy and cover-up in the assassination. This is one of the best documentaries ever produced on this subject. This first episode sets the stage for all the others by laying a solid foundation of the cover-up and the depths of the conspiracy that concealed nearly all the facts in this case for decades.

Turner, N. (Producer) (1988). *The Men Who Killed Kennedy: The Forces of Darkness*

The second episode covers the many enemies that President Kennedy had back in 1963 and which ones may have wanted him eliminated.

Turner, N. (Producer) (1991). *The Men Who Killed Kennedy: The Cover-Up*

In this episode, Nigel Turner tells us what he knows about the massive cover-up that in many ways continues to this day.

Turner, N. (Producer) (1991). *The Men Who Killed Kennedy: The Patsy*

This episode covers the facts surrounding the life of Lee Oswald, many of which may surprise you. They make one point very clear: Oswald was not the one-dimensional character that the Warren Commission made him out to be.

Turner, N. (Producer) (1991). *The Men Who Killed Kennedy: The Witnesses*

So what did the witnesses really see that day? The witnesses were ignored by the federal authorities. The real witnesses never made it into the Warren Report; these are their true statements based on their experiences and what they saw. It is clear after watching this just how many times the Warren Commission distorted or ignored the statements of several key eyewitnesses.

Turner, N. (Producer) (1995). *The Men Who Killed Kennedy: The Truth Shall Set You Free*

This is an excellent documentary, like all of them. Episode 6 covers some powerful truths, such as the death of Commander William Bruce Pitzer and further analysis of the photographs and motion pictures of the assassination.

Turner, N. (Producer) (2003). *The Men Who Killed Kennedy: The Smoking Guns*

Wow, what an episode! It is packed with information on little-known facts. This is a hard-to-get video, but it is still out there. It includes information on a local Dallas mortician who may have helped alter some of the president's wounds after the murder.

Turner, N. (Producer) (2003). *The Men Who Killed Kennedy: The Love Affair*

This is a powerful episode that covers the fact that Oswald was, in fact, working for American intelligence and had nothing to do with the murder of the president. They also claim that Oswald had a lover while he lived in New Orleans, and she tells the world just how Oswald, Ruby, Banister,

Ferrie, and Clay Shaw were all tied together. Garrison had it all right back in the 1960s.

Turner, N. (Producer) (2003). *The Men Who Killed Kennedy: The Guilty Men*

This episode points to the involvement of the Texas connection in the murder of President Kennedy and includes solid witness statements. It also addresses the story about the mysterious fingerprint found in the sixth floor window connected to a henchman used by Lyndon Johnson.

Ventura, J., Russell, D., and Wayne, D. (2013). *They Killed Our President: 63 Reasons to Believe There Was a Conspiracy to Assassinate JFK*

Amazon book review: Unless you've been living under a rock for the past fifty years, you're aware of the many hypotheses that the assassination of President John F. Kennedy was not done by one man. Whether you've read one or a dozen of the books on this topic, it's nearly impossible to fully grasp the depth of this conspiracy—until now.

For the first time ever, *New York Times* best-selling authors Jesse Ventura, Dick Russell, and David Wayne have teamed up with some of the most respected and influential assassination researchers to put together the ultimate compendium that covers every angle—from the plot to the murder—of JFK. *They Killed Our President* will not only discuss the most famous of theories, but will also bring to light new and recently discovered information, which together shows that the United States government not only was behind this egregious plot, but took every step to make sure that the truth would not come out.

Weberman, A. J., and Canfield, M. (1992). ***Coup D'État in America: The CIA and the Assassination of John Kennedy***

This is an excellent work first completed in 1975; it really focuses on the CIA's involvement in the murder of President Kennedy. At the time the book was written, the authors did not have the benefit of the AARB's investigation in the 1990s, and the deathbed confession by E. Howard Hunt who was a longtime operative for the CIA and who confessed to being involved in the conspiracy in Dallas. The authors did a fantastic job of noting Hunt's involvement long before he ever confessed. Remember, Hunt and Sturgis were also Watergate burglars; they were ordered by Richard Nixon to commit yet further felonies by breaking into Democratic headquarters, thereby beginning the downfall of President Nixon. Many researchers believe that we still have not understood Nixon's total involvement in the Kennedy conspiracy, and I totally agree!

Resources

ABC News (Producer) (2007). *JFK Assassination Plot in Chicago*. Retrieved from http://www.youtube.com/watch?v=NBKcJAwwKrQ

Anderson, J. (Producer) (1988). *American Exposé: Who Murdered JFK?* Retrieved from http://www.youtube.com/watch?v=oDbodTKnTjc

A Primer of Assassination Theories. Retrieved from http://kenrahn.com/JFK/Conspiracy_theories/Primer/Primer_of_assassination_theories.html

Baker, M. (2013). *Travel Channel's America Declassified: JFK Assassination*. Retrieved from http://www.youtube.com/watch?v=Atq7yfaHKXE

Baker, R. (2009). *Family of Secrets: The Bush Dynasty, America's Invisible Government, and the Hidden History of the Last Fifty Years*. New York: Bloomsbury Press.

Barbour, J. (1992). *The JFK Assassination: The Jim Garrison Story*.

Becker, D. (2011). *The JFK Assassination: A Researcher's Guide*. Bloomington, IN: AuthorHouse.

Belzer, R., and Wayne, D. (2013). *Hit List: An In-Depth Investigation into the Mysterious Deaths of Witnesses to the JFK Assassination*. New York: Skyhorse Publishing.

Benson, M. (1993). *Who's Who in the JFK Assassination: An A–Z Encyclopedia*. New York: Carol Publishing Group.

Blakey, R. G., and Billings, R. N. (1981). *The Plot to Kill the President: Organized Crime Assassinated JFK*. New York: Times Books.

Bolden, A. (2008). *The Echo from Dealey Plaza*. New York: Three Rivers Press.

Bowen, R. S. (1991). *The Immaculate Deception*. Carson City, NV: American West Publishers.

Brown, W. (1995). *Treachery in Dallas*. New York: Carroll & Graf Publishers.

Callahan, B. (1993). *Who Shot JFK?: A Guide to the Major Conspiracy Theories*. New York: Simon & Schuster.

Canal, J. (2000). *Silencing the Lone Assassin: The Murders of JFK and Lee Harvey Oswald*. St. Paul, MN: Paragon House.

Chambers, G. P. (2012). *Head Shot: The Science behind the JFK Assassination* (Expanded ed.). New York: Prometheus Books.

Childs, A. (2013). *We Were There: Revelations from the Dallas Doctors Who Attended to JFK on November 22, 1963*. New York: Skyhorse Publishing.

Corsi, J. R. (2013). *Who Really Killed Kennedy?* New York: WND Books.

Craig, R. (1971). *When They Kill a President*. Self-published.

Crenshaw, C. (1992). *JFK: Conspiracy of Silence*. New York: Penguin Books.

Curry, J. (1969). *JFK Assassination File*. Dallas: American Poster and Printing Co.

Dankbaar, D. (Producer) (2012). *Confessions from the Grassy Knoll: The Shocking Truth.*

Dankbaar, D. (Producer) (2012). *I Shot JFK: The Shocking Truth.*

De Mey, F. (2013). *Cold Case Kennedy.* Tielt, Belgium: Lannoo.

Duffy, J. P., and Ricci, V. L. (1992). *A Complete Book of Facts: The Assassination of John F. Kennedy.* New York: Thunder's Mouth Press.

Duffy, J. R. (1989). *Who Killed JFK? The Kennedy Assassination Cover-Up.* New York: Shapolsky Publishers.

Epstein, E. J. (1966). *Inquest: The Warren Commission and the Establishment of the Truth.* New York: The Viking Press.

Escalante, F. (2006). *JFK: The Cuba Files: The Untold Story of the Plot to Kill Kennedy.* New York: Ocean Press.

Fetzer, J. (2000). *Murder in Dealey Plaza: What We Know Now that We Didn't Know then about the Death of JFK.* Chicago: Catfeet Press.

Fetzer, J. (2009, May 1). "Arlen Specter and the 'Magic' Bullet." *OpEdNew.com.* Retrieved from http://www.opednews.com/articles/1/Arlen-Specter-and-The-Mag-by-Jim-Fetzer-090429-78.html

Fetzer, J. H. (1998). *Assassination Science: Experts Speak Out on the Death of JFK.* Chicago: Catfeet Press.

Fiester, S. P. (2012). *Enemy of the Truth: Myths, Forensics, and the Kennedy Assassination.* Southlake, TX: JFK Lancer Publications.

Fischer, E. (Producer) (2010). *Did the Mob Kill JFK?* [Television episode, air date February 10, 2014, the Military Channel].

Fulsom, D. (n.d.). *Richard Nixon's Greatest Cover-Up: His Ties to the Assassination of President Kennedy.* Retrieved from http://surftofind.com/mob

Furiati, C. (1994). *ZR Rifle: The Plot to Kill Kennedy and Castro.* Melbourne: Ocean Press.

Giancana, G., Hughes, J. R., and Jobe, T. H. (2005). *JFK and Sam: The Connection between the Giancana and Kennedy Assassinations.* Nashville, TN: Cumberland House.

Giancana, S., and Giancana, C. (1992). *Double Cross: The Explosive, Inside Story of the Mobster Who Controlled America.* New York: Warner Books.

Groden, R. J. (1993). *The Killing of a President.* New York: Penguin Books.

Groden, R. J. (1995). *The Search for Lee Harvey Oswald.* New York: Penguin Books.

Groden, R. J. (Producer) (2003). *JFK Assassination Files: The Case for Conspiracy.*

Groden, R. J. (Producer) (2003). *JFK: The Case for Conspiracy.*

Groden, R. J. (2006). *JFK: The Case for Conspiracy: The Killing of a President* (Memorial ed.). Dallas: New Frontier Publications.

Hinckle, W., and Turner, W. (1992). *Deadly Secrets: The CIA-Mafia War against Castro and the Assassination of JFK*. New York: Thunder's Mouth Press.

Hoffman, E. (1980). *What They Saw: Ed Hoffman*. Retrieved from http://www.youtube.com/watch?v=veVqYo9I5gg&feature=fvwrel

Horne, D. (2009). *Inside the Assassination Records Review Board: The U.S. Government's Final Attempt to Reconcile the Conflicting Medical Evidence in the Assassination of JFK* (Vol. 1–5). Self-published.

Hurlburt, C. E. (2012). *It's Time for the Truth: The JFK Cover-Up*. Self-published.

Hurt, H. (1985). *Reasonable Doubt: An Investigation into the Assassination of John F. Kennedy*. New York: Henry Holt & Co.

Janney, P. (2012). *Mary's Mosaic: The CIA Conspiracy to Murder John F. Kennedy, Mary Pinchot Meyer, and Their Vision for World Peace*. New York: Skyhorse Publishing.

Jones, H. (2003). *Death of a Generation: How the Assassinations of Diem and JFK Prolonged the Vietnam War*. New York: Oxford University Press.

Kaiser, D. (2008). *The Road to Dallas: The Assassination of John F. Kennedy*. Cambridge, MA: The Belknap Press of Harvard University Press.

Kroth, J. (2003). *Conspiracy in Camelot: The Complete History of the Assassination of John Fitzgerald Kennedy*. New York: Algora Publishing.

Krusch, B. (2012). *The Case against Lee Harvey Oswald* (Vol. 1–3). Self-published.

Kurtz, M. (2006). *The JFK Assassination Debates: Lone Gunman versus Conspiracy*. Lawrence: University Press of Kansas.

Lane, M. (1966). *Rush to Judgment: A Critique of the Warren Commission's Inquiry into the Murders of President John F. Kennedy, Officer J. D. Tippit, and Lee Harvey Oswald*. New York: Holt, Rinehart & Winston.

Lane, M. (Producer) (1966). *Rush to Judgment*.

Lane, M. (Producer) (1967). *Rush to Judgment*. Retrieved from http://www.youtube.com/watch?v=6FncG5WwO3Y

Lane, M. (Producer) (1987). *Two Men in Dallas*.

Lane, M. (2011). *Last Word: My Indictment of the CIA in the Murder of JFK*. New York: Skyhorse Publishing.

Letterbox. (Producer) (2009). *Dark Legacy: George Bush and the Murder of John F. Kennedy*. Available from www.thedarklegacy.com

Lewis, R. (1993). *Flashback: The Untold Story of Lee Harvey Oswald*. Roseburg, OR: Lewcon Publishing.

Lifton, D. (1980). *Best Evidence*. New York: McMillan.

Lifton, D. (Producer) (1990). *Best Evidence: The Research Video*.

Livingstone, H. E. (1993). *Killing the Truth*. New York: Carroll & Graf Publishers.

Livingstone, H. E. (1995). *Killing Kennedy and the Hoax of the Century*. New York: Carroll & Graf Publishers.

Maier, T. W. (2012, July 2). Deathbed Confession: Who Really Killed JFK? *Baltimore Post-Examiner*. Retrieved from http://baltimorepostexaminer.com/deathbed-confession-who-really-killed-jfk/2012/07/02

Marrs, J. (1989). *Crossfire: The Plot that Killed Kennedy*. New York: Carroll & Graf Publishers.

Martin, O. (2010). *JFK: Analysis of a Shooting: The Ultimate Ballistics Truth Exposed*. Indianapolis: Dog Ear Publishing.

McBride, J. (2013). *Into the Nightmare: My Search for the Killers of President John F. Kennedy and Officer J. D. Tippit*. Berkeley, CA: Hightower Press.

McClellan, B. (2003). *Blood, Money, and Power: How LBJ Killed JFK*. New York: Hanover House.

Mellen, J. (2005). *A Farewell to Justice: Jim Garrison, JFK's Assassination, and the Case that Should Have Changed History*. Washington DC: Potomac Books.

Morley, J. (2008). *Our Man in Mexico: Winston Scott and the History of the CIA*. Kansas City: University Press of Kansas.

MPI Media Group. (2006). *The Murder of JFK: A Revisionist History*.

Noyes, P. (2010). *Legacy of Doubt: Did the Mafia Kill JFK?* 2nd ed. P&G Publications.

North, M. (1991). *Act of Treason: The Role of J. Edgar Hoover in the Assassination of President Kennedy*. New York: Carroll & Graf Publishers.

Oglesby, C. (1992). *The JFK Assassination: The Facts and the Theories*. New York: Penguin Books.

O'Leary, B., and Seymour, L. E. (2003). *Triangle of Death: The Shocking Truth about the Role of South Vietnam and the French Mafia in the Assassination of JFK*. Nashville, TN: WND Books.

O'Reilly, B., and Dugard, M. (2012). *Killing Kennedy: The End of Camelot*. New York: Henry Holt and Company.

Palamara, V. M. (2013). *Survivor's Guilt: The Secret Service and the Failure to Protect President Kennedy*. Waterville, OR: Trine Day LLC.

PBS (Producer) (1993). *JFK, Hoffa, and the Mob.*

Pierson, J. (2007). *Camelot and the Cultural Revolution: How the Assassination of John F. Kennedy Shattered American Liberalism*. New York: Encounter Books.

Piper, M. C. (1993). *Final Judgment: The Missing Link in the JFK Assassination Conspiracy*. Washington DC: The Wolfe Press.

Polasek, R. J. (2010). *Powers behind JFK Assassination*. 2nd ed. Raleigh, NC: Lulu.

Prouty, L. F. (1992). *JFK the CIA, Vietnam and the Plot to Assassinate John F. Kennedy*. New York: Carol Publishing.

Prouty, L. F. (2011). *The Secret Team: The CIA and Its Allies in Control of the United States and the World*. New York: Skyhorse Publishing.

Remington, R. A. (2005). *Falling Chips: A Deconstruction of the Single-Bullet Theory of the JFK Assassination*. Bloomington: Xlibris Corp.

Rike, A., & McSween, C. (2008). *At the door of memory: Aubrey rike and the assassination of president kennedy*. (1 ed.). Southlake: JFK Lancer Productions & Publications, Inc.

Russell, D. (2008). *On the Trail of Assassins: A Groundbreaking Look at America's Most Infamous Conspiracy*. New York: Skyhorse Publishing.

Russo, G. (1998). *Live by the Sword: The Secret War against Castro and the Death of JFK*. Baltimore: Bancroft Press.

Sale, K. (1975). *Power Shift: The Rise of the Southern Rim and Its Challenge to the Eastern Establishment*. New York: Random House.

Sauvage, L. (1966). *The Oswald Affair: An Examination of the Contradictions and Omission of the Warren Report*. New York: World Publishing Co.

Scheim, D. E. (1988). *Contract on America: The Mafia Murder of President John F. Kennedy*. New York: Shapolsky Publishers.

Scott, P. (2013). *Oswald, Mexico, and Deep Politics: Revelations from CIA Records on the Assassination of JFK*. New York: Skyhorse Publishing.

Sloan, B., and Hill, J. (1992). *JFK: The Last Dissenting Witness*. Gretna: Pelican Publishing Co.

Smith, M. (2008). *JFK: The Second Plot*. 2nd ed. London: Mainstream Publishing Co.

Spartacus Educational Publishers Ltd. (2012, June 12). *In the Eye of History: Disclosures in the JFK Assassination Medical Evidence*. Retrieved from http://www.spartacus.schoolnet.co.uk/JFKoconnorPK.htm

Stone, O. (Producer) (1991). *JFK*.

Stone, O., and Sklar, Z. (1992). *An Oliver Stone Film: JFK: The Documented Screenplay*. New York: Applause Books.

Swike, J. (2008). *The Missing Chapter: Lee Harvey Oswald in the Middle East*. Self-published.

Tague, J. T. (2003). *Truth Withheld: A Survivor's Story*. Dallas: Excel Digital Press.

Talbot, D. (2007). *Brothers: The Hidden History of the Kennedy Years*. New York: Free Press.

Turner, N. (Producer) (1988). *The Men Who Killed Kennedy: The Coup D'État*.

Turner, N. (Producer) (1988). *The Men Who Killed Kennedy: The Forces of Darkness*.

Tuner, N. (Producer) (1991). *The Men Who Killed Kennedy: The Cover-Up*.

Turner, N. (Producer) (1991). *The Men Who Killed Kennedy: The Patsy*.

Turner, N. (Producer) (1991). *The Men Who Killed Kennedy: The Witnesses.*

Turner, N. (Producer) (1995). *The Men Who Killed Kennedy: The Truth Shall Set You Free.*

Turner, N. (Producer) (2003). *The Men Who Killed Kennedy: The Smoking Guns.*

Turner, N. (Producer) (2003). *The Men Who Killed Kennedy: The Love Affair.*

Turner, N. (Producer) (2003). *The Men Who Killed Kennedy: The Guilty Men.*

Ventura, J., and Russell, D. (2010). *American Conspiracies.* New York: Skyhorse Publishing.

Ventura, J., Russell, D., and Wayne, D. (2013). *They Killed Our President: 63 Reasons to Believe There Was a Conspiracy to Assassinate JFK.* New York: Skyhorse Publishing.

Waldron, L., and Hartmann, T. (2009). *Legacy of Secrecy: The Long Shadow of the JFK Assassination.* Berkley, CA: Counterpoint.

Warren Commission. (1964). *The Warren Commission Report: The Official Report of the President's Commission on the Assassination of President John F. Kennedy.* Washington DC: US Government.

Weberman, A. J., and Canfield, M. (1992). *Coup D'État in America: The CIA and the Assassination of John Kennedy.* San Francisco: Quick Trading Co.

Wecht, C.H. (1993). Cause of Death. New York: Penguin Books.

Weisberg, H. (1994). *Case Open: The Omissions, Distortions and Falsifications of Case Closed.* New York: Carroll & Graf Publishers.

Weisberg, H. (1994). *Selections from Whitewash.* New York: Carroll & Graf Publishers.

Zirbel, C. I. (1991). *The Texas Connection: The Assassination of John F. Kennedy.*

About the Author

Ed Souza with Chief Gates

Professor Ed Souza is a former Los Angeles police officer who has spent twenty five years in the fields of law enforcement, investigations, and education. Currently, he is a senior professor and program lead of criminal justice and criminal investigations. Professor Souza earned a bachelor's degree in political science from California Polytechnic State University in San Luis Obispo. He also earned a master's degree in criminal justice from Kaplan University and is completing his dissertation in the studies of criminology and public safety.

Index

D

E

F

G

H

I

J

K

L

M

R

S

T

V

W

X

Y

Z

Printed in the United States
By Bookmasters